ROME

a thousand years of power and glory

CIVILIZATIONS THAT SHAPED OUR WORLD

ROME

a thousand years of power and glory

CONDENSED VERSION OF *HISTORY OF ROME*
PUBLISHED BY FABER AND FABER

Reader's
Digest

THE READER'S DIGEST ASSOCIATION, INC.
PLEASANTVILLE, NEW YORK / MONTREAL

CIVILIZATIONS THAT SHAPED OUR WORLD *was developed by Reader's Digest.*

ROME—*a thousand years of power and glory*

is part of the **Civilizations That Shaped Our World** collection

Editorial
GÉRARD CHENUET, PATRICE MENTHA, EMMANUELLE CAGNAC-VALETTE, ALBERT MALAIN, RÉMY COTON-PÉLAGIE, CAMILLE DUVIGNEAU, THOMAS VON JOEST, JEAN-MARIE MONOD

Design
DOMINIQUE CHARLIAT, VÉRONIQUE ZONCA, COLMAN COHEN

Illustrations
PHILIPPE BIARD

Cartography
EDITERRA

Picture Editing
DANIELLE BURNICHON, MONIQUE TRÉMEAU

U.S. READER'S DIGEST PROJECT TEAM

Contributing Project Editor
FRED DuBOSE

Contributing Editor
THOMAS A. RANIERI

Designer
JENNIFER R. TOKARSKI

Production Technology Manager
DOUGLAS A. CROLL

Art Production
PATRICIA HALBERT

Translation
MOLLY STEVENS

Proofreading
JANE SHERMAN

Indexing
NAN BADGETT

READER'S DIGEST BOOKS

Editor-in-Chief
NEIL WERTHEIMER

Editorial Director
CHRISTOPHER CAVANAUGH

Senior Design Director
ELIZABETH L. TUNNICLIFFE

Associate Marketing Director
DENNIS MARION

Vice President and General Manager
KEIRA KUHS

GLOBAL BOOKS & HOME ENTERTAINMENT RIGHTS & PERMISSIONS

Director
ALFREDO G. SANTANA

Asssociate Director
LISA GARRETT-SMITH

READER'S DIGEST ASSOCIATION, INC.

Editor-in-Chief
ERIC W. SCHRIER

President, North American Books and Home Entertainment
THOMAS D. GARDNER

READER'S DIGEST EDITORIAL, INTERNATIONAL

GARY Q. ARPIN, IAIN PARSONS

FIRST EDITION

© 2002 The Reader's Digest Association, Inc.
© 2000 Sélection du Reader's Digest, S.A.

This volume includes material from HISTORY OF ROME © *Michael Grant Publications Ltd., 1978, 1979, 1993. The original edition of this book was published in 1978 by Weidenfeld and Nicolson, London. The present revised edition was published for the first time in 1979 by Faber and Faber Ltd., London. The condensation in this volume was completed by Reader's Digest and published with permission from the author and Weidenfeld and Nicolson.*

ISBN 0-7621-0414-7

Address any comments about *Civilizations That Shaped Our World* to:
Editorial Director, Reader's Digest Home Division
Reader's Digest Road, Pleasantville, NY 10570-7000

To order additional copies of *Civilizations That Shaped Our World*, call 1-800-846-2100.

You can also visit us on the World Wide Web at **rd.com**

Printed in the United States of America

UK 0074/G–US   1 3 5 7 9 10 8 6 4 2

TABLE OF CONTENTS

BODY TEXT FOR *ROME* IS CONDENSED FROM
HISTORY OF ROME BY MICHAEL GRANT.

Large Fresco from the Villa of the Mysteries, *in Pompeii, depicting initiation rites of the Bacchic cult.*

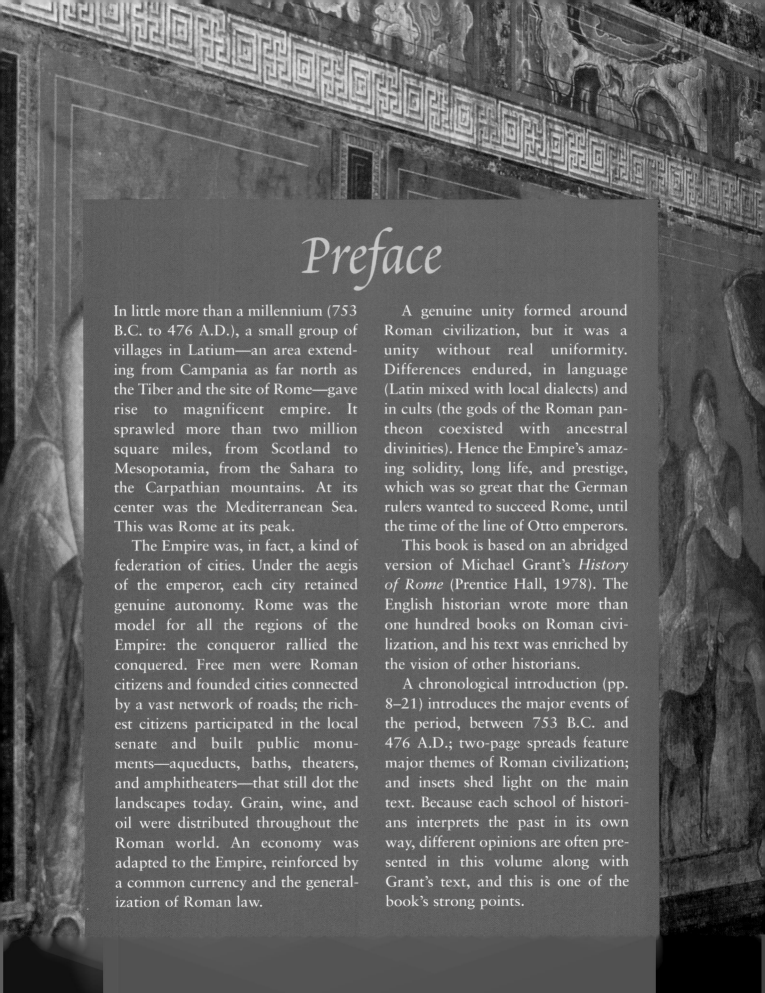

Preface

In little more than a millennium (753 B.C. to 476 A.D.), a small group of villages in Latium—an area extending from Campania as far north as the Tiber and the site of Rome—gave rise to magnificent empire. It sprawled more than two million square miles, from Scotland to Mesopotamia, from the Sahara to the Carpathian mountains. At its center was the Mediterranean Sea. This was Rome at its peak.

The Empire was, in fact, a kind of federation of cities. Under the aegis of the emperor, each city retained genuine autonomy. Rome was the model for all the regions of the Empire: the conqueror rallied the conquered. Free men were Roman citizens and founded cities connected by a vast network of roads; the richest citizens participated in the local senate and built public monuments—aqueducts, baths, theaters, and amphitheaters—that still dot the landscapes today. Grain, wine, and oil were distributed throughout the Roman world. An economy was adapted to the Empire, reinforced by a common currency and the generalization of Roman law.

A genuine unity formed around Roman civilization, but it was a unity without real uniformity. Differences endured, in language (Latin mixed with local dialects) and in cults (the gods of the Roman pantheon coexisted with ancestral divinities). Hence the Empire's amazing solidity, long life, and prestige, which was so great that the German rulers wanted to succeed Rome, until the time of the line of Otto emperors.

This book is based on an abridged version of Michael Grant's *History of Rome* (Prentice Hall, 1978). The English historian wrote more than one hundred books on Roman civilization, and his text was enriched by the vision of other historians.

A chronological introduction (pp. 8–21) introduces the major events of the period, between 753 B.C. and 476 A.D.; two-page spreads feature major themes of Roman civilization; and insets shed light on the main text. Because each school of historians interprets the past in its own way, different opinions are often presented in this volume along with Grant's text, and this is one of the book's strong points.

The Roman world

*The Roman Empire was at its greatest reach at
the beginning of the second century A.D. It embraced
most of Europe, North Africa, and a great part of what is
now known as the Middle East, and had a population of
between 50 and 60 million people.*

THE ROMAN MIRACLE
*The world has long been
fascinated by the sweeping
and long-lasting Roman
conquest. Historians have
considered this period
unique in history,
a genuine miracle.*

Italy before Rome

- *Since 1500 B.C.: settlement of the Ligurians.*

- *Between 1400 and 1300 B.C.: Celts appear in northern Italy.*

- *Between 1300 and 1200 B.C.: settlement of the Italiotes.*

- *Around 1150 B.C.: according to legend, Aeneas and his Trojans settle in Latium. Ascagnus, Aeneas' son, founds Albus.*

- *Around 1000 B.C.: beginning of the Iron Age. Civilization known as Villanovan (from Villanova, near Bologna).*

- *Around 900 B.C.: settlement of the Etruscans between the Tiber and the Arno.*

- *Between 800 and 600 B.C.: Etruscan civilization expands, toward the north in the Po plains and toward the south in Latium and Campania. Founding of a confederation of twelve cities.*

Map labels

Antonine's Wall
Hadrian's Wall
BRITAIN
Germania Inferior
Rhine
BELGICA
GERMANIA
Lugdunensis
Danu...
GAUL
Germania Superior
Raetia
Noricum
Aquitainia
(Grees Alps) Pennines Alps
Cottian Alps
Pann...
Narbonensis
Maritime Alps
ITALY
Dal...
HISPANIA
Tarraconensis
Corsica
Lusitania
Baleares
Sardinia
Baetica
Sicily
ATLANTIC OCEAN
Mauritania Tingitana
Mauritania Caesarinensis
Africa
Numidia
(Pracons)
M...

GREATEST REACH OF THE
ROMAN EMPIRE *(from the second century)*

PRINCIPAL ROMAN EMPERORS

**27 B.C.–14 A.D. Augustus,
first emperor**

JULIO-CLAUDIAN DYNASTY
14–37 Tiberius
37–41 Caligula
41–54 Claudius I
54–68 Nero

FLAVIAN DYNASTY
69–79 Vespasian
79–81 Titus
81–96 Domitian

ANTONINUS PERIOD
96–98 Nerva
98–117 Trajan
117–138 Hadrian
138–161 Antoninus Pius
161–180 Marcus Aurelius
180–192 Commodus

SEVERUS DYNASTY
193–211 Septimus Severus
211–217 Caracalla
218–222 Elagabalus
222–235 Alexander Severus

**GALLIENUS AND THE
ILLYRIAN EMPERORS**
259–268 Gallienus
268–270 Claudius II
270–275 Aurelian
284–305 Diocletian

**ROME UNDER
THE KINGS**

717–617 B.C.
Latino-Sabine king...

616–510 B.C.
Etruscan kings
(Tarquinius Superb...

Pages 10–11

Timeline

1500 B.C.
- Mycenaean civilization in Greece
- The Celts from Central Europe settle in Europe
- Hittite civilization in Asia Minor
- New Kingdom in Egypt

1200 B.C.
- Invasion of the Sea Peoples
- The Hebrews fight for the Promised Land

1100 B.C.
Greek Diaspora

1000 B.C.
- Iron Age in Europe
- Kingdom of David and Solomon
- Phoenician colonization

900 B.C.
- Arrival of the Etruscans
- *The Iliad* and *The Odyssey*
- 814: Foundation of Carthage

753 B.C.
Foundation of Rome

509 B.C.
The Republic

Elsewhere in the world...

INDIA AND CHINA

Because of the luxury goods trade and the famous Silk Road, Rome had ties with India as early as Augustus's era, and with China in the second century A.D. At the time, India was divided into several independent kingdoms. In the north, the union of five tribes formed the Kushan kingdom. Its King Kanishka favored Buddhism and trade development. In the second century, China was a powerful empire. Under the reign of the eastern Han Dynasty, sea routes from Canton were created and an outlet in the Persian Gulf from Turkestan was opened. Paper was invented around 100 A.D.

GERMANIC POPULATIONS

Germanic people could be divided into three groups: northern Germans, who stayed in Scandinavia; eastern Germans (Vandals, Burgundians, Goths, etc.), who emigrated to areas east of the Elbe; and western Germans (Batavi, Chatti, Francs, Saxons, Suevi, Lombards, Marcomanni, etc.), who settled along the Rhine, the Weser, and the Elbe. Living off agriculture and animal husbandry, the Germans had been trading with Mediterranean countries since the Bronze Age. Organized by tribe and clan, they were led by kings and princes surrounded by loyal soldiers.

THE PARTHIAN ORIENT

The Parthian Empire, which extended across the entire Iranian plateau, was formed in the third and second centuries B.C. by annexing the Seleucide provinces. Although essentially agricultural, it also traded with the Far East: Produce was transported through caravan routes toward Syria and the Roman Empire. Armenia very quickly became what was always at stake in battles between Rome and Parthia; in the first century, the Parthians were able to defend the frontiers of their territory, which was bordered by the Euphrates. But, in the second century, Rome repeatedly attacked the capital, Ctesiphon, which weakened a monarchy that was already threatened by internal struggles. This tumult benefited the Persians under King Ardashir I. They settled in Iran as early as the third century.

SUB-SAHARAN AFRICA

With few historical records, non-Roman Africa, was not well known. The Romans themselves imagined it to be populated by mysterious beings— half-man, half animal. Only the Moor tribes, which relentlessly advanced into Roman territory, were pacified and quartered on top of the limes system (military roads). We do know that there was trading across the Sahara. Slaves and hides could be transported from the Ivory Desert to Leptis Magna, in Tunisia. This age-old trading route was revitalized during the Roman period, when dromedaries began to be used. Another trade route existed between Nubia and the Nile Valley.

SARMATIA

BLACK SEA

Dacia

Moesia

Thrace

Bithynia and Pontus

Cappadocia

Asia

Galatia

Lycaonia

Cicilia

Euphrates

...donia

...chaia

Cyprus

Syria

Crete

Arabia

Palestine

...RANEAN SEA

Italy after Rome

- 455: Vandals seize Rome.

- 476: End of the Western Roman Empire. Odoacer, a lieutenant under Attila, becomes king of Italy.

- 488: Odoacer is killed by Theodoric.

- 493–553: Theodoric's Ostrogoth Kingdom, led by Zeno, Byzantine emperor.

- 553–568: Emperor Justinian gradually reconquers Italy.

- 568–774: Lombard Kingdom (northern and central Italy; Pavia is capita), Byzantine Italy (Rome, Ravenna, southern Italy, and Sicily).

- 773–774: Charlemagne, King of the Franks and Lombards.

- Until 887: The Carolingian Kings of Italy.

THE REPUBLIC AT ITS PEAK

51 B.C. – Law known as Twelve Tables

343–291 B.C.
...ars against Samnites

264–146 B.C.
Punic Wars

Pages 12–13

FROM THE GRACCHUS CRISIS TO AUGUSTUS

133–123 B.C.
Gracchus brothers reforms

73–71 B.C.
Spartacus's Gladitorial War

44 B.C.
Caesar killed

Pages 14–15

PROSPERITY AND THE EMPIRE IN CRISIS

64
Fire rages through Rome

79
Mount Vesuvius erupts and Pompeii is destroyed

276–279
String of Barbarian invasions

Pages 16–17

THE LATE EMPIRE

330
Constantinople, new capital of the Empire

410
Alaric sacks Rome

Pages 18–19

---

133 B.C.　　0　14 A.D.　　　　476 A.D.　　　　800 A.D.

The Greeks　　The Empire

End of the Third Century (Diocletian)

End of the Roman Empire

End of Antiquity

- The Merovingians in France, the Ostrogoths followed by the Lombards in Italy
- Byzantine Empire
- Islam emerges and Arab Empire is built
- Start of Carolingian Empire

Roman Civilization

Rome under the kings 753–509 B.C.

Founded in the middle of the seventh century B.C., Rome at first was but a small town, governed by a succession of kings of Latin or Sabine origin. They were the ones who gave Rome its first political and religious institutions. But the Etruscans, who took power in the seventh century, had a deep cultural influence on Rome, turning it into a genuine City-State.

ETRUSCAN GODS AND GREEK GODS

Etruscan civilization strongly influenced religious domains. The Etruscans gave the city its first stone and square temples (including the Temple of Jupiter on Capitoline Hill) decorated with terra cotta motifs. They also left us with statues of gods, fabricated in the Caere or Veii workshops. Apollo, the Greek god, proves that there were cultural exchanges between the Etruscans and the Greek cities in the south of Italy. As early as the seventh century, Rome reaped the benefits of this twofold heritage.

THE TRANSFORMATION OF WRITING

Alphabetic writing, which was borrowed from the Greeks, was also passed on to the Romans by the Etruscans. Most of the inscriptions discovered in excavations are either ritual or funeral texts or bits of script on everyday objects (bowls, clasps, etc.) with the names of their owners or donors. Because they are very short and essentially consist of proper names, these texts have not been much help to historians striving to reconstitute the Etruscan language.

753 B.C.   Founding of Rome

753–717   Reign of Romulus
*First senate established.
Abduction of the Sabine women.*

717–617 B.C.   Reign of the Three Latino-Sabine Kings

717–673   Numa Pompilius *First religious institutions*

672–641   Tullus Hostilius, warrior king *Battle of Horatii and the Curiatii: fall of Albus*

639–617   Ancus Marcius *Development of the right of war. Foundation of Ostia. Settlement of the Aventine Hill by the Latins.*

THE FIRST HOMES *This bronze urn found in the Vulci necropolis tells us about burial customs in Villanovan civilization (Etruscans from the ninth to the eighth century B.C.). The ashes of the deceased were placed in clay or bronze containers that were reproductions of the homes of the living. These objects therefore allow us to imagine the first Roman houses — the huts with cob walls and wooden beams, round or oval, that dotted the Quirinal and Palatine Hills.*

THE LEGEND OF THE FOUNDING *This famous bronze she-wolf recalls the legend of the founding of Rome by Romulus and Remus in 753 B.C. It is most likely the first representation of this myth, which was at the peak of its popularity in the middle of the Republican era. Although it was probably not installed on the Capitol until 296 B.C., its style, which is typically Etruscan, suggests that it was made two centuries earlier. The twins were added during the Renaissance, but nevertheless must have existed in the original sculpture.*

INSPECTION OF INNARDS *This bronze mirror, which attests to the quality of Etruscan craftsmanship, depicts an important ritual in Roman religion: the inspection of the innards of a sacrifice with a haruspex. The priest is checking that the liver looks normal. This method of divination, the purpose of which was to assure that the gods would approve of the offering, was directly borrowed from the Etruscans; during the Republic, priests of Etruscan origin continued to be entrusted with this ritual.*

A LOCATION WITH AN ADVANTAGE *(background photograph) Because it was protected by hills, and especially because of the River Tiber, Rome had advantages that favored trade and conquest. The Etruscans contributed to this development by building essential foundations in the city: The swampland was dried out and the first forum became a public place; the Cloaca Maxima, the Great Sewer, collected used water; the streets were paved. The first roads and the first stone bridges made Rome a strategic point between central Italy and southern outposts.*

616–510 B.C.   Reign of the Three Etruscan Kings

616–579   **Tarquinius Priscus** *Major urbanization work in Rome*

578–535   **Servius Tullius** *Voting system based on poll tax. A surrounding wall is built around Rome*

534–510   **Tarquinius Superbus** *Temples of Jupiter, Juno and Minerva are built on Capitoline Hill. A sewer, Cloaca Maxima, is also built.*

509 B.C.   Tarquins Overthrown

Republic declared

Brutus and Collatin appointed consuls

The Republic at its peak
509–133 B.C.

Once the Tarquins were driven from Rome, principal Republican institutions could be established. After a long struggle, the commoners gained a fair share of power from the patricians, members of the great Roman families. Starting in 275 B.C., Rome created its first provinces; although the new conquests amassed wealth, they stirred troubles that foreshadowed tensions to come.

DOMINATION OF THE GREAT FAMILIES

At the beginning of the Republic, Rome was a genteel society, one dominated by large families. The patricians monopolized power, and their fame, sustained by renowned ancestors, was perpetuated through a burial custom. When a family member died, death masks of his or her ancestors were paraded through the city. This "right to images," reserved for patricians, passed down traditional values and gave birth to the art of the portrait.

ROME AGAINST CARTHAGE

The Carthaginian general Hannibal used elephants of war during the second Punic War (218–201 B.C.) just as Pyrrhus, King of Epirus, had done against Rome (279–275 B.C.). The conflict that pitted Rome and Carthage against each other for more than a century played an important role in Rome's conquest of the Mediterranean. Hannibal spent a long time in Italy. But this nevertheless had disastrous consequences on the rural economy, triggering a serious social crisis.

ROADS AND CONQUESTS

The construction of the great Roman roads in Italy and in the Empire dates back to the first conquests. These wide, straight, paved roads served not only the military—to deploy troops and send messages— but also traders. The first road, marked out in 312 B.C. during the Samnite war, was the Appian Way. It went from Rome to its colonies in Campania. The Road to Ostia (background photograph) was above all used to transport goods. It completed the port's development.

509 B.C.
Proclamation of the Republic

451–449
Law of Twelve Tables
(first written code)

396
Etruscan city of Veii is seized

390
Gauls sack Rome

367
Licinian laws
(consulship opened to the plebs)

340–337
War against the Latins
Roman supremacy in Latium Samnite Wars

343–291
Samnite Wars
Roman supremacy in central Italy

CENSUS OF THE POPULATION *This relief, executed by a Greek sculptor commissioned by Gnaeus Domitius Ahenobarbus, the consul, depicts an important act in Roman political life: the registration and classification, according to wealth, of all Roman citizens. The census was taken every five years by the censor and allowed the number of free men in the Empire to be counted. It played an important political role, since it determined how both the popular assemblies and the army were to be organized.*

THE MAGISTRATES IN POWER *Passed down by the Etruscan monarchy, the objects and symbols of power were closely linked to the magistrates who possessed them. The supreme power of the consuls (imperium), both civil and military, was symbolized by the fasces—an ax projecting from a long bundle of rods tied together with a red strap. The power of the curule magistrates (consuls, praetors, curule aediles), who raised troops, declared the law, and led the senate sessions, was represented by the curule chair—a folding chair made of ivory and upholstered with leather or fabric.*

COINS AND PROPAGANDA *Silver coins made economic exchanges between Rome and the Greek world easier. Coins also allowed the Romans to disseminate images that illustrated their institutions at work. Voting scenes were a recurring theme. Here we see a citizen, identified by his toga, casting his vote by putting a pre-inscribed tablet into the urn. The secret ballot, which was introduced at the end of the Republic, took away the pressure of vote-catching.*

272
Rome gains control of Italy
Tarentum seized

264–241
First Punic War

218–201
Second Punic War
(Hannibal in Italy)
Scipio victory in Zama Roman supremacy in the western Mediterranean

149–146
Third Punic War
Carthage and Corinth destroyed

133–123 B.C.
The Gracchus Reforms

From the Gracchus crisis to Augustus 133 B.C.–14 A.D.

The land crisis and the Gracchus period, the slave revolts, and then the Social War all weakened the Republic. Figures rose to power who used the army to establish their authority. and this threatened institutions. The civil war calmed only when Octavian came to power. Under the title of Augustus, he inaugurated the principate and pacified the Empire.

CAESAR IN POWER *Julius Caesar left both a political and an architectural mark on Europe. In addition to restoring several buildings in the Republican forum, he is said to have built an entirely new forum in Rome (background photograph), a long and narrow rectangular esplanade surrounded by porticos. After defeating Pompey in 48 B.C., he erected a temple here to Venus Genetrix, mother of Aeneas and the divine ancestor of the Julian family.*

SULLA'S DICTATORSHIP *The route to power of the Roman general Sulla illustrates the flimsiness of Republican institutions during the first century B.C. Mirroring Marius's ascent to power, Sulla took control through the military prestige he gained through the Social War and the Mithridatic War. A champion of aristocratic privileges, Sulla ruled over a short-lived monarchy that disempowered the masses and outlawed thousands of political enemies without a trial. This short period of absolute power paved the way for Augustus's new regime.*

PEACE IN ROME *Having restored the Empire's institutions and consolidated its borders, Augustus could boast that he enriched the city of Rome with marble monuments. The Altar of Peace of Augustus was one of the constructions meant to establish the ideology of the regime. The principal values associated with Augustus's reign—peace and prosperity—were represented in allegorical fashion. Here, a procession of the chief priests of Rome, the senate, and family members gather around the emperor.*

| 133–123 B.C. The Gracchus Reforms | 107 Marius reforms the army | 91–88 B.C. Social War (Italian confederates against Rome) Citizenship granted to all who wanted it | 73–71 Spartacus's Gladitorial War | 60 The First Triumvirate: alliance with Pompey, Caesar, and Crassus | 58–50 War with Gauls |

GLADIATORS AND SLAVES *Originally a Campanian funeral ritual, gladiator combats were a very popular form of entertainment at the end of the Republic. The participants, mostly slaves or prisoners of war, were actually educated and trained in schools. Spartacus was among them; he and his collaborators used weapons—Thracian daggers, helmets with visors, and long lances designed to fight animals—to challenge the Roman legions between 73 and 71 B.C.*

THE GLORY OF AUGUSTUS
In 27 B.C., Augustus emerged as the "savior of all citizens." In this name, he received the civic crown from the Senate, a military honor accorded to soldiers who saved a fellow citizen in combat. The Emperor immediately began using the crown in his propaganda. In many portraits (coins, cameos, busts), the military distinction became a symbol of the monarchy, a symbol that was reminiscent of the band worn by the Hellenistic monarchs.

POLITICAL DUELS
The stance and gesture of this figure suggest the stormy debates that upset the tribunates and political assemblies at the end of the Republic. Tracing its roots back to Ancient Greece, the art of oratory did indeed develop in Rome in the first century B.C. It thrived on both the influence of Hellenism and the turbulent political climate. From this moment on, rhetoric, which was taught in Latin in schools, was the mainspring of education for the young Roman elite. Famous men, like Cicero, used oratorical skills to establish their political careers.

49–31 B.C. Civil Wars

48   In Pharsalus, Caesar defeats Pompey's troops

44   Caesar killed

31   Battle of Actium. Octavian defeats Antony and Cleopatra

27 B.C.
Octavian named Augustus

Inauguration of the imperial regime

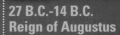

27 B.C.-14 B.C.
Reign of Augustus

15

Prosperity and crisis in the Empire 1–300 A.D.

During the first and second centuries, the Roman Empire, at its greatest extent, enjoyed a period of prosperity and relative stability. The emperors successfully ruled over the province that they had conquered. But by the third century, the Empire was in crisis. Socioeconomic problems and Barbarian upsurges along the borders gave rise to a rapid succession of emperors.

THE WORK OF AURELIUS *Several important events highlight the reign of Aurelius: his victories over Zenobia and Tetricus, the last emperor of Gaul, but especially the construction of a wall around Rome. Today, visitors can still admire large sections of it. He also issued a new coin that he hoped would improve the Empire's economy. Moreover, having developed a solar theology for which he was both a god and a disciple, the emperor had himself depicte on coins wearing a radiant crown.*

CULT OF MITHRA AND EASTERN CULTS *Originally from Iran, the cult of Mithra spread to the highly militarized regions in the Empire Divided into ranks, followers practiced the cult in underground sanctuaries. This representation shows the god slitting a bull's throat, its blood and semen to be used to populate the world. The cosmic elements—the moon and sun—point to the development of new religious hopes at the end of the second century, which ensured the success of Eastern religions.*

THE BARBARIAN THREAT *Images of Barbarians bowing down to the conquering mperor were widely used by monarchs to exalt heir magnanimous character. Marcus Aurelius s seen here receiving the conquered Barbarians fter attacking the Danube. At the end of his eign, however, the emperor was mostly concerned ith the people of Germania. The first Barbarian nvasions threatened Roman sovereignty and everely shook the Empire's confidence.*

–69 Julio-Claudian Family

43	Claudius conquers Britain
55	Tacitus, the historian, is born
64	Fire burns Rome

69–96 Favian Dynasty

70	Siege of Jerusalem by Titus
79	Mount Vesuvius erupts and Pompeii is destroyed

96–192 Antoninus Period

101–106	Trajan wars against the Dacians
122–132	Hadrian travels and builds the Villa Hadriana
162–165	War against Parthia. Seleucie destroyed

TRIUMPHAL ART AND PUBLIC MONUMENTS *Trajan's column, which celebrates Roman legion victories over the Dacians (the population of today's Romania), is decorated with reliefs. It was built in 133 A.D. in the middle of Trajan's forum, which also included two large libraries, a basilica, and a temple. Triumphal art—equestrian statues, triumphal arches, commemorative columns —developed during the Antoninus reigns and was meant to exalt the emperor's military triumphs. Rome was able to build many public monuments with the spoils it plundered during military campaigns.*

A PORTRAIT OF A FAMILY *This medallion was executed to spread the image of the Severus imperial family throughout the Empire. With his curly hair and philosopher's beard, Septimus Severus showed his desire to be associated with the Antoninus Dynasty. The presence of Julia Domna, the empress, points to the important role women played in the cortege of African emperors, as well as their close relationship to power. Young Geta's face was removed from the medallion when his brother, Caracalla, murdered him in 211 A.D.*

GUARDING THE BORDERS *(background photograph) The system that Hadrian established—the limes system for border fortification—greatly helped guarantee the stability and security of the Empire in the second century A.D. In the south of Scotland, the emperor had a stone wall built with several forts where troops could be permanently stationed to protect vulnerable points. Antoninus Pius added a second rampart to the wall, more to the north. The Germanian border, on the other hand, was protected by a wooden stockade that was some 350 miles long.*

The Late Empire 301–500 A.D.

Diocletian put the Roman world back on its feet, paving the way for a transformation in the fourth century. From that time forward, the Empire would be divided into two parts: the Eastern Empire and the Western Empire. After Constantine, Christianity became the official religion. In the fifth century, the Barbarian invasions intensified, up until Romulus Augustulus abdicated the throne in 476, putting an end to the Western Roman Empire.

JEWEL OF PALMYRA (background photograph) Incorporated into the province of Syria in 18 A.D., the oasis of Palmyra was successful in trade, permitting luxury items to be transported from India, China, and Arabia to the ports of Tyre and Sidon. It was crossed by a wide avenue lined with columns. In the third century, Odenathus, King of Palmyra, with the support of Emperor Gallienus, defended the eastern border against the Persians. At his death, his wife Zenobia created an independent kingdom, conquered by Aurelius in 272 A.D.

UNION OF TETRARCHS In 293 A.D., Diocletian divided the Empire into two parts—the Eastern and Western Empires—and chose caesars to act as junior emperors. This tetrarchy, a major reform of the Diocletian reign, was a success. The first tetrarchs—Diocletian, Maximian, Galerius, and Constantius I, represented here as two almost identical couples—illustrated the desire the four rulers had to unite. This porphyry sculpture is inset into the wall of Saint Mark's Cathedral in Venice.

CULTURAL PRESTIGE During late Antiquity, culture had great prestige. Beginning in the third century, the upper class, depicted as cultured, holding a scroll or dressed in a Greek cloak, believed that the study of literature and philosophy guaranteed them immortality. It was for this reason that the decurion Julius Longinus had the nine Muses, Apollo, and Minerva—gods associated with knowledge—sculpted on his headstone.

THE SPREAD OF CHRISTIANITY

Constantine is shown holding the sack of gold that would finance the construction of the massive Hagia Sophia in Constantinople. He played a personal role in the establishment and organization of Christianity, which became the official religion of the Empire in 313 A.D. The Christian doctrine spread throughout the schools of the great cultural capitals. The Council of Nicea, held in the imperial palace in 325 A.D., was the first in a long series of Episcopal synods. It reaffirmed the unity of the Church, which was threatened by constant theological debates.

THE SACRED ROLE OF THE EMPEROR

Only a few remains have been found from the Colossus of Constantine, which rose more than 30 feet tall. Seated, his raised right hand holding a scepter, the emperor looks like the god Jupiter. The disembodied form is such that only the eyes, with their deeply carved pupils, draw your attention. This exaggerated effect, which is partly due to the size of the statue, was also a turning point in sculpture, revealing an ideological evolution: From that time forward, the emperor was placed in a world beyond humans.

THE SPLENDOR OF THE COURT

This large silver plate was designed in 388 A.D. for the tenth anniversary of Theodosius's reign. It attests to the masterful technique of the silversmiths during the fourth century, and to the splendor of the Late Empire's imperial courts. By then the emperors had become sacred figures. Theodosius, enthroned amidst architectural perfection, is depicted with his two sons, Arcadius and Honorius. He returns his nomination tablets to a public official, who takes them with veiled hands. Germanic guards frame the scene.

History of Rome

BY MICHAEL GRANT

CHAPTER 1

Rome and Etruria

Rome and Italy

Italy's central position in the Mediterranean is a call to self-assertion, suggesting many promising opportunities. For instead of forming a barrier between the eastern and western reaches of the sea, the country serves as a link between them, open to maritime channels on either side. Moreover, the curiously elongated shape of the peninsula provides, next only to Greece, the longest coastline in Europe. Besides, Italy is significantly placed in relation to the continental lands to its north. It is far enough removed from them to escape many of their turmoils, yet near enough to gain a share of whatever cultural advances are in the making.

Three-quarters of Italy's territory consists of hills. They rise into the harshly ribbed vertebrae of the Apennines, which dominate the whole land, curving down from the northwestern seaboard to the eastern, Adriatic coast and then back again to Italy's toe. Yet there are also plains at the foot of this mountainous mass; they provide convenient inland corridors and enjoy a relatively temperate and humid climate, which in early times opened up possibilities of agriculture on a scale that no other Mediterranean country had.

The greatest of the plains is the Po Valley in the north between the Apennines and the Alps. However, that region, known to the Romans as Gaul this side of the Alps (Cisalpine Gaul), is part of the continental landmass rather than of the peninsula, once not even regarded as part of Italy at all. Yet in the south, too, even more fertile districts are to be found, especially along the west coast. On this shore there was above all the Campanian plain centered round the Gulf of Cumae (Bay of Naples) and to its north, the two hundred and thiry mile stretch of lowland Latium; and then, north of Latium, there was Etruria, separated from it by the Tiber, which, although smaller than the Po, is the largest river of peninsular Italy.

BRONZE HELMET *(second half of the 8th century B.C.) This helmet, graced by a crest and geometric designs, came from a tomb in Tarquinii. It covered a terra cotta urn that contained ashes and personal objects, and underscored its owner's involvement in war during his lifetime.*

PAINTING AND MYTHOLOGY *(left-hand page) This fresco from L. Caecilius Iucundus's house in Pompeii depicts young women playing Orestes and Iphigenia in Tauris. The Greek myth of Iphigenia, which is part of Euripides's tragedies, continued to thrive in Latin theater.*

Descending from the central massif, the Tiber becomes navigable in its lower reaches. And fifteen miles from the Mediterranean—far enough to provide warning of maritime raiders, but near enough to give it ready access to the sea—was the lowest of the river's feasible crossing points: at Rome. It was a crossing of vital importance, since it coincided with the most convenient longitudinal routes of Italy, a route which provided the main line of communications along the western flank of the country. Moreover, like London and Paris, the site commanded easy progress not only across the river, but along its course as well. Both upon its waters and by the road that lay beside it there was access to precious, rare salt-pans on the shore; and inland the continuation of the same road up the Tiber valley led into the central regions of the land.

Once the inhabitants of Rome became strong enough, they would be able to dominate these vital passages in all directions. However, people at an important junction are as likely to reap suffering as profit, and the men and women who came and lived here were open to aggression from all sides and needed all the protection they could get.

AVNORVM SATYRORVM ET SILENORVM DELECT

THE ROMANS, DESCENDANTS OF AENEAS

Concerned about justifying their conquests, the Romans of the 2nd century B.C. wrote their own history, inventing prestigious origins. Two centuries later, Virgil gave the legend its complete form in the *Aeneid*, a book commissioned by Augustus to legitimize his power; the emperor, the adopted son of Julius Caesar, appeared in it as the descendant of the goddess Venus. As the story goes, in 1183 B.C., after ten years of attacks, when the Greeks seized Troy, Aeneas (son of Venus), escaped from the carnage. Taking his son Iulus (also known as Ascanius), and his father, Anchises, he set out to found a new Troy. Despite the promises of the oracles, Aeneas was buffeted by storms. He finally landed in Africa, where a queen from Phoenicia, Dido, built a splendid city, Carthage. Fascinated by the stories of the hero, the unhappy woman was consumed with passion, and destiny united her with Aeneas in a cave. Alas, the gods forced the Trojan to abandon Dido, who then committed suicide. Aeneas set out for Italy, conquered native people, and married the daughter of King Latinus, in honor of whom he founded Lavinia. His son, founder of Alba Longa, gave birth to the clan of Julia and thus gave Augustus, the future emperor, a divine ancestry.

They got it from the cliffs on which they planted their settlements, for the river lay in a deep trough at this point, and the settlers came to live on the hills above its southern bank. These heights were between a hundred and three hundred feet above sea level—a series of flat-topped spurs projecting, more sharply than now, towards the Tiber, and safely raised above the floods to which its valley was exposed. Ravines divided the hills from one another and from the main plateau of the hinterland as well.

The site of Rome enjoyed a good water supply and was within easy reach of fertile soil. It had seen human occupation, at least at sporadic intervals, from a very early date. But in about 1600 B.C., men and women with unfamiliar customs made their first appearance in Italy. They buried the bodies of their dead, practiced a seminomadic pastoral economy, and made excellent bronze work and decorated pottery. These settlers lived on either side of the Apennines, to the north in the valley of the Po, and to the south in Etruria, which extended down as far as Rome's river the Tiber. Early in the last millennium B.C., new groups of migrants gradually moved to this location. These were the descendants of men and women who had probably been settled for some generations in the area later called Latium, which extended from the borders of Campania as far north as the Tiber.

These settlers spoke a primitive dialect related to Latin. They engraved bronze skillfully, but supplemented this talent by a growing familiarity with the use of iron. In contrast to their predominantly pastoral forerunners, they plowed the soil with light plows and did not bury but cremated their dead. They form one of the main streams of Iron Age history.

One of the nuclei of these Latin communities was the Alban Mount, thirteen miles southeast of Rome. The Alban Mount was a former volcano that had ceased to be active. However, its eruptions had guaranteed the future wealth of the area by covering the marshy clay plain for miles around with layers of new soil containing phosphates and potash that made the sodden clay especially fertile when drained.

By the early years of the first millennium, the Iron Age settlers moved into Rome. Groups of shepherds and farmers gradually moved across from the Alban region until they came to the Tiber and built their huts upon the Roman hills, which were particularly attractive because they provided communications with Etruria beyond the river. First of all, groups of these people settled on the level summit of the isolated and well-protected Palatine Hill, and in the marshy, moat-like valley of the Forum, which lay between the Palatine and the Quirinal, Esquiline, and Capitoline Hills. Next, in the ninth and eighth centuries B.C., more immigrants came and settled on the Quirinal; and then others established themselves on the Esquiline as well. The precipitous Capitoline and the Caelian, rising northwest and east of the Palatine respectively, also received inhabitants in an early period.

And these people not only dwelt on the hills and the Forum that lay between them, but also deposited the remains of their dead near their dwellings. Cremation and inhumation, the two types of interment characteristic of the two groups of Iron Age settlers, are both found. The cremators dug small, deep, circular pits, within which they placed large jars that had stone slats as lids. Inside the jars were urns in which the ashes of the dead person were laid. The inhumers buried the bodies in hollowed-out logs or rough stone sarcophaguses, which they laid in long trenches, sometimes lined with stones. Whether the practitioners of these two customs differed from one another in race we cannot say. But the two groups, whoever they were, gradually mixed and amalgamated both with each other and with whatever sparse populations they already found living on the hilltops when they arrived.

Rome, according to tradition, was founded in 753 B.C. But the date is mythical—too late for the first regular settlements, too early for the time of true urbanization. When we seek to reconstruct the early history and chronology of Rome, its myths and legends have to be distrusted. And yet those are the only literary material we possess for all these centuries before any reliable historical facts are available. The myths tell us what later generations of Romans believed about their country. But to find out what actually happened, we are compelled to have recourse to archaeological excavation.

THE SARCOPHAGUS OF THE SPOUSES *(ca. 520 B.C.). Preserved in the Etruscan Museum of the Giulia villa in Rome, this masterpiece made of terra cotta from Caere is in fact a funerary casket. The way in which the couple on top is rendered—long faces, the man's beard, almond eyes, the woman's braided hair and cap— shows the influence eastern art had on the Etruscan aristocracy of 6th century B.C.*

The Etruscan city-states

In the years around 700–675 B.C.—at a time when Asia Minor and the lands beyond it were suffering from especially troubled conditions—a succession of small bands of immigrants from some unidentified eastern territory, following perhaps in the wake of reconnaissances by earlier traders, arrived upon the shores of Etruria. Running their ships aground on the flat, gray beaches, they seized the hill spurs nearby, fortified them with wooden palisades, and established upon them in due course the powerful city-states that we know as Etruscan. They did so with the collaboration, willing or forced, of the peoples whom they found already in residence there; for, despite the sudden upsurge suggestive of a new cultural element, there is also a strong measure of archaeological continuity on the sites.

The Etruscans owed to their eastern forebears, as well as to the Greeks when they subsequently got to know them, a marked talent for urbanization, and this was encouraged by the compulsion, imposed by Italy's geography, to cluster together on the relatively few sites that were eligible and attractive. And so the Etruscans created their cities, first near the coast, and then on inland sites towards the middle course of the Tiber. Traditionally there were twelve such communities in Etruria. Each of these cities seems to have been independent of all the rest. Indeed, they were not only independent but highly individual and distinguished from each other by sharp political, social, and cultural differences. Rome is likely to have been most greatly influenced by the southern communities, which lay so close to the Tiber. These south Etruscan cities, in close proximity to the coast, were livelier and more cosmopolitan, more open and receptive to Greek and other foreign contacts than their north Etruscan counterparts. They supplied the formative stimulus and inspiration that transformed Rome from a huddle of hut villages into a city.

THE SHE-WOLF SUCKLING ROMULUS AND REMUS
This mosaic, dating from the beginning of the 4th century, is evidence of the constancy of the myth of the founding of Rome in art of late Antiquity.

Earliest Rome

By the early seventh century B.C., the communities on the several spurs of the Palatine, Esquiline, and Caelian had joined together. The unit they now formed was the *Septimontium*, or Seven Hills (different from, and smaller than, the later Seven Hills of Rome). Then, perhaps in 625–620, the low-lying area later known as the Forum was systematically drained, and Rome's Great Sewer, the *Cloaca Maxima*, was dug through it. Thus the Forum was able to start its long career as a meeting place and market for the unified Roman hills. Within another quarter of a century, the momentum quickened still further. The Forum, and the Sacred Way that connected it with the other quarters of the town, received their first permanent pave-

24

CLOACA MAXIMA
Photographed at the spot where it opens into the Tiber, this large sewer, draining the valleys between the hills of Rome, allowed for the construction of the first forum. Built by the Etruscans, it was renovated under Augustus. Its size impressed even those in its own day. Pliny the Elder noted that one could "fit a chariot overflowing with hay through its galleries."

ments, and the *Forum Boarium* (cattle market) near the river was regularly laid out.

At about the same time, the Quirinal and Viminal Hills joined the growing community. This new and larger Rome of the Four Regions, as it was called, was a completely unified entity and was on the way to becoming an Etruscan town.

Etruscan Rome

What interested the Etruscans about Rome, in the first place, was not its own attractions but its position on the way south to the Campanian plain, incredibly favored by nature. Traversed by two rivers and fanned by moist winds, this territory of spongy volcanic earth enjoyed relatively mild and short winters. Moreover, its soil was capable of producing in some districts as many as three grain crops every year, in addition to a crop of vegetables as well.

AVNORVM SATYKORVM ET SILENORVM DELECT

THE LEGENDARY FOUNDING OF ROME

According to Livy, the historian, a coup ended the reign of Aeneas's descendants: Amulius deposed his brother Numitor and killed his sons, and then forced celibacy on his daughter Rhea Silvia, making her a vestal virgin. Seduced by Mars, she bore twins and was condemned to die buried alive. Meanwhile, Romulus and Remus were thrown into the Tiber in a trough. A swollen river carried them, a she-wolf suckled them, and a herdsman took them in. At 18, discovering their origins, the twins drove out the usurper and decided to found a city. But a king had to be chosen: the observation of birds in flight designated Romulus.

Alas, Remus jumped over the line that his brother had drawn for the placement of the city walls. Furious, Romulus killed him and became the king of Rome. The city grew, but soon lacked women. Romulus therefore invited the neighboring Sabines to a festival and abducted their females. A war ensued, but the Sabine women intervened and brought about peace; the two enemy populations united.

These legends explain the rites that were a prelude to the founding of Roman cities (consultation of the gods, bloody sacrifice, marking of a surrounding wall) and the fusion of populations that made up early Rome.

But the Greeks reached Campania before the Etruscans, for in the eighth century B.C., Greek colonists chose Cumae, on the coast just northwest of the gulf now known as the Bay of Naples, for their settlement on Italy's mainland. Cumae became a great center for the sale of grain and the diffusion of Greek influence over most of south Italy and Sicily. But before 600, travelers, or armies, from certain Etruscan city-states made their way into Campania to found the leading city of the fertile lowlands, Capua, seventeen miles north of Neapolis (Naples). From Capua the Etruscans extended their domination over the greater part of the Campanian plain.

They rapidly found it desirable both to create a land route to these new southern dependencies and to possess harbors on the way to them as well. That brought them into Latium, and during the seventh century many leading Latin towns became subject to Etruscan city-states. But it was impossible for the Etruscans to hold Latium without also taking Rome, which lay between Latium and themselves. Its river crossing was essential for their access to the Latin plain. There was also the added attraction of Rome's proximity to the salt-pans at the mouth of the Tiber, since they could not obtain salt from any other source.

These, then, were the reasons Rome came under Etruscan influence in the last quarter of the seventh century B.C. Nor was it long before influence took the form of overt political control, and Rome came under the rule of an Etruscan monarch.

Early Roman religion

What sort of place did the monarch find? Above all, a religious community. The Romans had from the earliest period cherished a powerful, pervasive religion, based on mutual trustfulness (*fides*) between the gods on the one hand and men and women on the other. The trust accorded by the gods, and their benevolence—what was called the peace of the gods (*pax deorum*), a balance of nature in which divine powers and human beings worked in harmony—could be secured by meticulous ritual and not so much by good moral behavior. Nevertheless, this idea of the divine peace indirectly exercised a moral influence, since the respect which it induced for vows made to the gods was extended to vows made to other human beings as well.

Yet the individual human being was not what mattered in the religion of the Romans, for they saw this as a group affair, not a matter for individuals. And indeed, the same applied to the whole of Roman life, in which individuality was submerged in family, clan, and state. The head of the family (*pater familias*), any male citizen who had no living ancestor in the main line, was absolute; there is nothing, perhaps, in any other culture quite as extreme as this long-lasting patriarchal assertion. In the home, his word was literally law—and so long as he remained alive his sons never came of age.

Thus he controlled, among much else, the domestic cult, which played a mighty part in daily life. The household deities were worshipped every day, and no important family event could take place without securing divine approval. Whether domestic or communal worship came earliest is disputed, but the latter was a magnified version of the former. Vesta, worshipped by her Vestal Virgins beside the Forum, in her round straw hut which later became a temple, was the hearth-goddess of the Roman state. But she was equally prominent in family cult as well, symbolizing the solidarity of the home as well as the nation.

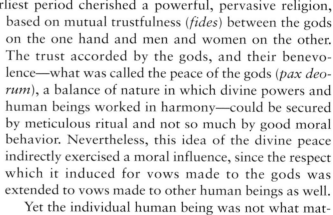

TEMPLE OF TRIUMPHANT HERCULES *(110 B.C.) This circular temple, located at the site of the Forum Boarium, is the oldest marble structure in Rome. Built by a rich Roman, it was dedicated to the god who protected oil merchants. Its design, and the provenance of the marble used for the twenty columns that surround the cella, point to a Hellenistic influence.*

26

ROME MAPPED
Opposite, Etruria and Latium during the seventh century B.C.; above, the site of Rome with the seven hills and the first Etruscan settlements.

ANCESTOR STATUETTE
(tomb of Five-Sieges, Caere, ca. 600 B.C.) Made for a large aristocratic family, this terra cotta statuette is typical of the period of Etruscan art that was influenced by the East.

In the earliest times, the Romans lacked the Greek taste for seeing their deities in personalized form, so that the temple of Vesta contained no image at all. Yet this concept gradually became modified from a very ancient date, when Greek ideas first began to come in. Vesta, even though she lacked a statue, was the same, etymologically and by assimilation, as the Greek Hestia. And Mars, the first god recognized by the Romans as chief of all the divinities, was identified with the Greek Ares.

The structure of the earliest Roman state

That Rome had originally been ruled by kings was unanimously asserted by its historians. Before Etruscan rule began, there had already been four non-Etruscan monarchs. Most or all of these are either of dubious historicity or are downright fictitious—notably the alleged city founder Romulus, which just means "the man of Rome." Yet the memory that Rome had been a monarchy was authentic.

CAVALRYMEN FRESCO
(ca. 520–490 B.C.)
The tomb of the Baron in Tarquinii contained one of the jewels of Etruscan painting. Reminiscent of Greek vases with red figures, its ochre silhouettes stand out against a light background, dotted with shrubs. The elongated lines and outlined shadows beneath flat areas of contrasting color lend a modern feeling to this ancient work of art.

FUNERARY URN FROM MONTESCUDAIO
(630–625 B.C.)
Atop this ancient urn, the deceased is shown feasting, served by a slave.

The Roman state was divided into three units, known as tribes (*tribus*). They may instead have been groups of clans without any clear ethnic differentiation. In any case, the threefold division is likely to have been made in the first place in order to facilitate military and financial censuses of the people.

These tribes may reasonably be ascribed to the earlier times of Etruscan influence, perhaps towards the end of the seventh century B.C. The three tribes were subdivided into ten *curiae,* or wards (from *co-viria,* "gathering of men"), each comprising a number of clans or groups of families. It was upon these *curiae,* and the tribes into which they were grouped, that the earliest Senate was based. These senators were selected by the kings from the *patres familias*—the heads of the clans and of their component families. The curial system also seems to have been the basis of Rome's most primitive military organization, an army or legion (*legio*) of three thousand infantry and three hundred cavalry. The names of the three tribes are Etruscan and ought to be synchronized with the fifth name on Rome's traditional king list, for he was Etruscan. He represents the Etruscan takeover of Rome, which is a historical fact. His name was said to be Tarquinius Priscus (i.e., the Elder, in contrast with his son Tarquinius Superbus, who became king later).

The traditional dates of Priscus's reign are 616–579 B.C., and here tradition harmonizes for the first time with the findings of archaeology, which ascribe the decisive stages of Rome's urbanization to the last quarter of the seventh century.
It was in this Etruscan period that the rulers of Rome built a citadel on the precipitous, defensible Capitoline Hill, while their followers settled between the Capitoline and Palatine in "Etruscan Street," the Vicus Tuscus.

How Etruscan did Rome become? As inscriptions show, there was a Latin-speaking population under an Etruscan-speaking ruling class. Nevertheless, there was deep fusion between the two ethnic and linguistic groups, and Rome did, at this time, turn into a more or less homogeneous Etruscanized city—scarcely surprising, since it was only due to the Etruscans that Rome had become a city at all.

"Servius Tullius"

Midway in the Tarquinian regime, legend inserted the mysterious King Servius Tullius, who was credited with a thorough overhaul of the institutions of the Roman state. The three original tribes of Rome were replaced by twenty-one new ones—four in the city and seventeen in Rome's rural appendages. These new tribes represented local, geographical divisions, and the urban tribes correspond with the Four Regions of Rome. They were instituted for census reasons and were basic units for raising levies and collecting taxes.

Moreover, under the same king, or at least at the same period, a completely new military system was inaugurated, according to which the size of the army was doubled to six thousand based on sixty "centuries" of one hundred men each. This change had important effects both of a political and military nature. On the political side, it meant that the Assembly of *curiae* was replaced by a new Assembly of Centuries, the *Comitia Centuriata*. This made for greater efficiency since the curial system, having been based on wards, had proved unadaptable to an expanding city; for example, it cannot have worked well when citizens moved. The *Comitia Centuriata* was a useful organ of the monarch's

LEGENDARY FIGURES

The reign of the first successors of Romulus (Numa Pompilius, Tullus Hostilius, and Ancus Martius) is essentially legendary. Roman historians had to fill in the period between the founding of Rome (753 B.C.) and the supposed arrival of the Etruscan rulers, some time during the 7th century. It was an opportunity to include uncommon figures, to which the main Roman institutions were linked and who illustrated major traditional virtues.

Numa Pompilius, Romulus's successor, gave the Romans their religious foundations. Pretending to receive advice from the nymph Egeria, he instituted the colleges of priests, established holidays and the calendar, and built temples. He turned his people into a model of scruples towards the gods.

Under the reign of Tullus Hostilius, the famous battle between the Horatii and the Curiatii took place. Of the Horatii, chosen by Rome, only one survived; but, in simulating escape, he fought one Alban champion after the other and was victorious.

So it was that Rome's rival was destroyed. Its inhabitants then settled on the Caelian Hill, significantly expanding Rome's population. This legendary episode illustrates the importance of war and warrior virtues.

authority and might have had some say in state decisions, but it still was not a particularly democratic institution. There was no question of "one man, one vote." Voting was not by heads but by groups, and the procedure was so organized that the richer groups were predominant. The new army on which the centurial Assembly was based consisted of property owners graded according to wealth. The wealthy or relatively wealthy filled more than half of the total number of centuries of which the Assembly was constituted.

This manning of the new army by property-owners, men rich enough to provide their own arms and armor, directly echoes changes in military organization that had been occurring in Greece and Etruria. From about 675, Greek military history had shown a slow and piecemeal adoption of a round shield, defensive metal body-armor, and a thrusting spear, with the tactical corollary that these heavily armed soldiers ("hoplites," from *hopla*, "arms") fought in a closely knit line or phalanx. They were all men who possessed sufficient property of their own to equip themselves with the full array of this personal armor. The hoplite shield began to appear in Etruria too, and during the sixth century, hoplite arms came into standard use among the Etruscans.

And so this military innovation arrived at Rome as well, and the men who provided Rome with its greatly enlarged reservoir of recruits were to achieve astonishing military triumphs. Each spring, before setting out to war, they sat and deliberated in the *Comitia Centuriata* and endowed it with a military *esprit de corps*; it was the Roman Army in Assembly, orderly obedience its second nature.

This was a middle-class army, containing the men whom the prosperity of Etruscan Rome had encouraged to flourish. But the eighteen centuries of cavalry (*equites*, "knights"), which formed the richest group, no doubt consisted chiefly of nobles.

Servius encircled at least part of his city of the Four Regions with a rampart. The earthwork was rather more than twenty-five feet high, with a ditch in front. It was erected on the vulnerable open plateau on the north side of the town, from the Quirinal along the brow of the Viminal towards the northern end of the Esquiline, so as to block the heads of the valleys leading from the interior of Latium to Rome.

Servius seems to have been an expansionist in the Etruscan tradition, and it may well have been in his time that Rome emerged as the leading power of northwestern Latium. The dominant feature of this land, the Alban Mount (Monte Cavo), had become a religious sanctuary for the Latin communities around. It was devoted to the sky-divinity Jupiter—*Diou-pater*, "the bright one."

While extending their rule in this northwesterly direction, the Romans also expanded the same distance southwestward as far as the coast and established the port of Ostia at the mouth of the Tiber in order to exploit the adjoining salt-beds.

Rome's first wooden bridge, the *Pons Sublicius* replacing the island ford, may well belong to the same time as Ostia. For when the salt had been collected at the river-mouth, it was hard work to convey it to the city by river, which meant taking it upstream. The Romans needed the bridge to move the salt across the Tiber, to its Etruscan purchasers and others beyond.

Servius Tullius again had the outside world in mind when he added an appendage to Rome of the Four Regions. This he did by building an important temple on the Aventine Hill, which lay just beyond the city's boundaries to the south. It was a shrine of Diana—"the bright one" like Jupiter, and at the same time a goddess of forests who helped women by giving them children.

The Aventine shrine was the possessor of a statue of the many-breasted type that was peculiarly characteristic of the ancient Greek city of Ephesus. Its introduction to Rome represented a decisive step towards the personal, anthropomorphic interpretation of gods and goddesses.

But another, even grander, new Roman shrine was more Etruscan than Greek—the temple of Jupiter the Best and Greatest, and of Juno and Minerva, on the Capi-

WARRIOR FROM CAPESTRANO *(6th century B.C.) This limestone statue (about 8.5 feet high), was found close to Picenum, on the Adriatic coast.*

toline Hill, beside the citadel where the Etruscan kings resided. Jupiter the sky-god was called Best and Greatest because, under Etruscan influence, he now succeeded Mars as the principal god of the Romans. Jupiter, Juno, and Minerva formed a triad, or trinity. The names were Italian, but the linkage of the three is Etruscan.

The most significant feature of the Capitoline temple was its extraordinary size and grandeur. It had a deep, Etruscan porch of three rows of six columns and a row of free-standing columns down each side. It measured one hundred and eighty feet in width and over two hundred feet in length, as its sixteen-foot-high stone platform, so characteristic of Italian as opposed to Greek temples, reveals. Much of this still survives, though little more of the original structure is now to be seen. These huge dimensions made it the largest temple of its time in the entire Etruscan sphere. And although in the Etruscan fashion the superstructure was only made of wood, the building was of marvelous splendor.

The fall of the monarchy

Almost immediately after the dedication of this glittering temple, the Etruscan monarchy of Rome fell from power. In other parts of Italy too, including Etruria, monarchies were losing their grip and collapsing in these last years of the sixth century B.C. Moreover, it was a period when the Etruscan city-states in Latium and Campania were generally in retreat, hard-pressed by their enemies the Greeks. There was a general collapse of Etruscan rule over wide areas of Latium. Latins and hill-tribesmen profited from the Etruscans' troubles to move in across their lines of communications.

Such then was the fall of Rome's Etruscan rulers. However, despite the equal misfortunes of their compatriots in Latium and Campania, they did not accept their ejection by the Romans as final. Lars Porsenna of the inland Etruscan city-state of Clusium (Chiusi), marched eighty miles southward upon Rome and attacked it in a sudden raid. Moreover, contrary to the patriotic legend enshrined in Thomas Macaulay's *Lay of Horatius*, defender of the Sublician Bridge, it appears that Lars Porsenna actually captured the city for a time. Nevertheless, no really serious attempt was made by any of the Etruscan states to recover Rome or Latium, or even the greater lost prize of Campania beyond. Yet their lack of perseverance in the south did not by any means signify that this remarkable people was exhausted. For the reason, strangely enough, why they were willing to turn away from Campania and Latium was that certain of their city-states were, at this very period, launching a massive fresh drive in the opposite direction, north of the Apennines in the region that the Romans later called Cisalpine Gaul. The main center of this northern sphere of influence was Felsina (Bologna).

This new, northern enterprise of the Etruscans, though it survived long enough to bring writing and civilization to continental Europe, did not last for more than a hundred years. But, for the time being, it increasingly absorbed their energy and attention, and Rome found itself able to enjoy a respite.

TERRA COTTA ANTEFIXES *(Caere, 5th century B.C.) These decorative terra cotta elements, meant to adorn the ends of each row of tiles on sloping roofs, earned fame for the Etruscan studios. The first temple of Rome, dedicated to the Capitoline triad, was known for this kind of décor.*

CHAPTER 2

The unification of Italy

Rome's hostile neighbors

The worst of the grim difficulties that descended upon the Romans after the fall of the Tarquins still remain to be described. For although the Etruscan menace declined, the city continued to suffer from other enemies eager to take advantage of its diminished position. In consequence, the greater part of the two centuries that now followed witnessed constant, uphill fights, sometimes fights upon which the very survival of Rome depended.

In the first place, its immediate neighbors, the Latins, immediately became recalcitrant. The town of Lavinium, near the sea sixteen miles from Rome, threw off its allegiance to the Romans and asserted its claims as common sanctuary of a group of Latin coastal towns. This union, or league, conflicted with Roman interests, and in 496 B.C a memorable battle was fought beside the volcanic depression of Lake Regillus. Regillus belonged to the territory of Tusculum (near Frascati), which took the military lead in resisting the Romans. However, in the engagement that followed, Rome's heavily armed infantry, supported by its mounted knights (*equites*), won a decisive victory. As a result, the Romans incorporated in their own religion two deities who had been worshipped in Tusculum—a borrowing characteristic of their religious practice, intended to transfer and attract to themselves the power of the divinities of defeated states. The twin gods thus acquired after Regillus were Castor and Pollux—horsemen who became the patrons of the cavalry, or knights, of Rome.

Soon afterwards the Romans made a treaty with the Latin towns. This harmony with the Latins was needed since the menace from the Apennines, to Latins and Romans alike, was severe. Their remote valleys and high plateaus fostered isolated shepherd communities, speaking Oscan. These pastoral peoples, living tough lives wholly lacking in Mediterranean amenities, greatly coveted Latium's access to the sea and superior fertility and winter pasture-land. And so, for a century and more after the downfall of the Tarquins, they attacked the Latins and Romans and engaged in many fluctuating seesaw struggles for the critical mountain passes.

The tribes which led these persistent onslaughts were the Volsci and Aequi. The chief interest of these petty, repetitive, and for many years inconclusive wars against the Volsci and Aequi lay in the invention by the Latin League in the 490s of federal Latin colonies. These were not whole territories like Britain's "colonies" in North America and elsewhere, but were towns with tracts of cultivated land around them—settlements of farmer-soldiers, to whom newly acquired or recovered lands were allotted. These colonies were intended to provide potential Latin bases against external enemies and to influence local life in favor of pacific agriculturalism. These were Latin and not Roman foundations, and the Roman citizens among their set-

THE ABDUCTION OF SABINE WOMEN
As depicted on the last coin of the Republican period, a Sabine woman intervenes between fighters. This legendary episode symbolizes the first attempt by Romans to annex neighboring territories.

tlers had to become citizens of the Latin League instead. It was not until a good deal later that the Romans borrowed for themselves this fruitful idea, which was to play such an immense part in their future development of Italy.

The enemies against whom the Latins and Romans joined forces also included the Oscan-speaking Sabines, who lived in independent Apennine hilltop villages north of Rome. They had long coveted the superior resources of the plain of Latium. A few years after the start of the Roman Republic, one of the leaders of the Sabines, Attus Clausus, was so eager for a share of Rome's amenities that he moved his whole clan of four thousand relatives and supporters to Roman territory, where he settled them and became the founder of Rome's great Claudian clan (ca. 505 B.C.). However, Roman hopes that by admitting these immigrants they had scotched the menace of the Sabines were disappointed, because their raids continued almost without intermission.

Then, in 449 B.C., Rome defeated the Sabines severely. Thereafter, during the next one hundred fifty years, hostilities with the Sabines diminished and vanished, and the amalgamation of the two peoples was gradually accomplished, to a large extent because of the mutual advantage of transferring sheep between summer (Sabine) and winter (Latin) pasturage.

It had been a major piece of good fortune to Latium and Rome (helped on by able diplomacy) that these hostile Volscian, Aequian, and Sabine neighbors were too poorly organized ever to unite effectively against them. And this was all the luckier because the gravest of all the threats to Rome's existence came at the very same time from another and all too familiar source—Etruria, just across the Tiber.

BRONZE LID HANDLE
This intriguing handle, portraying a wounded soldier carried by fellow fighters, adorned the lid of a bronze box found in Praeneste.

Victory over Veii

One Etruscan city-state, Veii, was intolerably close to Rome, only twelve miles away. This meant that neither could ever feel safe from the other. Veii was powerful and its geographical position extremely strong, for it was situated on a steep, sheer plateau and surrounded on three sides by a moat of running water. Originally, like Rome, a group of hut villages which amalgamated into a single Iron Age settlement, Veii had become by 600 B.C. not a symbiotic Etruscan-Italian community, such as Rome, but a purely Etruscan city, and a city of wealth and culture. Given such extreme proximity, competing demands for markets and land and coastal salt were bound to lead to serious clashes.

In the later 480s, the recently established Roman Republic had been mainly controlled by the clan of the Fabii. They were connected with Etruria and owned land towards Veii; in consequence they were the defenders of the Etruscan frontier,

THE NECROPOLIS OF CAERE
(*cemetery of Banditaccia,*
7th–6th century B.C.)
Large circular monuments, cut
into the rock and topped by
dome-shaped mounds, housed
the tombs of members of a
single family. Evidence of the
great wealth of aristocratic
families, they attest to the
importance of funeral rituals
in Etruscan civilization.

which they guarded with a private army. So it was now against the threat from Veii that the Fabii threw this semifeudal force into the field. At first the hostilities amounted to little more than cattle-raids, but by setting up a block house near the Cremera, to command the stream and adjoining roads, the Fabian clan transformed this minor skirmishing into open warfare. But in the disastrous battle of the Cremera which ensued (ca. 476–475), three hundred members and dependents of the Fabii perished, and the block house was destroyed by the enemy. The whole west side of the Tiber was now in the hands of the Veians.

But after the Etruscans' crushing defeat by the Greeks in 474, Veii made a truce with its Roman neighbors across the river. Then, after the middle of the century, the balance of power shifted in Rome's favor, and it began to prepare for a final showdown. One of the principal bones of contention was the town of Fidenae (Castel Giubileo) on the south bank of the Tiber. This place was the first station on the salt road (*Via Salaria*), and was a highly strategic post.

In about 425 B.C. the Romans occupied Fidenae. This meant full-scale war— probably the most fateful of all the wars they ever fought, since their very existence

34

depended on the outcome. It was they who took the initiative, and they placed Veii under siege. The fighting, conducted with unprecedentedly large forces, seems to have gone on intermittently for at least six or seven years. In the end, the Romans succeeded in advancing on the northward side of the walls and occupying the only neck of territory that offered level access to the city. This piece of land contained one of the agricultural drainage tunnels that irrigated the whole of this territory; coming in from the open country, it passed under the walls and thus entered into Veii itself. This tunnel, then, the Romans cleared, using it to move a small body of men into the middle of the city, which in this way fell into their hands.

The Romans severely damaged the captured stronghold, razing its defenses and turning out many or all of its inhabitants. This elimination of a city-state's independent existence was a sinister innovation in Rome's military history, and a sign of the critical gravity of the war. In keeping with the solemnity of their victory, the Romans, as on other occasions, took over the defeated enemy's patron deity as their own, establishing her cult on the Aventine Hill just outside the walls of their own city. She was Juno, who was already worshipped as an associate of Jupiter on the Roman Capitol but at Veii enjoyed an independent and magnificent cult. From now onwards she would no longer watch over Veii but over Rome.

The downfall of this first great Etruscan city to succumb to the Romans was a turning point, for not only did it remove an enormous, hampering obstacle to their progress, it almost doubled the size of their territory as well.

The Gallic invasion and its aftermath

However, a formidable setback was on the way, at the hands of the Celtic Gauls. In the seventh and eighth centuries, the Celtic-speaking peoples had moved out of central Europe; then, during the fifth century, they gradually crossed the Alps and expelled the Etruscan settlers from most of northern Italy, which was henceforward known as "Gaul this side of the Alps," or Cisalpine Gaul. Some of the Celts who spread through Europe lived peacefully and even luxuriously, and they developed a lively art, based principally on the free use of contemporary Greek and Etruscan models but also echoing Eastern influences, notably from Scythia (south Russia). But the Gauls who swarmed into the valley of the Po were warlike and had developed a frightening, if somewhat barbaric, military organization, including cavalry with iron horseshoes—an innovation in ancient warfare—and infantry carrying finely tempered slashing broadswords.

In about 387–386 B.C., under their king Brennus, thirty thousand of these immigrants drove southward from the Po valley into the Italian peninsula and moved rapidly down against Rome itself. Only eleven miles from the city, beside the Tiber's little tributary the Allia, they were confronted by an army of ten to fifteen thousand Romans. It was the largest force Rome had ever put into the field. However, in the battle that followed, the Roman phalanx of heavily armed soldiers was rushed by the much faster cavalry and infantry of the Gauls and outreached by their swords. The Roman army was routed, and most of its soldiers plunged into the nearby stream and were drowned.

Brennus and his men marched to the city, which they proceeded to overrun, setting its buildings on fire. Rome had fallen to its first Barbarian conquerors, something that was not to happen again for eight hundred years. The Romans never for-

THE GEESE OF
THE CAPITOL
This frieze fragment, which decorated the Ostia forum basilica, recalls the famous feat of the geese devoted to Juno. During the invasion of Gaul in 390 B.C., these precious fowl warned the Romans of the enemy's approach, saving the Capitol.

AVNORVM SAIYKORVM ETSILENORVM DELECI AVNORVM SAIYX

BEING A CITIZEN

As opposed to slaves and migrants (foreigners), a free man, the son of a citizen or emancipated slave, paid a direct tax up until 167 B.C., and had military obligations between age 17 and 60. He also, however, had civil and political rights: sacrificing and participating in public worship; owning and trading goods; forming a legal union; bringing legal action; and being a juror on call by the people for a criminal case. A citizen could also be elected magistrate and vote in assemblies, or *comitia*. The *Comitia Centuriata*, in which the population was divided into 193 centuries according to wealth, elected the high magistrates. The *Comitia Tributa*, in which the population was split into 35 tribes according to place of residence, elected the interior magistrates and voted on laws. The list of citizens was reviewed every five years during the census. Upon the declaration of the father of the family, the censors noted new citizens and evaluated their wealth and morality. On this occasion, a citizen could emancipate a slave, who, having become a citizen, took on the name of his owner. A citizen was identified by three names —first name, last name, nickname (Caius Julius Caesar); he could also wear a toga.

At first limited to inhabitants of Rome, citizenship was extended to others during the conquest. The residents of the closest regions immediately obtained citizenship. The most distant cities or more resistant ones acquired only partial citizenship, without political rights *(sine suffragio)*. In 49 B.C., at the end of the War of the Allies, all free men of Italy became Roman citizens. The Empire established citizenship *(civitas)* to the inhabitants of certain province cities. In 212 A.D., citizenship was extended to all free men residing in the Roman world, by the Edict of Caracalla.

got this horrifying and humiliating event. Yet the Gauls were soon bought off and departed, because they had received news that their own lands in the north were threatened by external foes. And henceforward, the Gallic peoples lacked the stability to offer a permanent threat.

In this crisis, the Romans owed a debt to their surviving Etruscan neighbor, the city-state of Caere. It was situated twenty miles from Rome, very close to the sea, where it possessed three little ports. The Caeritans had helped Rome, not only by giving refuge to the sacred objects from its temples but also by exerting military pressure to hasten Brennus's departure. They were glad to help the Romans, because Greek threats and raids that menaced their own seacoast meant that they needed Roman assistance in their turn.

Responding to this friendly attitude, Rome granted Caere a novel, privileged status (ca. 386 B.C.). This *hospitium publicum*, as it was called, entitled its people to come to Rome on terms of equality with Rome's own citizens in matters of private jurisdiction, as Romans would likewise at Caere. This proved a historic formula, because Rome later extended it, with adaptations, to many other cities.

After the onslaught of the Gauls, the Romans no longer considered their city sufficiently protected by the old earth rampart of Servius Tullius. So in 378 B.C., they erected a massive new wall, one of the great defensive works of the age; the large portions that can still be seen today bear the erroneous name of the "Wall of Servius Tullius." It was made of stone from recently captured Veii.

More than twelve feet thick and twenty-four feet high, the new wall enclosed a larger area than the previous rampart, including the historic Seven Hills of Rome: the Palatine and Caelian, and the adjacent and independently fortified Capitol; the whole of the Esquiline, Quirinal, and Viminal to the north; and the newly included Aventine to the south, together with the adjacent Circus Maximus, where chariot races were held. This fourth-century wall encompassed an area of over one thousand acres. This meant that the new Rome possessed by far the largest perimeter of any city in Italy, more than twice the size of recently demolished Veii and more than four times the dimensions of Caere.

The Romans in Latium and Campania

But the Romans' major problem was now with their Latin confederates. Between these ostensibly equal partners, the pendulum had already begun to swing in the direction of the Romans, and the sentiments of the cities of the Latin confederacy towards Rome were deteriorating. Several of the largest Latin towns now began to prefer independence to their Roman alliance. Thus in 381 B.C., the citizens of Tusculum, although wholly surrounded by Roman territory, seemed on the verge of hostile action. But Rome successfully wooed them with an offer of incorporation into its own state, and full Roman citizenship. This was a fruitful new idea for the future—a Latin city had been transformed into a Roman community, while nevertheless retaining its own city organization and self-government. The Tusculan nobles adapted themselves so enthusiastically to the new order that they henceforward supplied Rome with numerous consuls—a greater number, over the course of the years, than any other single city.

The Romans also took a decisive step by extending their sphere of influence into Campania. In about 343 B.C., the members of a league of Campanian cities, threatened by invasions from Samnium, took the fateful step of appealing to the Romans. Thereupon Rome decided to make its entrance into this large, rich area and responded to the Campanian appeal, an event which set up a whole series of chain-reactions affecting much larger areas.

At first, however, things did not go smoothly for the Romans, since their army mutinied at having to fight so far afield (342 B.C.). Moreover, the Latins had interpreted the Roman intervention in Campania as a menacing attempt to encircle them, and, when the operation seemed to be failing, they felt encouraged to ask the Roman government for a full restoration of their own previous parity and equality. These proposals were sharply rejected, and war between Rome and the Latins soon followed.

It was one of the bitterest wars the Romans ever had to fight—and the first in which they can be seen to have employed a well-planned, long-term strategy. This eventually brought catastrophe to the Latins and their Campanian allies, whose cavalry, fighting poorly, suffered a heavy defeat at Trifanum. The Campanians made a separate peace with Rome, and the Latin cities too were obliged to submit.

When the fighting had ended, the Latin League was broken up (338 B.C.). The day of the Latins was done, except as a component of Roman power.

But Rome now showed a gift for conciliatory organization that no important states of the ancient world, including those of the Greeks, had ever displayed before. The Romans dealt with the defeated Latins not in a spirit of vindictiveness, but with cool common sense; not by imposing any overall, bureaucratic solution, but by making piecemeal arrangements with each individual city, as the facts of every separate case seemed to require.

In the first place, Aricia and three other places near Rome were granted full Roman citizenship like Tusculum nearly half a century earlier; Roman territory was thus expanded to forty-five hundred square miles, with a population of at least a million. Secondly, Tibur and Praeneste, although deprived of some land, retained formal independence, and their earlier alliances with Rome were confirmed. The other ancient Latin cities were permitted to retain their former status, and Rome granted the male inhabitants of this category of city a new sort of right, "citizenship without franchise" (*civitas sine suffragio*). This was, in effect, a partial, halfway

BRONZE SAMNITE WARRIOR *(5th century B.C.) Descendants of the Sabines, the Samnites, portrayed in this votive statuette found in Sicily, were among the most dangerous foes of the Roman people.*

37

Roman citizenship, by virtue of which the men of these places, while not given the "public" right to vote in Rome's elections, were granted "private" rights.

It was an ingenious arrangement. These communities had to follow Rome's foreign policy and were also obliged, in the event of war, to raise and pay a quota of troops for "mutual defense." Yet these soldiers were allowed to serve in their own cities' contingents, under commanders of whom half were their own compatriots. The Romans avoided the Greek error of imposing standing garrisons and were secure in the knowledge that the Latin cities were ruled by landed nobilities allied with their own.

For a long time, this halfway Roman citizenship escaped the slur of inferior status, and it worked. The outstanding political acuteness of the Romans enabled them to get the balance right. Their aim was to maintain control without offending local feeling, and that is what they achieved over a prolonged period of time.

MARKING THE BORDERS OF A COLONY *(1st century) This exquisite carved relief from Aquileia reflects the ritual for founding a Roman colony —marking the city limits by plow. This is how the legendary Romulus founded Rome on Palatine Hill.*

The invention of the colonies

A further instrument of power invented in the later fourth century B.C. was the purely *Roman* colony. Colonies of this type were placed at strategic vantage points; for example, all the earliest foundations of this type were planned on the sea to serve as coastguard stations. These Roman colonies were linked directly to Rome by a continuous stretch of Roman territory, which meant that they needed fewer defenders and could operate with a much smaller quota of settlers than their Latin counterparts. Rome did not want to send too many potential fighters so far afield, and in any case, there were not all that many families willing to go to such places.

One of the first Roman colonies was at Ostia, beside the mouth of the Tiber. The colony's primary function was to defend the Tiber mouth from maritime enemies and pirates, thus saving Rome from the necessity of maintaining a permanent fleet.

By 218 B.C., the number of coastal Roman colonies had risen to twelve, and there were more than that number again maintaining guard over river crossings, exits from mountain passes, and road centers. Altogether, if we include individual allotments outside colonies, sixty thousand holdings were established between 343 and 264 B.C., so that the area occupied was multiplied threefold, to a total of some fifty thousand square miles; the settlers who manned them provided a mighty contribution not only to agriculture but also to defense—and futher aggression.

The Samnite Wars

Outstanding among the enemies whom these colonists had to confront were the Samnites, warlike peasants and herdsmen who lived in unwalled villages throughout the landlocked valleys and gray limestone uplands of the Apennines. The Samnite nation in this central Italian homeland was divided into four large tribes, which were linked together in a loose but sometimes militarily effective league. In the middle of the fourth century B.C., these Samnites were Italy's largest political unit, possessing twice the territory and population of the Romans.

Pressure of population had brought some of their compatriots down into Campania. But now the separate confederacy which they formed in that country had been overwhelmed by Rome, and this the Samnites in central Italy could not tolerate. The Latin colony of Cales also provoked them, and so did another established in 328–327 B.C. at Fregellae on the River Liris, which was their border with the Romans. So the Samnites occupied the ancient Greek foundation of Neapolis (Naples) with a garrison—which the Romans drove out, thus precipitating the long and complicated Second Samnite War (327–304 B.C.).

Rome now created a potent new instrument of warlike policy by building the Via Appia (Appian Way) traversing the one hundred and thirty-two miles from Rome to Capua, mostly across the coastal plain. For the more ancient Via Latina, following an upper inland route, was vulnerable to attacks from Samnium, to which the new Via Appia was not exposed. The forerunner of so many other Roman roads in three continents, weapons of peace as well as war, this "Queen of Roads" was constructed on a straight course, with bridges or paved fords to carry it across rivers, while viaducts spanned marshy territory. By such means, the second Samnite War was eventually won by the Romans. Their success left their enemies firmly excluded from southern Italy and much inferior to the victors in land and population alike.

But a Third Samnite War (298–290 B.C.) was still to follow. In 296 the Samnite commander broke out northward to join forces with a frightening combination of anti-Roman allies—Gauls, Etruscans, and Umbrians. Hostilities continued for six years. Fortunes varied, but finally the territory of the Samnites was penetrated by the Roman forces and ravaged from end to end, so that they had to give in.

Rome's success in this war decided the whole future fate of peninsular Italy. It had been a ferocious, patient struggle, in which the Samnites had clung to valley after valley with dogged determination. But the Romans had learned to split the enemy into isolated blocks, and the Latin

AUNORVM SATTRORVM ET SILENORVM DELECT

ROADS AND BOUNDARIES

Having conquered Italy and the areas surrounding the Mediterranean, the Romans organized the terrain of their territories with a profound sense of rationalism and order.

Using basic but efficient tools, their surveyors laid down straight lines and right angles across landscapes. As a result, camps pitched every night by active armies were formed by perpendicular routes. Modern cities have often retained these for their streets.

When colonies were founded, rural areas were divided according to the centurion's rules: streets at right angles to each other

forming blocks or in line with rectangular fields that were identical in size.

Mostly for strategic and commercial reasons, the Roman Empire was covered by an extraordinary network of roads along the frontiers, between Italy, Gaul, Spain, Brittany, North Africa, and to a lesser extent, Greece and Asia. Flattened, paved, bordered by ditches, and straight, the Roman roads—with the Appian Way the greatest achievement—organized landscapes and allowed for relatively fast transportation, which could not be improved upon until the 18th century.

colonies that they had continued to found served the same purpose of dividing the central Italian tribes one from another.

In the process, the Roman army had become a good deal larger than before. It was now subdivided into two legions. Each legion contained a group of thirty smaller units (maniples), each of which could maneuver and fight separately either in serried ranks or open order, thus combining compactness with flexibility. Moreover, every maniple was formed into three lines, each of which could advance in turn through the line ahead, replacing it and enabling it to draw back for rest and replenishment. This new manipular legion, tested to the uttermost against the Samnites, was to prove the key to Rome's future success.

Earlier in the century, the Roman state had begun to provide standard weapons and equipment, an important stage towards the creation of a professional army. All legionaries wore helmets, breastplates, and leg guards (greaves) and carried swords; thrusting javelins had been superseded by javelins for throwing, more than six feet long, half wood and half iron. The Samnite wars had forged the army into a terrible weapon.

It was perfectly suited to the dour perseverance that characterized the citizens of Rome, enabling them to respond efficiently to each successive external threat. The Romans were so amply fortified by their religious leaders with the belief that all their ways were just that they could never suppose that the military measures they were taking might be morally wrong. And they were not generally reluctant to employ force when they felt that force was needed.

They were also capable of atrocious cruelty. But what made the Romans so remarkable was the combination of these unpleasant traits with a talent for patient political reasonableness which was unique in the ancient world. They had displayed this gift before, and now they showed it once again, for the defeated Samnites were offered the same treaty terms that had been proposed to them at the end of the second war. Rome's treaties with other states were either "equal" or "unequal." But the latter formula, explicitly stating the inferiority of the other party, was increasingly the choice the Romans preferred, and this type of "agreement" was accorded to the Samnites. In 280 B.C., the Romans also made treaties with seven Etruscan cities in order to make them part of the defense system against the Gauls.

SMALL MASK
(4th century B.C., region of Capua) This forbidding terra cotta mask had an apotropaic purpose—that is, it was believed to protect against the evil eye.

Such treaties, intended for peoples not close or reliable enough to be accorded the half-citizenship of the Latins, were an essential part of Rome's Italian system and explain why its dependents and subjects were regularly known as "allies" (*socii*). Like the Latins, these allies had to provide troops if requested. Yet their aristocracies were generally known personally to the Roman governing class and regarded by them with sympathy; this sort of friendly relationship with local governing classes was Rome's blueprint for its imperial future. The Romans protected the rulers of these allied towns and left them alone to rule their own peoples, and the peoples in question were, without having to pay taxes to Rome, securing from it protection and peace. Besides, from about 289 B.C., drawing on their extensive spoils of Italian bronze, the Romans developed a coinage to meet the common commercial and industrial needs of the area. In this, as in other respects, association with the Romans proved beneficial.

40

After the Samnite Wars ended, a network of one hundred and twenty Italian communities with which Rome had formed alliances extended across central Italy.

The whole Roman approach was empirical, working from precedent to precedent according to each individual case, the relationship with every community in turn being considered on its own merits. This complex multiplication of differing agreements seems like a classic example of the cynical principle, "divide and rule." And so it was. But like the earlier understandings with the Latins, it was reckoned and weighed out so acutely, with that instinctive, hard, practical Roman genius for common-sense statecraft, that the system proved successful for generation after generation. That was how the Romans accomplished their first major historical achievement, the creation of Italy.

THE APPIAN WAY
(outskirts of Rome)
The first Roman road, the Appian Way was built during the second Samnite War for strategic reasons. It stretched for 132 miles, from Rome to Capua.

CHAPTER 3

The class struggle

The early Republic

During these one hundred and seventy years of almost incessant fighting, the Roman community had found itself racked by the gravest internal disturbances it was to experience for centuries.

When the Etruscan dynasty of the Tarquins was overthrown shortly before 500 B.C., the headship of the state passed from the expelled monarch to a pair of consuls elected every year. The character of consular office combined supremacy and limitation. The consuls were supreme in that each of them was invested with absolute *imperium*, the administrative power conferring command of the army and the interpretation and execution of the law. This corresponded with the Romans' marked respect for lawful public authority and their inherited conviction that it ought to be obeyed. And this large power vested in the executive obviously gave it a greater possibility of getting things done.

Yet although responsible to no one, and limited only by the law in the exercise of their duties, the consuls nevertheless were subject to two practical restrictions. In the first place, they were only elected for a single year. And secondly, they were subject to one another's vetoes. Since the power of each was all-pervading, neither one could prevail over the other.

The members of the Senate body, which retained its numerical strength of three hundred for nearly half a millennium, had gained more say in affairs after the monarchy was expelled. The Senate possessed no executive powers, but it advised the elected magistrates on domestic and

AVNORVM SATYROROVM ETSILENORVM DELECI

THE POWER OF THE MAGISTRATES

The Roman Republic was founded on the balance between people, senators, and magistrates—those invested with power.

The magistrates were elected (the people voted in the *comitia*) and their terms were limited (annually, for the most part). They were not paid and were collegial (that is, each magistrate had at least one colleague of his same rank). There were rules that established required age, the interval between two magistrate terms, and the order to be respected, from lowest to highest responsibility. This was called the *cursus honorum*. One could become one of the two consuls, supreme magistrates of the State charged with political and military affairs, after first being a *quaestor* (charged with finances) and then an *aedile* (police, supplies, games) and *praetor* (justice).

Besides these regular responsibilities, there were exceptional offices: The censors, elected every five years for 18 months, drew up the list of senators, took the census, and guarded customs. Until 202 B.C., in times of crisis a dictator could receive all the powers for six months or more. Eventually, to thwart the exorbitant power of the consuls, the ten plebeian tribunes, protected by religious-like immunity, defended the plebeians.

foreign policy, finance, and religion, and counseled them on legislative proposals as well. And the consuls on their side, despite their extensive constitutional powers, were likely enough to defer to the Senate's advice because the brief annuality of their own office made them vulnerable after it was over. Besides, the senators were

endowed with redoubtable prestige, due to their positions and family traditions and achievements. The Latin word for this prestige, *auctoritas*, conveyed a very urgent call for respect and deference, and the individual *auctoritas* of each senator combined to form a corporate influence that remained strong enough to survive and keep on guiding policies for centuries.

That is not, of course, to deny that there were dissensions within the ranks of the Senate. But any disagreements that arose did not greatly inhibit the effectiveness of the Senate as a whole, even in the face of a whole host of foreign and internal oppositions and problems.

Since the Senate remained, in law, purely advisory, it was not the body which elected the consuls year by year. This was the Assembly of Roman citizens (*Comitia Centuriata*). However, candidates for the consulship were proposed to the Assembly *by the senators*, from their own ranks.

The Assembly, it is true, enacted laws, declared war and peace, and conducted trials. Yet the senators, with their superior prestige and wealth, controlled its votes on all such occasions. In many respects, therefore, the legal appearance of democracy was sharply corrected by what in fact happened.

This curious gulf between fact and appearance was created by one of the most important factors in Roman life, which continued to influence it profoundly for centuries. This was the institution of *clientela*. Roman society was a structure composed of powerful *patroni* and their dependent *clientes*. The client was a free man who entrusted himself to the patronage of another and received protection from him in return. The client helped his patron to succeed in public life and furthered his interests by every means in his power, and in return the patron looked after his client's private affairs and gave him financial or legal support.

THE CURIA *(Roman forum) The Curia monument (at right) that stands today dates back to Diocletian. Two buildings preceded it: the Curia Hostilia, which burned down in 52 B.C., and the Curia Julia, made of brick. The building's great height was in response to acoustic demands. A rostrum in the rear was reserved for the president of the session; the senators sat in three tiers.*

AVNORVM SATYRORVM ETSILENORVMDELECT

THE PRESTIGE OF THE SENATE

The governing body called the Senate was born during the era of the kings. At first only bringing together the *patres*, or heads of the 100 most important families, it soon grew to 300 in number, and then to 900 members by the end of the Republic. The roster of senators was drawn up once every five years by the censors, who registered all the former magistrates by order of seniority.

Sessions were held at the Curia, at the Forum, or in temples. Every senator could address the body, from his seat, and there were no time limits. The austere simplicity of the Senate was impressive enough to cause the ambassador of Pyrrhus to say that he felt himself to be before an assembly of kings. Consulted by the magistrates, who respected its authority, the Republican Senate intervened only in finances, foreign policy, and the administration of the provinces, for which it appointed governors. It also decided about war and ratified treaties.

Identified by a wide purple band bordering their tunics (the *laticlavis*) and by special shoes, the senators and their families formed the most respected class of society. Under the Empire, however, they lost power to the emperor and knights.

Such mutual arrangements are not unparalleled in other societies, but the Roman institution was remarkable for its all-pervasiveness and binding cogency. *Clientela* was hereditary; it was also heavily charged with feeling and emotion. A man was supposed to rate his clients even before his own relations by marriage. *Clientela* had attained a powerful quasi-religious force by long and universally respected custom. The keynotes of this force were *fides*, mutual good faith—worshipped as a goddess, according to tradition, from the dimmest early past—and *pietas*, the dutiful respect owed to patrons just as it was owed to parents and fatherland and gods.

It might be said that a poor client's relationship to his patron, based on inescapable ties of good faith, gave his life a meaning and security which poor people in other countries have frequently lacked. Nevertheless, *clientela* acted as a powerful brake on democratic development—and indeed, it helped to prevent it from ever taking place.

Patricians and plebeians

DENARIUS COIN *The coins of the Republican period often represented divine figures. Ceres, goddess of the harvest, was protector of the plebeians. She is easily identifiable here because of the ears of corn she holds in her hands.*

For one thing, this relationship between patrons and clients reflected the basic division of Roman society, existent when the Republic started or earlier still, between patricians and plebeians. After the beginning of the Republic, the Senate came to include not only heads of families (*patres familias*) but other prominent personages as well. And since these were very often the sons or relatives of the *patres familias*, they became known as *patricii*.

The patricians exercised power not only through their clients but also by virtue of a monopoly, hallowed by custom, of inherited religious rights, including the administration of major cults and the power to consult the gods (*auspicia*). During the fifth century B.C. some fifty-three patrician clans (*centres*) are known, a closed body of not more than one thousand families.

However, these patricians comprised less than one-tenth of the total citizen population of Rome. The remaining large majority of the inhabitants (apart from a number of slaves, a normal feature of ancient societies) were the plebeians, and the sharp political and social distinction that separated them from the patricians was the outstanding feature of early Republican social history. To some extent *clientela* kept the plebeians happy. But although all clients were plebeians, not all plebeians were clients. Besides, the most that a patron could do was not always enough to prevent discontent. For one thing, the plebeians were completely excluded from influential positions, including the consulships and, initially, from membership of the Sen-

44

ate. This point irritated the more powerful and prosperous of the plebeians—who alone among that order could afford the costs of holding office, so they were often seen leading movements of plebeian protest.

But there was a great deal more to the internal disturbances of the early Republic than that. While exclusion from office was frustrating for a few prominent plebeians at the top, the remaining plebeians, who covered a very wide spectrum of the social scale, did not want power so much as protection from the abuses of power that were being committed by others. Many of these men had suffered grievous impoverishment from the abrupt fall in Rome's prosperity after the expulsion of the Etruscan monarchs. When this happened, the city had sunk back to the status of a purely agrarian community operating at a low subsistence level, and there was not enough tolerable soil available, on the small territory of the early Republic, to give everyone a living. Even if a plebeian did possess land, he often had to go and fight in one of the unceasing frontier wars, and when he came back his farm had gone to ruin in his absence.

In these conditions, crippling grain shortages brought famines, and to ward them off, the Romans founded a temple of the grain goddess Ceres. The worship of Ceres was essentially a cult of the plebeians. It was borrowed from the Greek city of Cumae, where her Greek counterpart Demeter was one of the leading divinities. This Greek origin was significant since the Roman temple was located beneath the Aventine Hill, in an area near the cattle market and the river wharves that was a center for Greek traders. And it was to the Greeks that the poor of Rome looked for ideas of democracy. The economic situation in the fifth century was grim, due not only to the shortages and famines but also to the shattering epidemics which came in their wake. And in the hope of removing these troubles, the Romans continued their religious borrowings by taking over the great Greek healing god Apollo, in whose honor they built a temple in about 431 B.C.

The Twelve Tables

In these desperate circumstances of famine, pestilence, and savage frontier warfare, the plebeians, who bore the brunt of the miseries and the fighting, felt more discontented than anyone else, out of the conviction that nothing substantial had been done to relieve their social and economic miseries. Nor did they really know, legally speaking, how they stood, since the laws were not written down and were interpreted by the college of priests (*pontifices*), who were all patricians. This issue played a dominant part in the plebeians' next demands, and these demands became so violent and pressing that in 451 B.C., the normal appointments to consulships were temporarily suspended and a commission of ten patricians, the *decemviri,* was appointed to write down a collection of laws. The product of their labors was enacted by the Assembly as a statute and openly published on tablets that were set up in the Forum—the Twelve Tables.

In demanding that such a step should be taken, the plebeians were inspired by the Greek ideas they had heard around the Aventine, for the establishment of a code of laws was very familiar to the Greeks.

The contents of the Tables form a strange mixture of widely ranging principles and minor details of law (private, public, and criminal), of rules about matters

STATUE OF APOLLO *(1st century B.C.) This bronze statue illustrates the Hellenistic influence on Roman culture.*

TIBERINE ISLAND
The crossing point between north and south, this island allowed for the first bridges of Rome to be built—in particular, Pons Sublicius, which joined with the city of Etruria and was built in the 7th century. It was made from wooden beams and posts.

ranging from communal hygiene to personal safety. What is quite clear, however, is that the men who originally framed and drafted their short gnomic sentences were hard practical thinkers who were able to express themselves in almost painfully exact language, and who possessed in full measure that unparalleled talent for precise legal definition, which is one of Rome's greatest gifts to humanity.

The impact of the Twelve Tables upon later generations was enormous. The original tablets were destroyed in the invasion by the Gauls some sixty years later, but they were meticulously reconstructed and remained legally valid. Indeed, they were traditionally seen, with a measure of respectful exaggeration, as the source of much or most of Roman law; for century after century they retained a dominant position in the education of every Roman citizen.

Paradoxically, the initial publication of the tables was extremely badly received by the plebeians. For the decemvirs had not, to any significant extent, regarded it as part of their job to introduce into their compilation any new measures to improve the plebeians' lot. Their duty, as they interpreted it, was merely to reduce to visible statute form the most important regulations of the already existing customary law. By carrying out this task, they believed they had done enough to satisfy plebeian demands. But plebeian contentment was not forthcoming.

Nevertheless, we who scrutinize the tables today find it impressive that a people at such a relatively early stage of development were so clearly able to disentangle law from religion, deriving their sanction from a sense of justice and equity. The Twelve Tables also show a surprisingly precocious clarity of conception in dealing with contract and property. Moreover, in the measures regarding marriage, archaism is tempered by liberalism. In the earliest days, Roman matrimony granted every husband the same rights over his wife as his status as father of the family gave him over their children. But a slight weakening of the husband's authority was already sanctioned by the Twelve Tables, according to which his wife, after she had reached the age of twenty-five, retained possession of her property. The *mater familias* enjoyed, by custom, great respect and influence, being required to supervise, for example, the education of her young children. On the lips of men, there was much stress on women's place and duties in the home. But women lived and went out and about with a liberty that far exceeded the conditions of their Greek counterparts. The Twelve Tables give some idea how far this emancipation had gone. By another law of the Tables, a wife could avoid her husband's legal control by passing three nights each year away from his house. In due course there also developed free marriage, based on mutual consent, which gave the husband no authority over his wife.

Social appeasement

The decemvirate continued into a second year of office, during which a veto on intermarriage between patricians and plebeians was apparently confirmed. But then the decemvirs fell from power, and the normal succession of consulships was restored.

In 454 B.C., the succession of consuls may have been broken when groups of army officers were appointed instead. This was primarily for military purposes. But the new system, which continued for nearly eighty years, also served the cause of the plebeians, who were able to gain an occasional place among these military officers that they had not yet succeeded in gaining among the consuls. But the most prominent member of the new leadership was the winner of the war against Veii, Camillus, who was a patrician.

Towards the end of Camillus's career, however, the consulate was restored; after a prolonged struggle, two tribunes of the people, Licinius and Sextius, reelected, it was said, for as long as ten years (376–367 B. C.), carried a proposal that one of the consuls could henceforward always be a plebeian. Very soon, individual ple-

ROMAN WOMEN

Legally, women in Rome were minors, with no political rights and no personal property. In all matters of business, a woman had to be assisted by a person in charge. She had no name other than her father's surname, which was made feminine. Traditionally, she stayed at home and, among other domestic duties, was responsible for spinning wool. Many examples exist of arranged marriages or separations in the interest of money and without the consent of the woman.

The situation was more complex than it seems, however, for the Roman woman was educated. Take for example, Cornelia, the mother of Gracchus; Sulpicia, a poet who wrote at the same time as Tibullus; Calpurnia, the wife of Pliny; Sempronia, Catilina's partner; or Agrippina, Nero's mother. Furthermore, Romans enjoyed celebrating courageous women: Lucretia or Clelia in the Etruscan period, and Arria, who was stronger than her husband in the face of Domitian's tyranny. One could almost measure the importance of the matrons in the society by the ineffectiveness of the laws that aimed to limit their expenditures. Even stripped of rights, the Roman woman seems to have been able to exert her influence both privately and publicly.

beians were attaining positions of great and long-lasting political power, and only twenty-five years after the Licinian-Sextian measure, the inclusion of a plebeian among every pair of consuls became obligatory. The censorship, too, became accessible to plebeians by 351 B.C. at the latest, and it was decreed that one censor must always come from their ranks. The effect of these changes was to create a new ruling class, no longer an entirely patrician aristocracy but a nobility consisting of those men, patrician and plebeian alike, whose ancestry had included consuls or censors or dictators—which is what the term "noble" came to mean.

Plebeians of lesser rank were aided by the creation of a new office of state, the praetorship, in 366 B.C. This "urban praetor" was to undertake legal and other civilian functions in order to leave the two consuls free for military duties. But the interests of the underprivileged were benefited by the successive praetors' yearly "edicts." Higher officials of the Roman state were accustomed to proclaim by edict, on annual appointment to their office, the major policies that they proposed to follow as its occupants. Among such edicts, those of the praetor were of special significance for the development of private law and ultimately became even more important than the Twelve Tables. It was true that praetors were merely supposed to apply regulations that were already in force rather than institute new ones, but in fact their edicts formulated a multitude of new rules and improvements adapted to the increasing complexity of society.

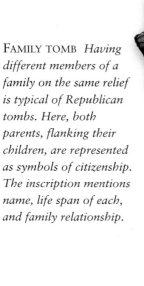

FAMILY TOMB *Having different members of a family on the same relief is typical of Republican tombs. Here, both parents, flanking their children, are represented as symbols of citizenship. The inscription mentions name, life span of each, and family relationship.*

The endeavors of Licinius and Sextius, dim figures though they are, to ease the conditions of the plebeians were unprecedented and impressive—the most important internal reforms since the foundation of the Republic. The next decades witnessed further perceptible advances in social progress and unity, so that Rome went into its decisive struggle against the Latin cities with a reasonable degree—if not of concord, at least of public acquiescence. Whatever the deficiencies of the system from a democratic viewpoint, it proved of decisive importance for the future that Rome, convulsed by these social dissensions at the same time as it was attacked by foreign foes on every side, had prevented the internal strife from reaching suicidal proportions; it was thus given a free hand to suppress each of its foreign enemies in turn, vastly expanding its territory and resources in the process.

In 298 B.C., the third and last Samnite War began, and it lasted for eight years. The ferocious struggle ended in victory, but also in financial exhaustion. The plebeians serving in the army had done so, like many before them, at the cost of the prosperity of their farms, which often fell into decay, so that they fell heavily into debt. So restless did they become, and so grave was the consequent friction, that in accordance with the constitution a dictator, Quintus Hortensius, was appointed (287 B.C.) as a temporary expedient to meet the emergency.

What economic measures Hortensius took, we are not sure. But he at least passed a law of a constitutional nature in favor of the plebeians, providing that the resolutions of their Council, the *Concilium plebis*, should have the force of law and be binding upon the whole community, patricians and plebeians alike. Thus a right that had been claimed for more than one hundred and fifty years was conceded, and the decisions of the plebeians were now every bit as valid as those of the executive. At very long last, the struggle between the orders had ended.

By ancient and modern standards alike, the Roman class struggle had been impressively peaceable, carried on for long years with a minimum of physical violence and through due process of law. The absence of continuous social progress is hardly surprising given the highly conservative character of the Roman people—patricians and plebeians alike—whose whole society depended fundamentally upon *clientela* and the habit of obedience to authority and group and community. But this system, patched together by what may seem to us a peculiar and unsatisfactory series of compromises, at least passed the pragmatic test, because it worked. Indeed, it continued to work, with relatively little change, for as long as any politico-social system has ever worked in the history of the Western world. And in the process, despite all its manifest faults, this system enabled Rome to face its mortal enemies with an imposingly united front.

SOCIAL HIERARCHY

The Roman city was hierarchical and unequal. Originally, the oldest 100 families formed the patricians, who revered the same ancestor, celebrated the same cult, and held all political rights. The plebeians had none of these privileges, and couldn't marry patricians. Seceding several times (they withdrew from Aventine Hill in 494 B.C. and established their own institutions), the plebeians eventually obtained the same exact rights as the patricians, notably access to the consulate (in 300 B.C., through Lex Ogulnia).

Servius Tullius, the legendary king, began a system based on tax qualification: Citizens were divided into five classes according to wealth, then subdivided into centuries, which determined their role in the army and the weight of their vote in assemblies.

The wealthiest citizens lived off the profit their land yielded and devoted themselves to political life; they formed the senatorial aristocracy. Knights, on the other hand, focused more on business at the bank. Under the Empire, the senatorial order—composed of families who had at least one consul ancestor —retained an honorary role, whereas the equestrian order was granted a growing number of official offices by the emperors.

The Romans and their gods

CULT OF ISIS *Coming from Egypt, the cult of Isis gave women an important role; its priestesses in the Roman world were numerous.*

The Romans lived surrounded by gods. Every one of their actions, every moment of their lives, was linked to a specific divinity. Furthermore, with each conquest, the Roman pantheon grew richer in new divinities. For the Roman religion, which was polytheist, was all the more open. Greek and Asian divinities in particular—Dionysus, the Greek god of wine; Cybele, the Anatolian goddess symbolizing fertility; Isis, Egyptian mother goddess; and later Mithra, Persian sun god—were very popular.

At the top of the hierarchy there reigned a group of three gods, established on the Capitol: Jupiter, the supreme god, Minerva, the goddess associated with war, and Juno, protectress of women and custodian of prosperity. At the end of the Empire, new religious aspirations, focusing on personal salvation, triggered the development of Christianity and philosophical movements.

The Roman priests did not form a caste; they were citizens elected by their peers or by the people, grouped into colleges and brotherhoods. At the top of the hierarchy, the pontiffs (there were nine of them in 300 B.C., 16 after Caesar) counseled the magistrates or the Senate on cultural traditions and sacred law, established the calendar, and controlled sacred places and necropolises. The *rex sacrorum* celebrated the rituals that dated back to the monarchy. The fifteen flamines, or high priests (including the three most important flamines of Jupiter, Mars, and Quirinus) celebrated the cult of divinity, from which their name derives. During the Empire, the emperor was named the great pontiff and controlled religious affairs as a whole.

The central element of the public cult was the sacrifice, which accompanied every political act. Celebrated before the temple, near the altar, it was offered by the magistrate, priest, or emperor, who was assisted by slaves. After the procession, the offering of incense and wine, and the invocation of the honored divinity, the victim (a sheep, a cow, or a pig) was sacrificed, then divided among the gods and men, who ate its meat during a sacrificial banquet.

Aside from public worship, there was also a private religion, presided over by the father of each family. Each family event (birth, marriage, birthday, etc.) was accompanied by prayers and a sacrifice to the gods who protected the home and the spirit of the master of the house.

PRIESTESSES OF VESTA
The college of Vestals consisted of female priests, all of whom were young girls of the Roman aristocracy. The Vestals guarded the permanence of the State by maintaining the fire of Rome.

HOUSEHOLD ALTAR
In the atrium of the house of the Vettii, a stucco altar depicts the master of the house surrounded by two lares (household gods). The serpent symbolizes the master's genius.

A LIVER FOR GUIDANCE *This bronze sheep liver served to guide the haruspex diviners. Each part of the liver corresponds to a part of the heavens and to a particular divinity.*

SACRIFICE *The presence of a pig, sheep, and cattle in this procession, which opened the ritual of a sacrifice, is evidence that this sacrifice is for the major divinities.*

MAISON CARRÉE IN NIMES
Built by Agrippa, this Roman temple is typical in that it is square-shaped, perched on a podium, and has a narthex and a cella, which house the cult statues.

DIVINATION

The goal of divination was not to predict the future, but to interpret signs sent by the gods. The *augur* performed auspices by observing the behavior of birds. Equipped with his rod, he symbolically traced a sacred space in the sky. If birds entered on the right side, the omen was favorable; a flight from the left meant divine disapproval. The *haruspex* examined the entrails of the sacrificed animal: if they did not suit his specifications, the sacrifice would have to be made again. Another means, better suited to a mobilized army, involved observing the appetite of sacred chickens. Beforehand, the *pullarius* starved his fowl; he then opened the cage and tossed in grain. If the chickens rejected it, the gods were angry. Finally, if there was a major crisis (natural catastrophe, epidemic, military failure), a college of 15 men, influenced by Greek culture, consulted the Sybilline Books, written in Greek and in mysterious verse, to find some way to appease the gods.

CHAPTER 4

First wars against foreign powers

The invasion of Pyrrhus

PYRRHUS, KING OF EPIRUS
The Roman victory over Pyrrhus in 275 B.C. allowed Rome to establish itself in Magna Graecia (Greater Greece)— the collective name for the Greek cities in southern Italy.

The Greek cities, which so abundantly filled southern Italy and Sicily that they were described as Magna Graecia (Greater Greece), did not have much to do with the Romans before 300 B.C. But the end of the Samnite Wars brought Rome's subject allies far down towards the south, within range of these Greek towns. The most important of them, on the mainland, was Tarentum, now Taranto, on the gulf of that name. Tarentum lay astride an isthmus, between a shallow protected bay and a tidal lagoon. Larger than Rome in the early third century B.C., the city based its great prosperity on the wool from its winterland, dyed with the purple of the murex mussels in the city's harbor. From this port the dyed wool was exported to Greece and elsewhere. The city possessed the largest fleet in Italy and an army of fifteen thousand men, but often supplemented this force by hiring mercenaries.

The Tarentines had an old agreement with Rome, according to which it undertook not to send ships into their gulf. Nevertheless, an eventual confrontation looked inevitable after Rome, in 291 B.C., during the last days of the Samnite Wars, founded a large colony at Venusia, near the far end of defeated Samnium. Venusia was fewer than ninety miles from Tarentum, which regarded its establishment as a strong provocation.

This growing tension came to a head in 282 B.C., when the Greek city of Thurii, on the southern side of the Tarentum gulf, was attacked by Lucanian raiders and appealed to the Romans, and who, after hesitation, duly sent a fleet to place a garrison in Thurii. Tarentum viewed this as a breach of the agreement not to send ships into its gulf. The Tarentines sank the Roman fleet and drove the offending garrison out of Thurii, jeering at the bad Greek spoken by envoys sent by Rome. They also applied for help to a Greek military adventurer, King Pyrrhus of Epirus just across the Adriatic. Pyrrhus, who claimed descent from Alexander the Great, was one of the foremost of the minor rulers and rent-an-army generals who had proliferated since Alexander's death half a century earlier. Accepting the invitation from Tarentum, he set sail for south Italy, taking with him twenty-five thousand mercenaries, the most highly esteemed professional soldiers of their day. And so the Romans had to prepare for the first battles they had ever fought against a Greek army.

The basis of Pyrrhus's force was a phalanx of twenty thousand men. In battle, lined up in depth, they displayed a front that bristled with the heads of their long lances, as impene-

52

AVNORVM SATYRORVM ETSILENORVMDELECTA

THE REPUBLIC'S ARMY

The organization of the Republic's army mirrored the organization of Roman society itself. Only the wealthy between ages 17 and 46 were subject to mobilization. The century (military unit of 100) who existed for voting in the *comitia* was eligible for the army, by order of the centurion. Officers were military tribunes, and the general was an elected magistrate (consul or praetor).

In combat, two centuries were paired into a maniple; three maniples constituted a cohort. A legion (in theory) included ten cohorts—a total of approximately 6,000 men.

According to their age and experience, the legionaries formed three staggered groups of five and mobilized in successive waves: the *hastati,* the *principes,* and the *triarii.* Along with this heavy infantry, there were light troops (foot soldiers, archers, and sling bearers) and the cavalry, often provided by allies.

During the march, the legionary bore his arms, tools, whatever was needed to build camp, and food for at least three days.

In 107 B.C., an important reform issued by Marius established pay and opened recruitment to lower classes. This created a professional army. Under the Empire, the army, which was entirely devoted to its sergeant, played a growing role in the choice of an emperor.

trable as barbed wire; their task was to hold the Roman army while their cavalry on the wings turned its flank. Pyrrhus also brought with him twenty frightening Indian war-elephants, which he used not frontally like tanks, as was the custom, but laterally, so that they could join the horsemen in attacking the enemy's flanks.

His first battle against the Romans was fought at Heraclea, a coastal colony of Tarentum lying to its west. The legions stood up well to Pyrrhus's phalanx. But his elephants routed the Roman horses and then charged the flank of the legionaries, putting them to flight, though at a heavy cost of Epirote as well as Roman lives. In the next year, with a larger force, he won another of his costly victories, known henceforth as "Pyrrhic," in a battle in northern Apulia. The Romans resisted his phalanx for a day. But on the following day, with the help of his elephants, he forced them back, though they avoided total disaster by regaining their fortified camp.

Next, in autumn 278 B.C., Pyrrhus moved on to Sicily, seeing the island as a base for further Mediterranean conquests. Three years later, he returned once again to the Italian mainland. There he engaged a Roman army in western Apulia. But the result of the battle was at best inconclusive and damaging, because the Romans had by now discovered that his elephants, if wounded by javelins, got out of control and could be made to trample their own soldiers. After this engagement, Pyrrhus drew back to Tarentum, and from there, before long, returned to Greece, where he was killed two years later by a tile thrown down from a housetop by a woman.

The outcome of the war had demonstrated that the Greek states of south Italy could no longer stand against Rome, and in 272 B.C., the Tarentines accepted the alliance that was proposed to them. The Romans were becoming conscious of their imperial responsibilities; it was probably in this decade that a south Italian mint produced the first silver coinage to be issued in their name, followed in about 269 B.C. by issues minted at the capital itself.

And so, within four generations after the lowest point in the Romans' fortunes, the whole of peninsular Italy down to the southernmost regions had come under their control. Moreover, this victory won by the Republic in its first war against a Greek army had been noted in the wider Greek lands of the east. For the first time,

Rome was recognized among these nations, and one of the great successor kingdoms of Alexander—Egypt of the Ptolemies—established diplomatic relations with its government by a treaty negotiated in 273 B.C.

Carthage—the other power

Rome's war with Pyrrhus brought it into much closer contact than before with the largest western Mediterranean power, Carthage in north Africa, in what is now Tunisia. The problems threatening the peaceful coexistence of the two powers rapidly multiplied.

During the eighth century B.C., when most Mediterranean trading was in the hands of the Phoenicians, one of their leading cities, Tyre (Sur), founded an offshoot far to its west; they called it the "New City" of Carthage. Carthage was of exceptional importance because of its position at the narrow waist of the Mediterranean.

For three-quarters of a century Carthage was a colony of Tyre, but from then onwards it became an independent republic. By the early third century B.C., its population was three times that of Rome. By 650 B.C., Carthage had taken over and greatly enlarged the old Phoenician trading posts all around the western Mediterranean and created many new posts, too.

Above all, like their fellow Phoenicians before them, these Carthaginian seafarers urgently wanted metals. The country best able to provide them was Spain. But to sail due westwards without any intermediate stopping places would have incurred all the hazards of an unwelcoming north African coast and a hostile current, so they needed bases upon the islands along the way. A vital link in this chain

THE RISE AND FALL OF CARTHAGE

Founded near present-day Tunis in the 8th century B.C., Carthage soon became a rich and powerful city that controlled both coastal cities and agricultural areas inland. The Carthaginians, who were mostly merchants, colonized the south of Spain, a country of mines. There they founded New Carthage and set out through sub-Saharan Africa and Cornwall in search of gold and pewter.

The aristocratic makeup of the city meant a few families dominated, including the Barcas (Hamilcar, Hannibal). There were two suffetes (supreme magistrates) elected for a year and monitored by a Senate that was appointed for life. Lacking a large enough population to recruit an army, Carthage maintained mercenaries. Faithful to the Phoenician religion, it venerated the gods Tanit and Baal, with sacrifices of children. Roman propaganda quickly exploited such cruelty.

First a Roman ally against the Greeks, Carthage was its enemy during three Punic Wars (264–241 B.C., 218–202 B.C., and 149–146 B.C.), after which the city was destroyed. Caesar and Augustus went on to establish colonies on its site, which gave rise to the second largest city of the Empire, populated by a sizable Christian community.

was western Sicily, where Carthage assumed leadership of the existing Phoenician colonists, establishing its main base at Panormus (Palermo), which commanded a superb harbor and fertile hinterland.

For three hundred years, it remained the firm policy of the Carthaginians to retain this Sicilian foothold. In Sardinia, too, they inherited and developed at least four ports. These possession of these island bases also enabled them to keep the Greeks away from Spain, where Carthage was consequently able to take over and develop important Phoenician settlements. The Carthaginians' strong points in Sardinia also gave them access to a second important source of metals, namely Etruria. They even had a share in two of the ports of Etruscan Caere. At one of them, Pyrgi, bilingual Etruscan and Phoenician inscriptions have been found. The other was called Punicum—the Latin word for "Carthaginian."

54

The first Punic War

It was only a matter of time before this empire came into conflict with the new Mediterranean power of the Romans. Carthage was only one hundred and thirty miles across the strait from Sicily, and its settlements at the harbor of Etruscan Caere were barely thirty miles from Rome. The breaking point came when the local ruling group at Messana (Messina), situated on the straits separating Sicily from the Italian peninsula, invited the Carthaginians to occupy their city and help them suppress the opponents of their regime—and the invitation was accepted. This upset the Greek cities of south Italy that had now become allies of Rome. When, however, the men in charge of Messana changed their minds and appealed to Rome instead, and the south Italian cities added their own urgent persuasion, the Roman government accepted the challenge (264 B.C.); the Senate was hesitantbut was overruled by the Assembly, which wanted plunder. So, with Rome as well as Carthage having responded to Messina's appeal, the Romans transported two legions across the strait to occupy the city, and the Carthaginian admiral who had failed to stop them was crucified by his own government.

But the focal point of this initial phase of the First Punic War was the Greek city-state of Syracuse, on the east Sicilian coast. It was for protection against the king of Syracuse, Hiero II, that Messana had initially appealed to the Carthaginians, and it was in order to thwart his expansion that they had accepted the appeal. It is

CARTHAGE
Overlooking the Mediterranean Sea, Byrsa hill, the former citadel of Carthage, retains ruins of Punic structures.

55

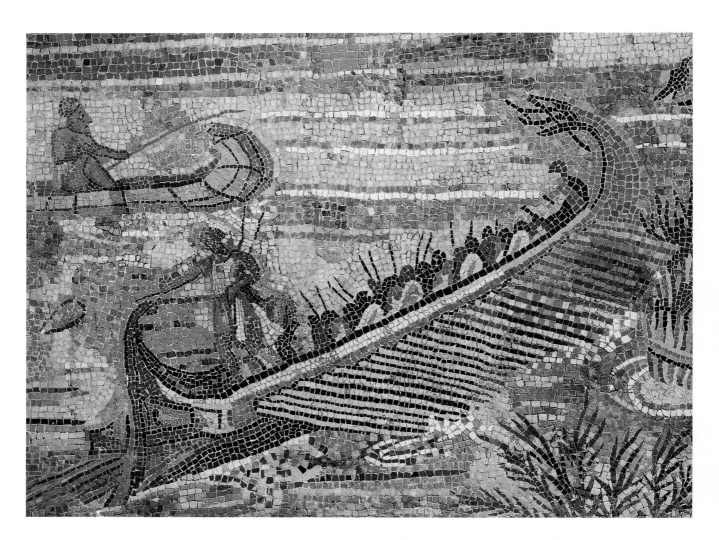

MOSAIC OF PALESTRINA
(ca. 80 B.C.) The First Punic War forced Rome to assemble a fleet. As early as 260 B.C., a naval construction policy created a squadron of 100 vessels, each manned by five rows of rowers, and 20 vessels with three rows. The invention of the grapnel, a small anchor very useful in naval battles, also dates from this period.

therefore surprising to find that Hiero, at the outset of the First Punic War, entered into an alliance with Carthage against Rome. Hiero must have believed Rome to represent a greater peril. However, driven back by a strong Roman military offensive, he almost immediately went into reverse and sought peace with the Romans after all. They responded prudently, conceding him a fifteen-year alliance. He remained Rome's loyal ally until his death forty-eight years later, and a new institution had come into being: the foreign "client" kingdom beyond the frontiers of the Roman state but its dependent—an extension of the custom according to which, within the Roman community, individual clients depended on their patrons.

The Romans rapidly came to the conclusion that a satisfactory peace could only be achieved by driving the Carthaginians out of Sicily altogether. Yet this could only be done if they had a navy, which they did not possess. So they proceeded to construct a fleet from virtually nothing, built of the timber that Italy provided in far greater quantities than Carthage. This enterprising decision to challenge the naval supremacy of the Carthaginians was the most extraordinary feature of the war.

In 260 B.C., the Romans began by constructing a flotilla one hundred and forty strong. The ships they built were massive quinqueremes, carrying marines and a crew of three hundred sailors divided into groups of five to an oar. To frustrate the superior naval dexterity of the enemy by making sea fights much like land battles, they equipped their craft with "ravens" *(corvi)*, gangways tied to the mast and hinged so that they could be released and dropped on the enemy's decks. The Roman fleet embarked on the second phase of the war, which witnessed the largest naval engagements that the Greco-Roman world had ever seen. The first of these engagements was at Mylae off the coast of Sicily. The ravens worked well, and fifty enemy ships were destroyed (260 B.C.). Then, four years later, off southern Sicily, they won the most grimly contested naval battle ever fought in ancient times in western waters.

This victory threw the north African shores wide open to the Romans. Their general, Regulus, made an unopposed landing and advanced to within a single day's march of Carthage itself. He offered them peace, but his terms were so stringent that the fighting continued. Then, in spring of 255 B.C., Regulus's force was annihilated and he himself was taken prisoner. A Roman fleet came to relieve the situation but was unable to rescue him. On the way home, it was wrecked by a storm.

After these disasters, the attempt to invade north Africa was abandoned, and hostilities dragged on for another thirteen years—largely because of the Romans' further enormous losses from storms due to the inexperience of their admirals. Eventually, however, Rome raised yet another fleet; this time the ships were lighter quinqueremes, without the *corvi* which had proved perilously top-heavy. This was the very last fleet the Romans could have afforded to raise, but it proved successful. With its help, they completed the investment of the main surviving Carthaginian strongholds in western Sicily, then they won an easy, total naval victory near the off-shore Aegates (Egadi) Islands. Thereupon Carthage was forced to accept peace (241 B.C.). Soon afterwards, fittingly enough, the unit of the Roman bronze coinage began to display a ship's prow as its design.

Defeated Carthage was not yet removed from the face of the earth. But it was forbidden to send ships into Italian waters ever again and was obliged to evacuate Sicily altogether. So, with the exception of Hiero II's state of Syracuse and a few other cities which remained independent client allies, the Romans now proceeded to annex the whole of the island. This was a fateful step, for it brought the Romans outside Italy and gave them their first overseas province. An entirely new and lasting stage in Roman history had begun—the epoch of imperialism outside the mother country. It was appropriate enough that some forty years later, a Latin poet named Naevius chose this war among all others as the theme of his epic glorifying the power of Rome.

THE PORT OF CARTHAGE
The two ports of Punic Carthage—one military and the other commercial, which is today a single oval pond— were connected by a channel. The military port harbored a mighty fleet of warships, divided among 140 docks along the port. The round island in the middle was home to the admiral's siege tower.

The loss of Sicily was the gravest of the damages imposed on the Carthaginians after their defeat. Yet they found themselves involved in new disasters the very next year after the First Punic War. Twenty thousand of their mercenary troops broke into violent mutiny because their pay was in arrears. This polyglot mass of warriors, from more than half a dozen different peoples, marched upon Carthage itself, and it was not until after three years of the most savage fighting and most inhuman atrocities ever recorded that the mercenaries were finally annihilated.

Immediately afterwards, in Sardinia, the fellow soldiers of these rebels broke into revolt against the Carthaginians and appealed to Rome (238 B.C.). The Roman government proceeded to send troops to the island to help the dissidents—and seize control of the Carthaginian fortresses. Carthage could do nothing, and the Romans went on to annex Sardinia and Corsica.

An age of innovations

In a bid for popularity, designed to keep up morale at the outset of the First Punic War, the government of Rome had introduced an institution of horrifying brutality which retained an enormous following throughout the whole of the subsequent history of the city: the gladiatorial combat—a national sport and a psychological safety valve.

At a funeral in the Cattle Market in 264 B.C., two sons of the dead man exhibited three simultaneous gladiatorial combats—a figure which was to rise, within the next half-century, to twenty-two such contests staged on a single occasion. The ferocious cruelty of these sports betrays the existence of a streak of sadism in the ancient Roman character.

But the First Punic War also witnessed, paradoxically enough, many novel humanizing influences derived from the Greek world. The war provided many new contacts with south Italy and Sicily and brought from those parts a considerable number of Greeks, who contributed an influx of Greek culture.

For example, Livius Andronicus, a Greek who had come from Tarentum, became the first teacher of Greek literature at Rome and virtually invented Roman poetry as well. Adjusting the clanking Latin tongue to Greek verse forms, he wrote tragic dramas based on classical Athenian models.

Advances in Roman law

The period of the First Punic War also produced two landmarks in the evolution of Roman law. The first started from what seemed an insignificant happening. In 253 B.C., the chief priest (*pontifex maximus*) Titus Coruncanius—the first plebeian to hold that office—commenced the practice of admitting his students to his legal consultations and therefore began the training of the first men who would practice as Roman lay jurists (*iuirisprudentes*).

These personages, whose long line was thus inaugurated, did not usually practice as advocates, but were advisers. They exercised their legal influence at every point, counseling praetors and other officials and judges, assisting citizens in a variety of matters, and giving answers on questions of law. The jurists sat in on trials and judgments. They became the central figures of Roman law for many successive generations, during which time they did much to create the way of life that the Western world has followed ever since.

In 242 B.C., a second praetorship was established at Rome to supplement the much older city praetorship. This new official was *praetor peregrinus*. It was his task to deal with legal cases in which at least one of the contestants was a non-Roman (*peregrinus*). Hitherto Roman law had dealt exclusively with the relations between one Roman citizen and another. The new post represented a major enlargement of Roman viewpoint, and stress was laid on the law's universal implications rather than narrowly national aspects.

AVNORVM SATYRORVM ET SILENORVM DELECT

THE INFLUENCE OF GREEK CULTURE

Though Rome was a military power with a remarkable sense of organization and an amazing legal spirit, its cultural dependence on Greece was huge. Rome seized the main Hellenistic kingdoms after the disintegration of the Alexandrian Empire in Macedonia, Syria, and Egypt. But after taking Taranto and the occupation of Sicily, Latin literature inspired by Greece proliferated—epic and elegiac poetry, theater, philosophy. Teaching in Rome was conducted in two languages, Latin and Greek.

Studies were completed in Greek. Works of art imported from Greece flooded Italy and were copied. The scientists and practicing doctors in Rome generally had Greek origins. Only mistrust and resistance coming from within senatorial circles could thwart this cultural movement. (It was the politician Cato, the great denouncer of Hellenism, who brought the Italian poet Ennius to Rome).

Centered around Scipio Africanus (Hannibal's conqueror) there was a pro-Hellenism circle that welcomed two eminent Greeks: the philosopher Panaetius and the historian Polybius. Could there be a better symbol of this fusion of civilizations than Titus Pomponius (also known as Atticus), a friend of Cicero who lived in Athens as a patron of the arts?

The creation of this new office contributed to the evolution of the "law of nations" (*ius gentium*), which has extended right up into our own times as public international law. This *ius gentium* demonstrated that a body of law could be acceptable to the members of different peoples and races, and it brought Roman law nearer to universal applicability than any others that have ever been devised.

CHAPTER 5

The Invasion by Hannibal

Carthaginians in Spain

In the 220s B.C., the Carthaginians once again offered a grave menace to Italy. This time the threat came from the armies they maintained in Spain. Their dominant position in that peninsula was the revival of an old phenomenon, for Carthage had earlier possessed a Spanish coastal empire. When it lost the First Punic War and was expelled from Sicily, Sardinia, and Corsica, it had also been deprived of almost the whole of its former Spanish dominions. But after putting an end to the mercenary revolt, the Carthaginians achieved a startling revival and built up a Spanish empire all over again. The agents of this recovery were the most able family Carthage ever produced: the house of the Barcids, who settled themselves for several decades in Spain, establishing a hereditary line of semi-independent governors.

The first of the family to set himself up there was Hamilcar Barca, who had played a distinguished part in the First Punic War. When he had again fulfilled a leading role in the suppression of the rebellious mercenaries, he was authorized to recapture territories in Spain. His successes were impressive, and the Spanish territories he had occupied were larger and richer than the Carthaginians had ever ruled before. The Spaniards, men of Celtic and Iberian stock famous for their physical endurance, provided him with a new army—the best Carthage had ever possessed.

In 229 B.C., however, Hamilcar was drowned. His son-in-law Hasdrubal, who succeeded him, moved his headquarters farther south to New Carthage (Cartagena), on a peninsula commanding one of the best harbors in the world. Hasdrubal pushed the frontier of the new Carthaginian Spain to the north, halfway up to the Pyrenees, and deep into the interior.

Then Hasdrubal was murdered (221 B.C.), and the command passed to his brother-in-law Hannibal. Hannibal pushed still farther inland. However, one coastal town, Saguntum, decided to resist him. The Saguntines appealed to Rome, and Rome took the fateful step of responding favorably. Before long, its delegates were on their way to Hannibal at Carthago Nova to transmit the Senate's command to keep his hands off Saguntum. Hannibal rejected the ultimatum and pressed on with the blockade of Saguntum. The Romans ordered the Carthaginian government to hand Hannibal over to them—a demand that was predictably turned down. But their refusal to surrender Hannibal meant war. The curtain was now going up for the most terrible of all Rome's struggles, and the most far reaching in its results—the Second Punic War (218 B.C.).

The real, underlying motive for the Romans' action was a profound suspicion of Hannibal. As to his own attitude, he must have known that his siege of Saguntum involved a serious risk of war against them. The legend, which may be true, was that his father had once made him swear eternal hatred towards the Romans.

But in any case, he evidently felt determined to avenge his country's defeat in the First Punic War, and he believed that the new Spanish empire gave him a wonderful opportunity to carry out these plans of vengeance and reversal.

The victories of Hannibal

But the Romans, too, were confident, and so now they declared war. They intended to send forces to Spain, but their designs were forestalled by Hannibal's audacious decision to invade Italy by the difficult land route. He took with him forty thousand men, comprising well-trained Spanish infantry and excellent African (Numidian) cavalry, with thirty-seven elephants. And he hoped to augment this army in north Italy by winning over anti-Roman Gauls and Rome's Italian subject allies.

In April 218 B.C., he transferred his army across the Rhone, and in the early autumn he crossed the Alps. The mountains were treacherous going because of premature falls of snow, but Rome's belief that this would stop an army from getting through them proved mistaken. Nevertheless, when Hannibal came down into the Po valley, he had only twenty-six thousand men left, and the Senate's generals hoped to wear him down. But they were almost at once defeated in two successive battles, on a northern and then a southern tributary of the Po. And so, within only two months, Hannibal had overrun almost the whole of northern Italy. He had lost most of his elephants, yet as a result of his victories, he was able to increase his force to a total strength of fifty thousand.

Meanwhile, at Rome itself, the plebeians were infuriated by the bungling which had lost the north Italian land. Their appointment of the reformist "new man" Flaminius to a consulship in 217 B.C. was a criticism of the Senate's conduct of the war.

Flaminius tried to block the Carthaginian army's southward advance, but early in the year they evaded him and pressed on through marshy country, in such rough conditions that Hannibal, riding on the sole surviving elephant, lost the sight of an eye through exposure to icy cold. However, he drew Flaminius after him and, on a foggy April morning, trapped his army in a defile between the hills and Lake Trasimene. Most of the soldiers of these two Roman legions were killed, and Flaminius himself was among the fallen. This victory presented Hannibal with an undefended road to Rome. However, he did not take the opportunity. He lacked siege equipment, and in its absence the walls of Rome could not be breached by any attack. So Hannibal swerved aside from the city and instead decided to seek allies in the southern part of the peninsula.

In the following year, the Roman generalship was bestowed on two inexperienced consuls, who were placed in joint command of the largest army Rome had ever put into the field. In an effort to end the war in a single blow, they accepted battle on a smooth open plain near Cannae, a small fortress near Italy's heel. Believing that their numerical superiority would tell, they attacked, and Hannibal allowed his convex crescent to become concave under the pressure of their center. But the prevailing hot sirocco wind blew blinding clouds of sand into their faces, and they found themselves caught in a pincer movement by the enemy's light troops on either flank and cavalry in the rear. Wedged tight in these hopeless conditions, the Roman army

BUST OF HANNIBAL
(2nd century B.C.)
This bust was commissioned by Hannibal's father, Hamilcar Barca, in New Carthage, Spain. Having lost Sicily after the First Punic War, Hannibal was forever seeking revenge.

61

ELEPHANT VASE
This terra cotta vase testifies to the legendary fame of the elephant, which the Carthaginians used extensively in battle. Pyrrhus, King of Epirus, also made use of elephants in warfare.

was almost wholly destroyed. This battle, the bloodiest defeat they ever suffered, provided an unprecedented example of a smaller force successfully enveloping a larger one on both sides—a tactic that required perfect coordination and was admired by the German general von Schlieffen at the outset of the First World War in 1914.

One of the consuls was killed in action, but the other received a courteous reception at Rome from his fellow senators, who thanked him for not despairing of the Republic—for in the city, despite this catastrophe, morale remained indomitable. Indeed, even before the end of the year, Rome's terrible losses were already more than made good by further recruitment, so that Hannibal's victory had failed to repair his numerical disadvantage.

In 212 B.C., Rome emphasized its status as a major power by issuing for the first time its historic silver coin, the *denarius*, which provided a much improved means of meeting the state's financial needs. Nor was it of any avail, in 211 B.C., for Hannibal to advance to the outskirts of Rome. Accompanied by a cavalry, he rode around the walls on his black horse, watched by the inhabitants on the walls. At that very moment, the site of his camp, three miles away, came up for auction in the city, and was duly sold. Nothing could have shown him more clearly that the Romans, in spite of all the disasters they had suffered at his hands, were determined to survive and to win.

The Scipios in Spain

Although the Romans had failed to keep Hannibal from crossing the Pyrenees and marching on Italy, they succeeded in preventing his younger brother Hasdrubal Barca, whom he had left behind to rule Carthage's Spanish empire, from sending him any reinforcements. This they did by making the decision to fight an active war in Spain itself, despite all the crises that they were undergoing in their homeland.

Rome's Spanish armies were commanded, for the first seven years of the war, by two men named Scipio, the father and uncle of the great Scipio Africanus. The Scipios gained control of the Mediterranean seaboard of the country, moving gradually southwards until, in 211 B.C., they captured Saguntum, the original bone of contention. But later that year both the brothers died in battle.

In 210 B.C., the Senate appointed a new and surprising general to command the Spanish armies. This was Publius Cornelius Scipio (later Africanus), son and nephew of the commanders who had perished in Spain the year before. Publius Scipio was only twenty-five, yet he was not untried in war, and his exploits had inspired the conviction that he was the right man for the job.

Once in Spain, he chose as his target the enemy headquarters at Carthago Nova. While assaulting the town from the land side, he profited by a squall, which had blown up and lowered the level of the lagoon, to send his troops through the shallow waters and scale the fortifications that were undefended on this side—and by this means Carthago Nova fell into his hands (209 B.C.). In the following year, he engaged Hasdrubal Barca's smaller army at Baecula. Scipio divided up his main force and, using his light troops as a screen, fell on the enemy's flanks. This striking demonstration of flexibility won him the battle.

Yet Hasdrubal Barca escaped and at last got out of Spain altogether, proceeding to Italy with the intention of joining his brother Hannibal. The departure of his army ensured final Roman success in the Spanish campaign. By the end of the year, Carthage had lost its Spanish possessions forever.

And so these most valuable portions of the Iberian peninsula had fallen into the hands of Rome, which annexed them and converted them into two new provinces: the eastern coastal strip of Nearer Spain, and beyond it, Further Spain. The Romans developed and expanded Carthaginian mining in the country, which was said to overflow with metals; at Carthago Nova alone, the silver mines subsequently employed as many as forty thousand workers at one time.

The triumph of Scipio Africanus

The removal of Hasdrubal Barca's army from Spain was Hannibal's gain in Italy. And it came at a very appropriate time, for the Romans were almost at the end of their resources. In 209 B.C., twelve Latin colonies out of the existing thirty had declared their inability to supply any more troops or money. They could fight no more. After crossing the Alps unopposed, Hasdrubal descended into the Po valley, where new Gaulish recruits raised his numbers to thirty thousand. Then the two Carthaginian brothers moved towards each other, intending to join forces. The Romans had an army in the north of Italy and an army in the south. At this juncture they benefited from a great stroke of luck: Captured dispatch-riders of Hasdrubal revealed to them that his meeting place with Hannibal was to be in Umbrian territory. On receiving this news, the southern Roman commander, Gaius Claudius Nero, undertook a rapid six-day march up the Adriatic coast to the Umbrian river Metaurus. On the following morning Hasdrubal heard a double bugle call from the camp of the Romans, which told him that their two armies had united. This meant that he was outnumbered by at least ten thousand men. In a desperate attempt to slip through and join forces with his brother, he moved up the Metaurus valley after nightfall. But he lost his way in the dark, was overtaken among the gorges and slippery crags, and died fighting—and almost all his men died with him.

For the first time during the entire long period of the war, the Romans had won a pitched battle in their homeland, and the end of Hannibal's occupation of Italy was now only a matter of time. He learned what had happened when his brother's head was hurled into his camp. Then he withdrew into the mountains of Italy's toe and stayed there, without emerging, for another four years.

When two of these years had passed (205 B.C.), Scipio, fresh from his Spanish victories, was elected consul and asked the Senate for permission to invade Africa and attack Carthage directly. The senators were reluctant, since they still felt appre-

BUST OF SCIPIO
It was after his victory over Carthage in Zama, in Tunisia (202 B.C.), that Scipio was named Scipio Africanus.

PUNIC BREASTPLATE
(3rd –2nd century B.C.)
A rare relic from the Punic
Wars, this extravagant
ceremonial breastplate,
made of gilded bronze,
can be seen at the National
Museum of Bardo, in Tunis.

hensive of Hannibal's continued presence in Italy and were anxious not to impose further burdens on the allied towns, but they eventually agreed. Scipio recruited seven thousand volunteers, bringing his total army up to thirty thousand, and with this force landed in north Africa. There he was joined by a neighboring prince, Masinissa, ruler of part of Numidia (eastern Algeria), with his excellent cavalry.

In the next year Hannibal returned from Italy, his fifteen-year-long invasion at an end. Carthage had begun negotiations for peace with the Romans, but Hannibal persuaded his government to break off these talks. Thereupon Scipio moved inland, and in 202 B.C., near Zama, seventy-five miles from the city, the final battle of the war was fought. It was not a real climax because the eventual outcome of the campaign could be in no doubt. But it achieved great fame owing to the caliber of the rival commanders—and before the engagement, the two men had a famous meeting about which nothing is known, except that it was unproductive.

When the battle began, neither side succeeded in outflanking the other, for both were by now thoroughly familiar with tactics of this kind. But the issue was decided by the horsemen of Rome's Numidian allies, who broke off their pursuit of the enemy's cavalry wings and fell on their rear, achieving total victory. There were few Carthaginian survivors, but Hannibal was one of them. He recommended to his government that peace should be made immediately, and this was done. The Carthaginians had already lost Spain, and now they had ceased to be a major power. So the Romans had completed the most decisive single phase of their rise to domination. The Second Punic War had made it certain that they would remain in control of the western Mediterranean for hundreds of years to come. For the west, therefore, with the possible exception of the struggles of the twentieth century A.D., the Second Punic War proved to have been the most momentous war of all time.

The career of Scipio, on whose initiative all this was done, revealed that the times when Roman leaders were almost anonymous representatives of a team had begun to come to an end. Scipio was a new phenomenon. He was an unfamiliar sort of Roman, replacing traditional prudence by a novel individualism, a spirit of adventure. It was symbolic that he was the first of Rome's generals to be known by the name of the country he had defeated—Africanus. His final triumph raised him to the most powerful position any Roman general had ever possessed.

The enemy Hannibal was a greater general than his father, Hamilcar, and greater even than Scipio; indeed, he was one of the outstanding commanders of all time. That he placed beyond doubt, first, by his initial successes in Italy and the brilliant methods he used to win them, and then by the almost incredibly daring feat of maintaining himself in that hostile country, so far from his home base, for fifteen years. And, above all, he was a leader of men so inspired that, throughout all those foreign years, he never experienced a mutiny.

Twenty-nine years old when he came to Italy, Hannibal was a wiry, athletic man, possessed of an iron self-restraint. Not only his talent but also the integrity of his personal character caught the fancy of subsequent ages, despite virulent Roman propaganda to the contrary. His final confrontation with Scipio in battle, preceded, it was said, by that mysterious meeting, could not fail to stir people's imaginations forevermore. He is one of the world's most noble failures, an altogether exceptional man who took on, in deadly warfare, a nation empowered with rock-like resolution—and that nation proved too much for him. It emerged hardened from the supreme test, and ironically, his most lasting achievement was to confirm and magnify its confidence and power.

The eclipse of the Greek kingdoms

The happenings of the third century B.C. had brought Rome into forcible contact not only with Carthage but also with Greece, with repercussions upon the future history of the Mediterranean, which within a remarkably short time became a Roman lake. The important Greek political units were three great monarchies carved out of Alexander the Great's (d. 323 B.C.) dominions after his death. The rulers of these were Antigonids in Macedonia; the Seleucids, whose dominions extended from the Aegean to the Hindu Kush; and the Ptolemies, who reigned over Egypt and the lands and seas around it.

The worst problem of these three Greek empires was the debilitating strife and tension that so frequently bedeviled their mutual relations. Philip V, the king of

ANTIOCHUS III
This portrait of the king of Syria (223–187 B.C.), from the Louvre, is a Roman replica of a Greek bronze original from the end of the 3rd century B.C.

THEATER OF THE
ACROPOLIS OF PERGAMUM
*(beginning of 2nd
century B.C.) This large
theater is an important
example of Hellenistic
architecture. Fanning out
on a hillside, it reflects the
urban concepts adopted
by the Attalus kings of
Pergamum, who wanted
to use the landscape to
set off monuments from
their surroundings.*

Macedonia, still deeply distrustful of the Romans, clearly perceived the perils of these inter-Greek tensions and therefore concluded a secret treaty with his Seleucid fellow ruler, Antiochus III.

In 203–202 B.C., Philip combined with Antiochus to make a joint attack upon the third major monarchy, Egypt of the Ptolemies, at that time ruled by a boy-king. Governed from its capital, Alexandria, the greatest commercial port and cultural center in the world, this Ptolemaic kingdom was run by an unparalleled system of centralized state control. It presented a particularly tempting target to attackers owing to its abundance of grain, gold, copper, iron, and building stones.

But this sinister alliance between Macedonia and the Seleucids greatly disturbed the Greek city-states, and particular alarm was felt by the two principal second-class powers of the time, Rhodes and Pergamum. They now turned to Rome and sought to make it share their anxieties.

The Pergamenes and Rhodians did not find it hard to convince the Roman Senate that if two of the major Greek powers could attack the third, they might feel inclined to combine again to attack Rome as well, and an ultimatum was delivered to Macedonia.

Philip rejected the demand as an impertinence, and so Rome's first important war on Greek soil was under way (200 B.C.). The first two years' campaigns brought little progress. But then it became clear that the Roman commander Flamininus, consul at the age of only twenty-nine, intended to eject the Macedonians from their three principal fortresses in Greece.

But Philip himself moved to the offensive, and at the ridge of Cynoscephalae (Dog's Head), now Karadag, in eastern Thessaly, forced a battle upon Flamininus. Philip's right wing charged successfully downhill but was then engaged in the rear by the Romans and routed, and the Macedonian cause was lost. In this first direct conflict between two different military traditions, the new flexibility taught by Scipio Africanus had made the legions more than a match for the tightly packed and relatively immobile Greek phalanx. In its defeat, the future of the east Mediterranean world could be read without too much difficulty.

Philip had to give up his fleet and his fortresses and accept the total exclusion of Macedonian influence from Greece. Flamininus filled the vacuum by declaring, at the Isthmian Games in the great mercantile city of Corinth, that the Greek cities were henceforth to be free. This famous Declaration of Freedom roused the Greeks to such excitement that the birds, it was said, were stunned by the shout of jubilation that arose. This joy was not, however, universal, since Rome's former allies, the Aetolian League, had given substantial assistance to Rome, and yet because of the general liberation had only been allowed to annex an insignificant amount of territory as a reward. In their disappointment, they invited Antiochus to bring a Seleucid army to Greece to drive out the Romans (193 B.C.).

At this time Antiochus's relations with the Romans were poor. What is more, Rome's ancient enemy Hannibal was now at the Seleucid court. After the Second Punic War, he had led Carthage into an impressive revival. But the Carthaginians had become tired of his strong leadership, and Antiochus allowed him to reside in Seleucid territory. Antiochus decided to accept the Aetolian invitation, whereupon in March 192 B.C., he invaded Greece, although by doing so he made it inevitable that the Senate would send armies to resist him.

Antiochus's conduct of the war found him no match for the Romans. Defeated heavily at the historic pass of Thermopylae (191 B.C.), he was forced to evacuate Greece. Then, in the following year, the Romans defeated him again, this time at sea. This enabled them to land troops in Asia, which they had never done before. And so came Antiochus's final confrontation with the Romans, a land battle at Magnesia in western Asia Minor (190 B.C.). Scipio Africanus's brother was the nominal Roman commander, but Africanus was there, too, as his adviser. The most heroic part was played by Eumenes of Pergamum, who broke the heavy armored Persian horsemen on the left flank of the enormous army of Antiochus. Then the Seleucid elephants, stampeded by javelins, charged backwards through their own central phalanx, and the Romans had won an overwhelming victory.

THE DYING GAUL
(Capitole Museums)
This well-known statue, found in the gardens of the historian Sallust, is a Roman replica of a statue from Pergamum. The original (3rd century B.C.) was displayed in Athena's sanctuary by King Attalus I to honor his victory over the hordes of Galatians (Gauls) in Asia Minor.

Within a very short time, the two most powerful Greek kingdoms had been separately engaged and invaded by the Romans, suffering extremely heavy reverses. Nevertheless, the setback experienced by Philip V of Macedonia had not proved final after all. In 179 B.C., Philip died and was succeeded by his thirty-five-year-old son Perseus. He renewed his father's treaty with the Romans, whom he had no desire to offend. But, at the same time, he took numerous steps to strengthen Macedonia's influence among all its neighbors. In 171 B.C., the Romans drifted once again into war against Macedonia. The feeble pretext was that Perseus had attacked some border chiefs who possessed ties of friendship with Rome. But the real reason was the fear that he might make a move to disrupt their settlement in Greek lands.

As in the previous Macedonian war, the first campaigns were irresolute and inconclusive. But by the fourth year of hostilities, the king had finally been obliged to withdraw from his frontier lines, so the consul Paullus was able to establish himself on the Macedonian plain itself, where he forced the enemy to give battle at Pydna. At first, the assault of Perseus's weighty phalanx of twenty thousand men drove the Roman legionaries back. But, as the phalanx charged, gaps opened in its line, and into these gaps small Roman units insinuated themselves, while others simultaneously enveloped the Macedonian flanks, where their slashing swords inflicted catastrophic losses on the opposing spearmen. The inferiority of the phalanx to the legions had now been demonstrated even more conclusively than before, and the Macedonian army had ceased to exist.

ISLAND OF DELOS
This island was chosen in 478 B.C. to store the treasure of the League of Delos, a military alliance of the cities along the Aegean Sea.

Imperialistic policies

Perseus surrendered, and his officials were deported wholesale from the country. Moreover, his monarchy itself was abolished, and the country was divided into four separate republics. This decision, overriding Macedonian nationhood in the roughest and most sweeping fashion, was momentous, for it was the first time that one of the three great successor states of Alexander had succumbed to total destruction at Rome's hands.

Within the space of a single generation the Greek world, hitherto dependent on the balance of power among three large empires, had been irremediably transformed and ruined by the utter defeat of two of those states—and their place was filled by the Romans, who had entered the lands surrounding the Aegean and were there to stay.

The division of the Macedonian kingdom into four autonomous but obedient republics had ensured that they should be too weak to do Rome any further harm. But it had also made it certain that they would be too weak to protect themselves—and so it turned out. In 150 B.C. a certain Andriscus announced, erroneously, that he was the son of the late King Perseus, and then, meeting only feeble resistance from the republican militias, he successfully reunited Macedonia and revived the kingship in his own person. The Romans had to intervene to expel him and run him down (148 B.C.).

At this point, they set their sights upon a major revision of policy. The whole concept of encouraging Greek communities to become their "free" but dependent clients now seemed ripe for abandonment. It was decided that the principle of direct annexation must be imported to these eastern regions. It had already caused widespread horror when Macedonia was destroyed in 167 B.C., and now there was a further shock when the republics into which that country had been divided were directly annexed by Rome. Within this new province a major road was constructed, the Via Egnatia, following an ancient route all the way from the Adriatic to the northern Aegean. This was the first important Roman road in the East. It linked the Macedonian cities to one another and to Italy.

On Macedonia's southern flank, in Greece itself, the Romans infuriated the members by allowing the city-state of Sparta, which the Achaeans had earlier compelled to join their confederation, to terminate its membership. This led to violent anti-Spartan and anti-Roman feeling at the league capital, Corinth, a large industrial harbor and key fortress, and when Roman envoys came to the city, they were beaten up. The Roman consul Mummius came down from Macedonia with four legions and captured Corinth (146 B.C.).

By order from his government, the whole place was razed to the ground and all its surviving inhabitants were sold into slavery. This drastic treatment of the city was partly intended as an insurance against social revolution, but it was a terrible sign of the new times that one of the most ancient and distinguished centers of Greek and Mediterranean civilization should be blotted out of existence. The Achaean League, too, was abolished, and Greece and its cities were amalgamated with the new province of Macedonia. The long centuries of Greek independence had been brought to an abrupt and violent end. And in the very same year, the independence of the Carthaginian state was likewise terminated by the Romans, and its ancient capital suffered the same fate as Corinth.

Rome's defeat of the Carthaginians fifty-five years earlier, while eliminating their international power, had not prevented them from making a remarkable recovery, initially under the guidance of Hannibal. But the fatal impediment to this revival proved to be Masinissa, the ruler of neighboring Numidia, who held his throne as a client of Rome and was eager to build up his empire. Throughout half a century following the Second Punic War, Masinissa encroached unscrupulously on Carthage's coastal colonies and wheat-lands. Finally, in 150 B.C., the Carthaginians, driven to desperation, took up arms against him, although their treaty with the Romans had forbidden them to engage in independent warfare. And when Masinissa appealed to Rome, the aged Cato insisted repeatedly to his fellow senators that Carthage must be destroyed, and war was declared.

The Carthaginians chose to offer a desperate resistance, which continued for four years. It was terminated in 146 B.C. by Scipio Aemilianus, who brought the siege of Carthage to a successful, bloody conclusion. Its survivors were sold into slavery; the whole city was demolished and salt scattered on the site so that it should remain barren and accursed forevermore. This was a measure of the traumatic effect Hannibal had exercised on the minds of the Romans. Masinissa had died, so they decided on a policy of annexation. Thus the Carthaginian homeland was converted into the province of Africa, corresponding with the northern part of Tunisia today. The new province possessed immense economic and agricultural wealth and was so overwhelmingly rich in grain that it gradually succeeded Sicily as the principal granary of Rome.

This ruthless obliteration of Carthage sent a shudder throughout the civilized Mediterranean world. Roman imperialism could now be seen by all, in its nakedly cynical form, but for all its moral defects, it had achieved astonishing practical results. Within the space of a few years, the Romans had become dominant in almost the whole of the Mediterranean—it was indeed *Mare Nostrum*, Our Sea.

COLOSSAL STATUE
Representing a barbarian captive, this statue comes from a façade from the Roman agora of Corinth. Destroyed by Mummius in 146 B.C.., Corinth became a Roman colony under Caesar. As capital of the province of Achaea, it abounds with temples and public buildings.

Games for gods and mortals

❧ ❧

ACROBATS
Between chariot races, entertaining interludes were presented for audiences: Fighters were introduced, exotic animals were exhibited, and acrobats performed.

As the high point of the religious celebrations that filled the public calendar, games *(ludi)* were a source of entertainment that the Romans, as well as their gods, enjoyed greatly. Circus games *(circenses)* and theater *(scaenici)* were a kind of offering, in fact, and closed each religious celebration. Under the Republic, the Great Games known as *Optimus Maximus,* which were devoted to Jupiter, the supreme god of Rome, lasted for half a month.

The theater and amphitheater, where the seating strictly reflected the social hierarchy, were the ideal places for city plebeians and authorities to meet; it was here that the emperor would regularly measure his popularity. The games could be offered by a distinguished person who wanted to attract more supporters in view of an election, or by the emperor, who, after a military victory, would show his generosity towards the people by doing so.

Chariot races were, from the beginning, an integral part of the circus (the oval track was an image of the cosmos) and adhered to a strict ritual. As soon as the magistrate gave the signal, the teams, riding on two- or four-horse chariots, would race around the track seven times. The drivers, who were organized into "factions," drew cheers from the crowd, made up of men and women who were seated together.

Gladiator combats, which first took place during big funerals to exhibit the cruelty of death, became part of Roman games as early as the end of the Republic. Under the Empire, each city administrative center had an amphitheater that could accommodate various kinds of entertainment. Gladiators—mostly slaves, and often professionals—would fight each other to the death with various weapons. Criminals or Christians would wrestle with wild animals. There were large hunts *(venationes),* which displayed the most exotic animals in fabulous settings.

The violence of this entertainment shocked many— Seneca and Augustine among them—and criticizing the games even became a recurring theme in the writing of the Fathers of the Church. Nevertheless, the ludi played an ever-growing role in the life of the Romans. It would not be until the reign of Emperor Honorius (395–423 A.D.) that gladiator combats were outlawed.

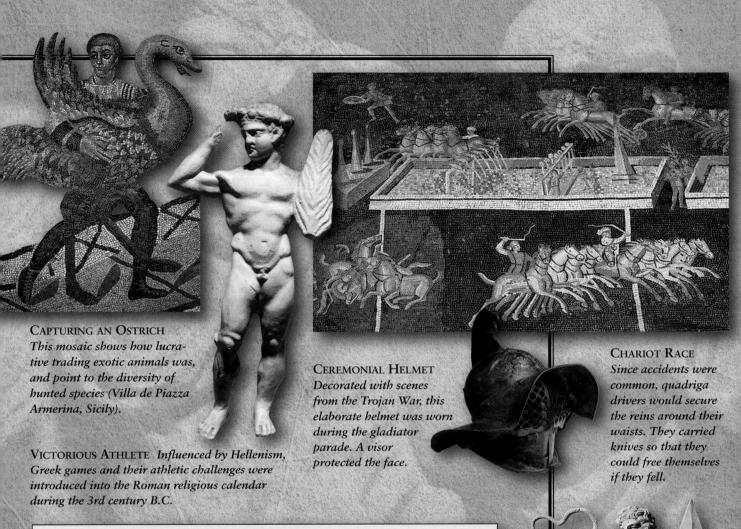

CAPTURING AN OSTRICH
This mosaic shows how lucrative trading exotic animals was, and point to the diversity of hunted species (Villa de Piazza Armerina, Sicily).

VICTORIOUS ATHLETE *Influenced by Hellenism, Greek games and their athletic challenges were introduced into the Roman religious calendar during the 3rd century B.C.*

CEREMONIAL HELMET
Decorated with scenes from the Trojan War, this elaborate helmet was worn during the gladiator parade. A visor protected the face.

CHARIOT RACE
Since accidents were common, quadriga drivers would secure the reins around their waists. They carried knives so that they could free themselves if they fell.

THE COLOSSEUM: A COLOSSAL ARENA

Begun under Vespasian and completed by his son Titus in 80 A.D., the Colosseum, the largest and most prestigious of all arenas of the Roman world, was built on the former site of Nero's reservoir. It replaced the wooden amphitheater that was destroyed during the fire that burned through Rome. A perfect oval, almost 625 feet long, the Colosseum served as a model for all amphitheaters thereafter. The monument could be filled with water to enact naval combats, called *naumachia*. An awning stretched over posts provided shade for the 50,000 spectators (seated on four levels); the arcades were decorated with statues of venerated gods. Under this vast arena, covered by a wooden floor, ran a maze of hallways. Through a system of hoists and trapdoors, machines brought the animals to the stage above ground.

GLADIATOR
If a gladiator proved courageous in fighting wild animals, he might be pardoned or even freed.

CHAPTER 6

The new society

Senate and nobles in charge

The foreign policy of these decisive first decades after 200 B.C., when ferocity and authoritarianism were on the increase all the time, was still directed by the Roman Senate and nobility.

During the Second Punic War, the Assembly had on rare occasions asserted itself against the Senate, most conspicuously by insisting upon the appointment of Scipio Africanus, but on the whole, the first two Carthaginian conflicts had greatly strengthened the oligarchy's control of affairs. As the third century passed into the second, the Senate's control of Roman policy remained as firm and thoroughgoing as ever, despite the occasional interventions by the Assembly.

This is confirmed by the statistics of elections: "New men," without consular ancestry, remained extremely rare, and government was virtually run by a close, clublike circle of about two thousand men belonging to fewer than twenty families.

These great aristocratic houses kept in their cupboards the wax masks of their ancestors who had held high office. The masks were arranged as a family tree and received religious worship; in family funerals, they were worn by actors engaged to walk in the procession.

So, guided by these men, the Senate reinforced its influence and, in the absence of any effective counterbalance, retained a position of virtually irresponsible supremacy, becoming even more exclusive and conservative in the process.

The rise of Latin culture

MASK OF TRAGEDY
(1st century B.C.) Because theaters were so large, making it hard for many to see and hear the actors, performers wore masks like this one to help them express the feelings of the characters and augment their voices.

In the literary field, too, the nobles and Senate became sensitive about suspected attempts to undermine their supremacy. One of those who suffered was the versatile poet Naevius (b. ca. 270–d. 201 B.C.). Naevius wrote patriotic works, of which only fragments survive today; they included original tragic dramas and a pioneer epic dealing with the First Punic War, in which he himself had served. But in about 204 B.C., he committed some fault for which he was imprisoned and then went into exile. Perhaps one reason was that the oligarchy still remembered the offense he had caused thirty years earlier when he criticized one of the greatest plebeian noble families.

Naevius's native ebullience also led him to write comic plays. But here he was outshone by Plautus (b. ca 254–d. 184 B.C.). With Plautus, we have already reached the precocious zenith of Latin verse comedy, and twenty of his complete plays have

survived. His models were the sophisticated products of the Greek New Comedy of fourth-century Athens, familiar to many educated Romans now that contacts with Greek south Italy and Sicily had multiplied. Yet Plautus wholly abandoned the subtlety of the original Greek comedies in order to give free rein to his own explosive genius for wild, quick-firing, slapstick buffoonery. His success in the centuries to come was enormous. And even during his lifetime, although his audiences comprised people at a wide variety of cultural levels, they were prepared to abandon the rival attractions of boxers, dancers, and chariot races in order to come and laugh at what they heard and saw on Plautus's temporarily erected stages.

Moreover, his plays are filled, for all their farcicality, with oblique but telling social criticism. Yet Plautus, unlike Naevius, escaped upper-class retaliation. He was careful to claim that his characters were not Roman but foreign and Greek, so that, superficially at least, it was not Roman institutions at all which were coming under fire. About fifteen years younger than Plautus was another poet, Ennius (239–169 B.C.). A poor man who enjoyed social life, he was said to have died of gout; "Unless I have gout," he had remarked, "I never write poetry." More industrious than this saying implied, he was the first professional literary man of Rome and the first to naturalize Greek literary culture. This was achieved, above all, by his rough, vigorous, colorful *Annals*, an epic poem in which, adapting the Greek

TRAVELING MUSICIANS *(Villa in Pompeii, 1st century B.C.) In this mosaic — attributed to a Greek, Dioscorides of Samos— musicians perform dance steps, accompanied by a flutist and a child who seems to be playing a small horn.*

73

heroic meter, he chronicled the entire course of Roman history up to his own day. His compatriots of later generations saw him as the father of Latin poetry, and he exercised a profound effect on subsequent historians and literary critcs.

Ennius had been brought back to Rome from Sardinia in 204 B.C. by Cato the Elder (234–49 B.C.), who was born at about the same time as Scipio Africanus. And although a "new man" without consuls among his ancestors, he became one of the outstanding politicians of his time. But Cato and Scipio were embittered rivals. Cato, taking his stand on antique tradition and rallying the support of many conservative landowners of the day, profoundly objected to the excessive personal reverence accorded to Scipio, whom he regarded as a careerist. Cato also deplored his interest in Greek culture (exemplified by his adoption of the Greek practice of close shaving). Ever since the Greco-Roman contacts of the Second Punic War, Cato saw Hellenism as an evil influence; it seemed to him outrageous when Scipio's brother brought back from the war against Antiochus the first bronze couches, bedcovers, ornate tables, fine cooking, and cabaret girls ever to be seen in Rome. And Cato had his way, for not long afterwards, in 184 B.C., he drove both the Scipios out of public life into retirement. Africanus died soon afterwards.

Cato's election to the censorship of 184 B.C. seemed a remarkable achievement for a "new man" and earned him the name of Cato the Censor ever afterwards; it also brought the term "censorious" into our language. The office enabled him to intensify his attacks on Hellenism, and he introduced numerous measures of moral and economic reconstruction and purification.

Cato was opposed to current tendencies towards the emancipation of women, complaining that wives tyrannized their husbands. Since the previous century, a much freer form of marriage had become habitual, and the influx of wealth meant that women began to dress and adorn themselves more luxuriously. They were also permitted to attend public entertainments and, in the more prosperous households at least, were taught not only the traditional household skills but more academic subjects, too. Thus Cornelia, the daughter of Scipio Africanus, in addition to managing her own estates, presided over a sort of intellectual salon.

AVNORVM SATYRORVM ETSILENORVMDELECT AVNORVM SATYR

THE ROMAN THEATER

As in Greece, the theater in Rome was religious in essence. Performances took place during certain festivities or to celebrate major events. Admission was free. A magistrate took on the costs, hiring a troupe leader who would buy a play from an author. The actors, who were men (except in mime), were slaves or emancipated slaves. They wore masks, since in the time of the Republic the profession was a source of infamy. Initially, stages were temporary ones made of boards. More permanent ones, housed in stone theaters, followed. Pompey built the first one in 55 B.C., after which many magnificent theaters were erected.

Unlike the Greeks, who built their theaters into hills, the Romans erected them on flat terrain. As popular entertainment, the theater first performed *attellans*—farces that dealt with standard characters like the old man, the braggart, the oaf, the glutton. A more sophisticated theater emerged after the conquest of Magna Graecia (Greater Greece). Whether tragic or comic, it most often involved Greek subjects, though sometimes a Roman subject was approached gingerly. These included historical episodes in tragedy and farces from the provinces in comedy. After the innovators—Livius Andronicus, Naevius, and Ennius—there were two great names in comic writing: Plautus (254–184 B.C.), who would later inspire some works by Molière, and Terence (190–159 B.C.), who was more sophisticated and psychological. Since audiences were not well educated, they tended to be more receptive to music than to narrative. Under the Empire, only mimes and pantomimes continued to be performed, but without words—first farces, then openly obscene pieces. Authors like Ovid and Seneca therefore preferred to read their works in public rather than have them performed.

Cato's disapproval of Cornelia's father, Scipio Africanus, was equaled by his distaste for enlightened women like herself. Indeed, his whole way of life was based on the single aim of protecting the traditional social values from contamination. He himself had been brought up in the country of the Sabines, to whose traditional harsh discipline and austerity he ascribed what seemed to him the best features in the character of all Romans—including, above all, their courageous endurance and loyal service to the state. This litigious and vindictive red-headed farmer with the piercing gray eyes was the epitome of puritanical reaction. But his obsessions were in vain, for his program could not, in the long run, succeed.

Apart from a work on agriculture, very little of what Cato wrote has survived. Yet his status as a writer is enormous. The gravest loss is his seven-volume *Origins*, a history of Rome. Written in Latin, not Greek like all its predecessors, it was the first major achievement in this field and virtually inaugurated Latin prose as a literary medium. Cato insisted that the Romans were basically different from the Greeks. In contrast to Greek states, he pointed out, Rome owed its successes not to a few individuals but to the combined genius of different people living and

TOILETTE CASE
Made of precious wood and decorated with bas-reliefs, this case held many ivory accessories, which the Romans used for their grooming. A polished bronze surface served as a mirror.

working together. So great was his distaste for the Scipio-type personality cult that in his *Origins*, he suppressed the names of great Roman commanders altogether, preferring instead, when describing the Second Punic War, to mention the name of a Carthaginian elephant, Surus.

Cato excelled at public speaking, which was the mainspring of Roman public life. As orator, statesman, and defender of austere but narrow morality, Cato remained greatly to the fore throughout these years.

In the campaign against Macedonia, one of the youngest Roman officers was Africanus's grandson by adoption, Scipio Aemilianus. He indulged even more than Africanus in the new Roman taste for Renaissance-style individualism that Cato so greatly deplored. And time after time in the years to come, it was to Scipio Aemilianus that the Romans turned in a crisis. It was he, in Cato's old age, who won the Third Punic War (146 B.C.), and for nearly twenty years of Rome's history he remained its key personality and outstanding statesman. He was a man of numerous contradictions—reputedly idle when young, yet formidably active in later years. As a speaker he was excellent, and although not a brilliant general like Africanus, he was an organizer with plenty of drive. But what was most important about him was his deserved reputation for decent behavior: He was regarded as a person of integrity in an age that needed this and knew it.

An intellectual sympathetic to Hellenism, Scipio Aemilianus had been educated by a variety of Greek tutors and was deeply interested in Greek literature and philosophy. Men who were in touch with him played a large role in the partially Hellenized Roman culture of the time, including the Latin dramatic poet Terence

(b. ca. 190–d. 159 B.C.), one of Plautus's successors on the comic stage. All six of Terence's plays survive. They display a constructional skill that left a strong imprint on the future theater of Europe. Their writer is seen to be not only gentler and more contemplative than Plautus, but also closer to his Greek models.

Roman wealth and new buildings

THE AEMILIA BASILICA *(179 B.C., Roman forum) Hellenistic in origin, this kind of building—the only remaining basilica from the Republican period— emerged in Rome during the 3rd century B.C. Divided into naves by rows of columns, this large covered space served as a forum during inclement weather. It housed the tribunates as well as political and economic activities.*

During these years, an ever-increasing stream of coin and bullion flowed into the Roman treasury from countries overseas. In 168 B.C., the three-day triumphal procession of the victor of Pydna, Paullus, included two hundred and fifty wagons of spoils and three hundred crowns made of gold. It was a metal that, for the first time, was becoming familiar in Rome, in this form of massive indemnities paid by its defeated foes. Rome already exceeded all the other cities of the Western world in size, and as this influx of foreign wealth continued, its buildings began to assume a monumental appearance. Greek influence was manifest in a new taste for freestanding porticoes and for the basilicas or public halls that replaced the old rows of shops beside the Forum.

In the first century B.C., these large halls were reconstructed with rounded arches instead of the rows of columns which had characterized the original basilicas. Although there had been timid attempts at the theme in Greece and Etruria, the arch was a preeminently Roman structural form. It could also be created in isolation from arcades and could even be detached from buildings altogether. The result of the latter process was another typical Roman creation, the free-standing monu-

AVNORVM SATYRORVM ETSILENORVM DELECTA

SPOILS OF WAR AND THE CONQUEROR'S TRIUMPH

During antiquity, an army in the field lived off requisitions and spoils. Every victory was a chance to pillage for the benefit of the soldiers and state. But in Rome, what was gathered was distributed according to very specific rules.

Although Roman soldiers in general were allowed to keep some of what they had seized, most of the plunder was sold to merchants who traveled with the army or was brought back to Rome in the war chest and put up for auction by the *quaestors* (procurators). The pillage was so great that after the defeat of the Macedonian King Perseus in a battle at Pydna in 167 B.C., the direct tax was eliminated.

Every so often, the senate authorized the conqueror to triumph—that is, to ceremoniously parade across Rome. The cortege would leave from the military esplanade, cross the Circus Maximus, go around the Palatine Hill, go down the Sacred Way to the forum, and go up to the Temple of Jupiter on Capitoline Hill. With politicians participating, the pillage would be shown, and both prisoners of war and animals to be sacrificed were displayed. The victorious army walked behind their general, dressed like the statue of Jupiter. At the end of the Republic, victory was also depicted in paintings and celebrated in inscriptions on soldiers banners.

mental arch. Its first recorded examples at Rome date from 196 B.C. They were the forerunners of the magnificent imperial triumphal arches.

These developments in the construction of arches and arcades, and of the curving apses, niches, and vaults which are likewise among the supreme architectural achievements of the Romans, were made possible by the discovery of concrete, which was the most revolutionary of all their structural inventions.

The Romans had detected the admirable properties of a material available in the soil, a natural, pulverized, volcanic blend of cinders and clay. When lime was mixed with this product in a kiln, the molten mass became an exceptionally consistent and coherent concrete. This was poured over a rubble "aggregate" made from chips of stone or pumice. The result was a compact, almost indestructible mass, extraordinarily resistant to strains and stresses. Successive generations of Roman architects would awaken to the potentialities of this concrete medium and employ it to build their soaring curvilinear marvels of the future.

In 144 B.C., a praetor built Rome's first aqueduct, the Aqua Marcia, which supplied the city with water from a source thirty-six miles distant. This was the first stage of a long process of such construction, at the end of which Rome's abundance of running water would be unequaled in its lavishness. There was also extensive building of Italian roads. In Rome itself, although nothing was done to increase their narrow width, the streets were paved with blocks of durable lava from the Alban Mount.

The growing population of the capital, however, was accommodated in rickety wooden blocks lacking adequate light, heat, or water supply and subject to frequent

SLAVES PRESSING GRAPES
On agricultural estates, the slaves who produced wine were treated relatively well.

fires and floods. For the houses of the rich, however, wall facings of dressed stone were coming into use. The houses presented plain façades to the street, with the rooms grouped around a central *atrium*—a blend of courtyard and front hall. The *atrium* housed the family altar and statues. Beyond it were the living and domestic quarters, which might include dining-rooms for summer and winter.

Agriculture and slavery

We learn about the agriculture of these years from Cato the Elder's *Treatise On Farming (De Agricultura)*, the earliest Latin prose work to have come down to us intact. To own a mixed ranch, insists this hard-bitten farmer-politician, and to work it scientifically, is much the best way to make money. And in this survey he provides a vivid picture of the novel enterprises of the day, which combined agriculture with commerce, banking, and various kinds of industry. The way to run these estates, Cato maintained, was by making good use of slaves. Enormous numbers of these were now available. As a result of the victorious campaigns of the third and second centuries B.C., slaves flooded into Rome.

Slaves lacked all human rights, and the dramatist Plautus, although expressing himself obliquely, indicated sympathy for their defenseless position in society. Yet household slavery could be relatively humane—and it provided one of the principal channels by which Greek culture came to Rome, supplying the city with its secretaries, teachers, and doctors. In the countryside, on the other hand, slaves fared a great deal worse. Cato estimated they ought to receive much the same treatment as farm animals. Often these rustic slaves were kept in chains, and when they became too old to earn their keep by working, Cato was prepared to let them perish. Yet he goes on to say that the most efficient principle of management is to treat *both* animals and slaves well enough to enable them to work as long as they can—which meant giving them more food than, for instance, a "free" Egyptian peasant was given.

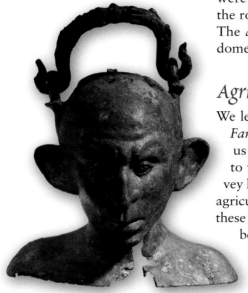

BRONZE PAIL
(2nd–3rd century B.C.) The accentuated features of this Syrian slave (the shape of the face, the size of the ears) are reminiscent of disparaging portraits of oriental slaves, such as the ones portrayed in Plautus's comedies.

AVNORVM SATYRORVM ETSILENORVM DELECT

THE LIFE OF A SLAVE

Slavery was a major factor of the history of antiquity. The economy of Classical Greece was greatly dependent on a servant workforce. This was also true for Rome, which needed its citizens to fight and participate in politics.

The great majority of the slaves of the Roman world were provided by conquest and by piracy. Though they numbered few at the beginning of the Republic, slaves arrived en masse starting in the 2nd century B.C. Stripped of freedom, they were sold in bulk in eastern Mediterranean markets, then resold to the state or to individuals. At this point, the slave lost his name and had no rights, either civil or political. His status was equal to that of personal property, and the father of the family decided on his life and death. His only chance of being emancipated was to be well-regarded by his master *(dominus)*.

Nevertheless, the lot of slaves varied greatly, depending on their value and knowledge. In the country, a slave without particular ability was chained and lived in harsh conditions. The situation was even worse in the mines. But qualified slaves, bought at a high price, were cared for; those who were professors, secretaries, and doctors, for example, were generally well-treated.

Other employers of slaves were as callous as Cato but less sensible, and subjected them to appalling ill-treatment. As a result, many slaves deserted their masters—one of the reasons why, at certain periods of the second century B.C., the whole structure of Classical Greco-Roman society seemed as if it might disintegrate. All over the Mediterranean, social strains were acute. But despite these troubles, it was the slaves who made Italy's agricultural plantations work and prosper.

CHAPTER 7

Reform and war in Italy

The Gracchi

Tiberius and Gaius Gracchus, young tribunes of the people, now made spectacular attempts to cure the many ills from which Rome and Italy were suffering.

Tiberius Gracchus was an idealist. He also entertained a private grudge against his cousin and brother-in-law Scipio Aemilianus. However, when Tiberius assumed his tribuneship in 133 B.C., Scipio was absent in Spain, so the new tribune was able to bring forward a measure, although Scipio regarded it as unduly radical. This provided for the creation of individual allotments to be carved out of the extensive Italian public land that had come into the possession of the Roman government since the Second Punic War. The relief of urban poverty may have formed part of Tiberius's intention, but his main purpose, against the alarmist background of contemporary slave uprisings, was to increase the number of free men possessing enough property to qualify them for military service.

The measure could not be described as overwhelmingly radical. However, he decided to short-circuit obstruction to his bill by presenting it directly to the Assembly, without prior reference to the Senate. This was not illegal but was contrary to custom, which played so great a part in Roman politics.

Moreover, when the measure was vetoed by a fellow tribune, Octavius, Tiberius induced the Assembly to depose him from his office, which was wholly without precedent. At all events, the agrarian bill was now passed, and in order to bring it into effect a commission was set up, including Tiberius, his younger brother Gaius, and Tiberius's father-in-law.

Then, in order to safeguard his legislation against the strong probability of subsequent annulment, Tiberius offered himself for immediate reelection to the tribunate. This, like Tiberius's way of presenting his bill, was a complete departure from custom. Moreover, as the time for the vote approached, it became clear that he had made too many enemies to win. People were beginning to suspect that his high-handed actions were directed towards seizing autocratic control of the state. When, therefore, the Assembly began its electoral meeting on the Capitol, a violent quarrel broke out. Physical brawling soon followed, and a crowd of senators and their clients clubbed Tiberius and three hundred of his supporters to death.

It was the first time for nearly four hundred years that blood had been shed in Roman civil strife—and this was a deeply ominous model for the future. In his brief period of activity, Tiberius Gracchus had initiated something that he surely did not want: the disintegration of the Roman oligarchic system.

A number of senators, including Scipio Aemilianus, who had welcomed Tiberius's fate, tried to terminate the activities of the land commissioners. But in this they did not succeed. The commissioners were able to carry on with their work, and their

THE SOWER
(1st century B.C.) This diminutive bronze comes from the villa of Lugugnana in Venetia, an ancient district at the head of the Adriatic.

achievements even did something to retard the ruin of the small farmers. Then one of the commissioners, Gaius Gracchus, was elected tribune for 123 B.C. Gaius was a most accomplished orator and used his oratory and diplomacy to win support from every direction. He was able to improve on Tiberius's record by securing his own immediate reelection to a second tribuneship unopposed.

Gaius began, apparently, by reaffirming his brother's agrarian enactment, supplementing it by a measure providing for the foundation of Roman colonies at centers including Tarentum and Carthage. The Carthaginian proposal was a complete novelty, since overseas colonization was a Greek idea unfamiliar to the Romans, and many of them found it unwelcome. Gaius also arranged for the passage of highly controversial bills concerning the law courts. Many officials had been far too readily acquitted by the court, since its jurymen, like the defendants, were all senators. In consequence, Gaius Gracchus promoted a measure providing that all the jurymen should be knights.

The rise of the knights had been a major phenomenon of recent years. In ancient times, they had been horsemen of the Roman cavalry, as their designation as *equites* indicated. But by the third century the knights had retained their social position but changed their function. They were roughly divided into two categories. The first consisted of prosperous landowners. The second group, however, engaged in financial opera-

AVNORVM SATYRORVM ETSILENORVMDELECT

THE LAND CRISIS

Until the 3rd century B.C., Rome was a nation of small landowners, mobilized almost every summer to defend the land or participate in the conquest of Italy. In the 2nd century B.C., the Italian economy was at a crisis point: Wars beyond the peninsula prevented small landowners from reaping the benefits from their land. With limited resources, they got into debt, while the agriculture yield of conquered countries brought tough competition.

At the same time, large landowners became richer by lending money at a high interest rate, by confiscating the land of ruined peasants, and by taking over seized land in conquered countries *(ager publicus)*. This land belonged to the state, but the Senate granted it in return for a symbolic sum. Development, facilitated by a growing servant workforce from the conquests, led to huge properties.

Several politicians attempted to stop this trend, which was emptying the countryside, enlarging the urban plebeian population and diminishing the number of men who could be mobilized. Two brothers, Tiberius and Gaius Sempronius Gracchus, attempted to redistribute the *ager publicus* (seized lands) and limit the size of land properties. But their reform efforts failed; both were assassinated.

tions. These financial knights had a good deal to do. The collection of public revenues was contracted out by the state to the highest bidder, and such bidders were normally knights; they were known as publicans.

Conflicts with the Senate sometimes arose, especially when the *publicani* tried to make too much money from these activities, thus leaving too little loot for the senators. Until the time of Gaius Gracchus, such attempts on the part of the knightly financiers were curbed without too much difficulty. An entirely new situation, however, was created by Gaius's new court consisting wholly of knights. Indeed, his action could be said to mark the beginning of what was later called the Equestrian Order as a separate and significant class, whose interests would inevitably clash with those of the senators so that the governing cadre of the state would no longer be a homogeneous whole.

Gaius then tackled a perilously heated question: the status of Rome's Latin and Italian allies. The allies had played a massive part in winning the Second Punic War, and after it was over, the time had been ripe for their admission to Roman citizen rights. But the Senate had no desire to bestow the Roman franchise on men whose votes it could not control, so nothing was done to improve their position.

An effort was made to appease the Italian allies by proposing that they should have a share of the small holdings now to be created out of the public land, but the government refused to allow the commissioners to take this step. Gaius decided that he could not evade the issue; and in the second year of his tribuneship (122 B.C.), he put forward a proposal. According to this scheme, Roman citizenship should be conferred upon all Latins, and in other Italian communities local civic officials should become Roman citizens. The status was thus a halfway house to the full franchise. But this statesmanlike measure was cunningly outbid by a conservative nominee, who passed a law with a far more ambitious policy than anything Gaius was proposing. No effort was made to carry this program out. But Gaius had been undermined, and when he went to supervise his new foundation at Carthage, malevolent rumors about the ill-omened site weakened his position still further.

In consequence, when he tried to secure reelection to a third tribunate in 121 B.C., he was rejected, and soon afterwards the end came. His political enemies now set out to cancel the Carthaginian colonization altogether, and when his supporters vociferously opposed this, a servant of one of the consuls, Opimius, was killed in a scuffle. Thereupon Opimius persuaded the Senate to pass a declaration of public emergency. On the strength of this injunction, he personally led a crowd of senators and knights in a physical attack on Gaius, who was killed, and then some three thousand of his supporters were executed after perfunctory trials. The decree that led to these actions, later known as the senatus consultum ultimum, was to become a feature of the many disturbed decades that now followed.

And so the two brothers left their ineffaceable and permanent mark on the history of Rome, with the result that within a hundred years after their brief careers, the Republic was no more.

Marius—a brief shining light

In the client kingdom of Numidia—flanking the Roman province of Africa—the successor of King Masinissa had died, and Rome divided the country between two young princes (118 B.C.). One of them was Jugurtha, who had served under Scipio Aemilianus. He was a noted athlete and horseman and a born soldier. The Roman partition had given him only the western and more primitive part of the country, and he not only rejected this but also ordered his troops to massacre the Italian residents in Numidia.

Rome declared war on him, but its first two expeditionary forces achieved nothing at all. A more competent general was dispatched (109 B.C.), but even he failed to induce his enemy, who became known as the lion of the desert, to surrender. Roman public opinion, not appreciating the difficulties of desert warfare, secured the appointment of one of his deputies over his head. This was Gaius Marius, a "new man" of middle-class origins who had amassed wealth as a knight and *publicanus* and had built up useful political support. Now, by fomenting the popular discontent against his own chief, he obtained for himself the consulship for 107 B.C. and the supreme command. In order to recruit troops for the war, Marius ignored the property qualifications for military service and called up propertyless volunteers on an extensive scale.

This inaugurated a period in which volunteer and conscript soldiers began to look to their general to use his own power to gain them rewards. On arrival in Numidia, Marius won impressive successes that showed him to be an exceptional military com-

PORTRAIT OF MARIUS
(end of the Republic)
This face, with its deep wrinkles and frowning eyebrows, is typical of Republican portraits, which emphasized severe features.

VIA DOMITIA
(121 B.C.) This road went from Italy to Spain, crossing the Narbo colony in Gaul from east to west. Its paving stones still bear traces of the horse-drawn carts that traversed it.

mander. In the end, however, Jugurtha was captured through the treachery of an African ally, and the Romans put him to death (104 B.C.).

Public impatience at the slow course of the Jugurthine war was heightened by alarming developments beyond the northern frontiers. The land defenses of Italy had become gravely threatened by two groups of German tribes, the Cimbri and Teutones. Marius crushed the Teutones in a bloody engagement at Aquae Sextiae (Aix-en-Provence), where three thousand of his men concealed on high ground won the day by unexpectedly launching an attack on their rear (102 B.C.). Then, in the next year, he fought the Cimbri on the Campi Raudii in north Italy, and inflicted shattering casualties on them. And that was the end of the German threat.

The war had instilled in the Romans a terror of the northern barbarians which they never again wholly lost. Moreover, it had brought about other consequences also. It had given Marius, elected consul year after year, the opportunity not only to achieve unprecedented power for himself but also to raise the Roman army's equipment and organization to a new level of efficiency. Each cohort now contained six centurions of different grades who provided continuity: men of formidable courage, experience, and initiative, generally promoted from the ranks, who combined the functions of a modern company commander and a senior sergeant. Each cohort had military standards of its own and was animated by a new feeling of *esprit de corps*: a feeling that was increasingly directed to the commander himself rather than to the state, so that his soldiers became known as "Marius's Mules."

Their dependence upon him was immediately put to the test. After their military service was ended, land had to be found to reward them, in the face of senatorial opposition. This became the task of a popular speaker named Saturninus, thus revealing the potentialities of an alliance between a military leader and a demagogue. Elected tribune in 103 and 100 B.C., Saturninus arranged for Marius's veterans to be assigned large allotments in north Africa and southern Gaul. But the most significant feature of his activity was the violence he organized at meetings and in the streets; this marked the beginning of a new epoch in which such disorders were to become habitual. Saturninus smoothed the way to his own reelection by hiring toughs to murder one of his competitors. But by now Marius had had enough and withdrew his cooperation. In support of the Senate's declaration of an emergency, Marius personally raised an improvised force and led it against Saturninus and his friends, who were arrested and shortly afterwards died by lynching in prison.

There now followed a period, the opening decade of the first century B.C., in which Marius, having offended both sides, was discarded and played scarcely any part in Roman politics.

The war with the Italians

It was a time in which the claims of the Italian allies, which had waxed so strong in the time of Gaius Gracchus, were strongly revived, while the Senate did virtually nothing to deal with the problem. In 97 B.C., Marcus Livius Drusus the Younger was elected to a tribunate. He now proposed a measure granting the full Roman franchise to the Italian allies, and they, in enthusiastic response, proclaimed that he was their patron. But neither the senators nor the knights supported his bill. His program was rejected, and an assassin fatally stabbed him.

The death of Drusus created feelings of such desperate disappointment among the already disaffected Italians that they now plunged the peninsula into an unparalleled and terrible war (90–87 B.C.), known as the Social War (from *socii*, allies). These peoples, for the most part, wanted full Roman citizenship. But the revolt was also joined by the Samnites, who still remembered their defeats by the Romans two centuries earlier.

The Romans were caught by surprise in the first year of the war, and their enemies were able to maintain the initiative, pursuing an effective strategy of exhaustion. The Romans fought back, but were increasingly racked by fears that the spread of the uprising would threaten their communications with Cisalpine Gaul. The Roman authorities therefore decided, in mid-war, that the major political concessions that they had so catastrophically failed to offer in time of peace could not be delayed any longer. So one of the consuls, Lucius Julius Caesar, brought forward a bill conferring Roman citizenship upon all Italians who had remained loyal, as well as on those who had revolted but were now prepared to lay down their arms. This concession halted the impetus of the rebellion, and the war petered out.

In the long run, the results of the rebellion were mixed, for whereas Lucius Caesar's law marked a large step towards the unification of Roman Italy as a nation, it also meant that the old city-state government had become obsolete. Moreover, the concessions proved, on closer inspection, to be inadequate and illusory. They had provided that the new citizens should be restricted to only eight or ten of the thirty-five tribes, thus ensuring that their voting power could always be defeated by the other Roman citizens.

In 88 B.C., the problem was tackled by the tribune Sulpicius Rufus. An orator of incomparable dignity, Sulpicius put forward a proposal that the newly enfranchised Italian allies should be distributed among all the thirty-five tribes. Not surprisingly, this measure encountered the fiercest opposition. So he turned away from his more conservative friends to Marius, who had been skulking disregarded in the wings. And he proposed, in exchange for political help, to secure for Marius the supreme command in an important Eastern war.

Sulla in the East

This was to be fought against King Mithridates VI of Pontus, in northern Asia Minor. A noted hunter, lover, and warrior, Mithridates was of Persian descent and had inherited from his father a policy of territorial expansion. He thus became an active, aggressive rival of the Romans, whose frontiers matched his own in Asia Minor.

In 88 B.C., Mithridates invaded the province of Asia. After gaining control of large regions of Asia Minor, he crossed the Aegean and occupied Athens, so that Roman military retaliation became an urgent necessity. The supreme command was entrusted to the patrician Lucius Cornelius Sulla, a man who had distinguished himself in the Jugurthine and Social Wars, and now assumed the consulship for 88. But the tribune Sulpicius Rufus, by forcible methods, secured Sulla's supersession by his own new ally, the half-forgotten Marius. However, Sulla, refusing to accept this dismissal, fled to the troops he had been destined to command in Asia Minor (his old soldiers in the Social War) and instead led them successfully upon Rome itself.

It was a fateful moment in history. This was the first march on the capital, the first civil war, and the first clear example of troops acting out of loyalty to their commander to defy the government. Moreover, Sulla created another precedent by declaring Sulpicius (whose legislation was rescinded) to be an outlaw, and Marius another. A price was set on their heads, and Sulpicius was hunted down and put to death. But Marius escaped and hid in north Africa.

MOSAIC OF PALESTRINA *(ca. 80 B.C.) This mosaic, which depicts the course of the Nile from its source to the delta—symbolizing the course of history—also commemorates the victories of Hellenistic rulers. Here, soldiers stand before the palace in Alexandria.*

84

Meanwhile, Sulla left for Greece, where he twice defeated a general of Mithridates and then captured the city of Athens. Next, remaining aloof from other Roman troops in the area—whose commanders were opposed to him politically—he crossed over into Asia Minor. But once there, instead of pursuing the fight against Mithridates, he negotiated an agreement with him at Dardanus, near Troy (85 B.C.). Sulla could not afford to expend his troops on prolonging the war, for Rome itself had fallen into the hands of his political enemies. Its government was led, for the next four years, by the patrician Cinna. Like Sulla, whom he now proceeded to outlaw, he had fought in the Social War, and as soon as Sulla had left for the East, he again followed in his footsteps by marching on Rome. Marius, too, came back from north Africa to join him and took the lead in political reprisals, comprising by far the bloodiest civilian massacres that Rome had ever experienced. Shortly afterwards, with his mind partly unhinged, Marius died (86 B.C.).

The dictatorship of Sulla

Four years later, Sulla, outlawed in Rome, openly rebelled and invaded Italy. The administration was supported by the Samnites—still smarting from memories of the Social War—and the combined force made a final stand against Sulla outside the Colline Gate of Rome (82 B.C.). But the outcome was catastrophic, and the Samnites fell to a man during the engagement and the butchery of prisoners that followed. Nor were they the only people to be slaughtered, since Sulla organized a mass murder of his enemies that left even Marius's precedent far behind. With the help of a bodyguard of ten thousand, he executed a total scarcely short of that number, including forty senators and sixteen hundred knights. Their lands, too, were avidly confiscated by Sulla, to be given to one hundred thousand of his retired legionaries, settled in numerous large Roman colonies.

For himself he chose the obsolete position of dictator so that he was completely immune from checks from any quarter. Yet he chose to pass his laws in proper form through the Assembly. They were numerous and almost uniformly conservative, for Sulla's solution for the troubles of the community envisaged the restoration of the Senate's flagging authority. To this end, he decided to break the power of the tribunes of the people, who had so often challenged senatorial control. Henceforth, they were not allowed to move any law whatever without the prior approval of the Senate.

But the most impressive and lasting of Sulla's prosenatorial achievements was the reconstitution of the law courts (*quaestiones*), of which the number was increased to seven, each dealing with a separate range of crimes. Gaius Gracchus had given the original court to the knights, but Sulla excluded them from it, making the *quaestiones* into a senatorial monopoly. But Sulla was not an enemy of the knights, and this blow was mitigated by the admission of many of them into the Senate, which he doubled in size to six hundred.

Sulla, remembering the illegalities of himself and others, took steps to bring provincial governors under firm senatorial control. In particular, they were forbidden to make war outside the province allotted to them, or to depart for any reason beyond its borders, without previous authorization from the Senate or Assembly. One of the principal lessons against those who strayed was a law of treason.

It seemed paradoxical that these measures to shore up the ancient oligarchy should be taken by a man who had revived the office of dictator, but Sulla stopped

SILVER DENARIUS
OF SULLA
Issued by the Cornelia clan, this coin depicts Sulla sitting on a platform. Before him, the king of Mauretania assumes a position of supplication (on his knees, branch in hand). Behind him, Jugurtha, king of Numidia, is held prisoner.

THE MERIDA THEATER
Emerita Augusta (current-day Merida, in Spain), built by Augustus in 25 B.C. for his veterans, became the capital of Lusitania. The theater, erected in 16 B.C., held some 6,000 people. The magnificent stage wall dates back to Hadrian.

short of absolutism. Instead, he decided to abdicate from his dictatorship, becoming consul in 80 B.C. and returning in the following year to private life in Campania, where he died a year later.

The memory of this mulberry-faced man, so energetic, easily moved to laughter and tears, who claimed he never forgot a friend or a foe, remained alive, but his elaborate constitutional scheme failed.

The rise of Pompey

The failure of Sulla's reconstruction was demonstrated without the slightest delay. When one of his former officers, Marcus Lepidus, a patrician with extensive noble backing, became consul in 78 B.C., he employed his term of office to bring forward an opportunistic program for the restoration of the tribunate. Lepidus staked his chances on a possible mass uprising of Italians dispossessed by the proscriptions. In 77 B.C., he led a considerable force of malcontents in a dash for the capital. His way was barred by an army of the government, he was defeated at the Milvian Bridge, and shortly afterwards he died.

Far more able was another anti-Sullan, Sertorius, a Sabine who set up an independent government in Spain. He maintained contact with Lepidus, whose followers fled to his colors after the collapse of Lepidus's uprising in Italy.

86

The Senate dispatched an army against them, but was forced at the end of 77 B.C. to supplement it by sending out substantial reinforcements under the command of a general only twenty-nine years of age. This was Pompey (Cnaeus Pompeius), who already enjoyed a considerable reputation. At first, he achieved no result. But finally, Sertorius was murdered at a banquet by his own lieutenant, whom Pompey then defeated without difficulty and put to death. In this somewhat unmerited fashion he increased his military renown.

Meanwhile, in Italy, an event had occurred that inspired great terror among the Romans. It was the last of the series of slave wars extending back to the previous century. But this was a special slave war because the principal rebels were professional gladiators. The outbreak was led by a Thracian named Spartacus, a man of courage and some humanity, who had served as a Roman auxiliary soldier. Slaves of all kinds flocked to join him, and within the space of two years they defeated no fewer than four Roman armies.

The Roman authorities entrusted the command against Spartacus to the ex-praetor Crassus; he was a former subordinate of Sulla, amiable and flattering, easy of access, a talented wire-puller. After meticulously training a force of forty thousand men, Crassus attempted in vain to catch Spartacus in the toe of the peninsula but finally cornered and killed him in Apulia, crucifying six thousand of his slave followers along the Appian Way (71 B.C.). Meanwhile Pompey had been summoned back from Spain to help conduct the operations and arrived just in time to take part in the final manhunt.

At this point the two ambitious men, each with his own army, might well

AVNORVM SATYRORVM ETSILENORVM DELECT

THE REVOLT OF SPARTACUS

Starting in the 2nd century B.C., the concentration of slaves on the large estates of Italy and Sicily led to a series of revolts in these regions. The largest of these was led by a legendary figure named Spartacus.

A Thracian prisoner of war, Spartacus was put into a gladiator school in Capua. In 73 B.C., he escaped with some collaborators and, by dint of his courage and charisma, soon became a leader. His companion, a prophetess, gave the troops confidence by promising a great future. With their gladiator weapons and the war equipment acquired during a military attack, they took refuge on Mount Vesuvius.

Plundering the region, they took in thousands of slaves from the area, and even the small landowners who had been ruined by the land crisis. With their ranks having grown to more than 100,000 men, they were, on several occasions, able to defeat the Roman legions. After raging throughout the north and south of Italy for more than a year, Spartacus fell victim to pirates who did not provide the boats promised to him to go to Sicily, and the rebelling slaves, blocked by Crassus's troops, suffered a terrible defeat. As tragic examples, some 6,000 survivors were crucified along the Appian Way between Capua and Rome.

have come to blows. They did not clash, but instead came to an understanding according to which they would jointly demand election to the consulships of the year 70 B.C. Legally speaking, both were unqualified because neither had disbanded his army as consular candidates were required to do. Pompey, who had not even taken his seat as a senator, was debarred on grounds of his youth. Nevertheless, the Senate had to give way, thus revealing how a resolute combination of ambitious men could frustrate the republic. Setting their disagreements aside, they devoted their year of office to overturning Sulla's constitution—a program that gained them considerable popularity, except, of course, in the Senate. They supported a bill reducing the senatorial membership of the jury panels to one-third, and a law proposed by Pompey relieved the tribunate of all the restrictions placed upon it by the late dictator. Almost the whole of Sulla's activity was therefore obliterated, and the old flexibility and anarchy of Roman politics had been fully restored.

During the years that immediately followed, Crassus remained content to stay at home, increasing his financial resources and political influence. But Pompey was waiting for a chance to effect some spectacular increase in his military reputation, and the opportunity was not long in coming.

After the peace of 85 B.C., Mithridates VI of Pontus had rapidly recovered, repelling the officer left behind by Sulla and building up stores of money and supplies, so that when Rome decided to annex adjacent Bithynia in 74 B.C., he had marched into that country to forestall them. Then the Romans sent out a general of great ability named Lucullus, who expelled the king from Bithynia and even from his own homeland of Pontus (74–70 B.C.), forcing him to flee to his eastern neighbor and ally Armenia.

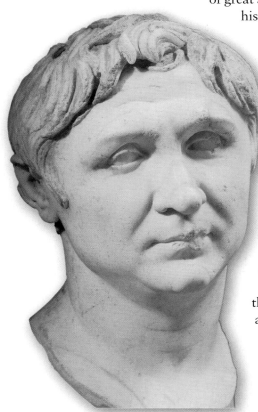

Lucullus occupied the Armenian capital, but in 68 B.C. his troops refused to carry on. He had foes at home who played their part in instigating the mutiny in his army. But on the spot, too, the weather conditions his soldiers had to contend with were intolerable. Above all, Lucullus, for all his military talents, was an aristocratic disciplinarian who lacked the ability to get on with the rank and file. In all these unfavorable conditions, his army virtually fell apart. One of the Roman leaders who had accelerated its disintegration from afar was Pompey, and he now took over the command.

On arrival in the field, he proved outstandingly successful. Mithridates was deserted by his Armenian allies, so that it was possible to defeat him immediately. He contrived to escape to the Cimmerian Bosphorus (Crimea), but there, faced by a rebellion led by his son, he committed suicide.

Pompey, after sensationally opening up the hitherto unknown region of the Caucasus (65 B.C.), now put into effect a sweeping settlement of the affairs of western Asia. Pontus was annexed and united with Bithynia to form a single province. In Syria, the last feeble Seleucid monarch was removed, and his country, with its great city of Antioch, was made a province, so that out of the three great successor states of Alexander, Macedonia, the Seleucids, and Egypt, only the last now remained independent. In the small Judaean kingdom, where there had been dynastic disputes, Pompey captured the ancient capital Jerusalem, causing great and lasting Jewish distress by walking into the Temple. But a member of the reigning Hasmonaean (Maccabee) dynasty was still allowed to rule, as one of Rome's dependent client monarchs.

This extension of Rome's ancient *clientela* principle to foreign states was nothing new. But Pompey enlarged its application greatly. His reconstruction of the Near East far exceeded anything of the kind that any Roman had ever performed before, showing him to be an administrator of the very first order. Indeed, although he still had fifteen years to live, this was easily the greatest achievement of his career, massively standing the test of time and forming the basis of all future reorganizations. His arrangements were immensely lucrative, both to himself and to Rome. As for his own gains, the spoils of war and gifts made him a richer man even than Crassus, who had hitherto been the wealthiest man of the day. And his settlement vastly enlarged the Roman treasury, raising the annual revenue of the state by no less than forty percent. The triumph at his homecoming was celebrated with unprecedented splendor.

BUST OF POMPEY
This marble bust is a copy dating from the reign of Claudius. The famous lock of hair, turned up on the forehead, recalls portraits of Alexander the Great, who had the same hair style. But the softness of the features and the good-naturedness of Pompey's round face differ greatly from Alexander's.

Cicero—politician and philosopher

While Pompey was away in the East, there had been an uneasy air of suspense at Rome, where people remembered the autocracy Sulla had established when he returned from the same lands. Intrigues multiplied, largely prompted by Crassus. He did not act directly against Pompey, but financed various needy characters. One such figure was Catiline, an impoverished patrician. As an undischarged prisoner on an embezzlement charge, Catiline was debarred from becoming a candidate for the consulship of 65 and 64 B.C., but he was admitted to the competition for 63 B.C. Crassus was willing to back him; but a wide range of senators were alarmed by the possibility that he might get in. He seemed to them a person ready for any kind of unscrupulous action.

In consequence, this group banded together to put up a candidate to stand against him. The man they selected was Cicero. Cicero came from a family that had never provided a consul before, and such "new men" found it notoriously difficult to gain the office. But he was an orator of unique brilliance in a society in which oratory was the major part of politics, and he duly won the consulship for 63 B.C.

At the elections for the consulships of the following year, Catiline made a further attempt to gain office, this time with a program sensational enough to confirm the worst fears, proposing not only a sweeping land distribution but a general cancellation of debts. The program was designed to appeal to bankrupt nobles, veterans, and urban poor—indeed, displaced and discontented persons of every sort. But such proposals scared off all conservatives and moderates, and when Cicero secured Catiline's defeat once again, that defeated and disappointed man began to move outside the law. His intention was that a force of his discreditable supporters in Etruria should march on Rome.

However, six days before the date fixed for the coup, rumors of its iminence leaked out, and the Senate passed its emergency decree. Nevertheless, in the absence of concrete proof, Catiline, protected by influential friends, was left at large in the city and went on plotting revolution. But when Cicero, in the first of his four magnificent Catilinarian Orations, proceeded to denounce his aims, Catiline felt it advisable to withdraw from the capital and left to take personal command of his followers in Etruria. Then, by a great stroke of luck. Cicero obtained written evidence of Catiline's revolutionary intentions. Thereupon he proceeded to seize five of the leading conspirators in the city, including men of very high rank, and obtained the Senate's approval of their execution, which was immediately carried out.

AVNORVM SATYRORVM ETSILENORVM DILECI

CICERO'S WAY WITH WORDS

Born in 106 B.C. in Arpinum, into a family of equestrian rank, Cicero showed talent at an early age and entered a career as a lawyer, as did many of his ambitious peers. His eloquence was quickly recognized, in particular during a scandalous trial started by the Sicilians against Verres, a governor who exploited them. Fifty-eight of his legal and political speeches survive out of the hundreds he delivered between 81 and 43 B.C. At the same time, Cicero launched a political career that led him to be elected consul in 63 B.C. Subsequently, he foiled the Catiline conspiracy, earning the nickname "Father of the country."

Withdrawing from the civil wars, Cicero revealed his rhetorical principles in his theoretical works and devoted himself to philosophy. He proceeded to edit the work of Epicurus, he studied Stoicism, and he developed neo-Platonic theses. Throughout his life, he was engaged in prolific correspondence (800 of his letters have survived). Returning to politics to support Octavian against Antony, Cicero was assassinated when the two enemies allied themselves temporarily.

The great care that was taken to copy Cicero's work during the Middle Ages testifies to how much it was respected by posterity.

In the final senatorial debate, preceding the execution of the plotters, two statesmen of the future expressed their views. Cato spoke up in favor of Cicero's proposal, and Julius Caesar against it. Cato, the great-grandson of the censor of the same name, was a man of thirty-two, formidable and uncompromising in his opposition to all who appeared not to measure up to the traditional system. Gaius Julius Caesar, five years older, was a patrician linked by marriage ties with Marius and Cinna. Caesar cast constitutional doubts on the propriety of putting the Catilinarians to death. His opinion did not prevail, but he gained valuable allies among those who were afraid of what such high-handed acts might lead to.

For the time being, however, Cicero's policy seemed vindicated, because Catiline moved into open rebellion at the head of his troops. But two armies sent by the government caught him, and he and his followers were destroyed near Pistoria (Pistoia) in January 62 B.C. Cicero was the hero of the hour.

Cicero owed his rise almost exclusively to one single quality. He was one of the most persuasive orators who have ever lived, in an age in which the very core of politics was oratory. The combination of his inborn talents with an elaborate education equipped him to speak and write that incomparably eloquent, rotund Latin that persuaded and overwhelmed his listeners and laid the foundations of the subsequent prose of all Europe. His speeches, of which fifty-eight survive, reflect all the stresses and strains of the crumbling Republic, in which for three decades he lived and worked. They also reveal Cicero, the man, and so, even more remarkably, do his eight hundred unique letters.

The person who emerges is humorous, warmhearted, and extravagant, as unable as the next man to see how to make a city-state govern an empire. Despite his occasional political successes, Cicero did not have the right temperament to be a first-class Roman politician. He possessed a fatal lawyerlike ability to see both sides of every question, and lacked the ruthless decisiveness that Roman public life required. Yet on two or three occasions in his lifetime he screwed up his courage to stand up against tyranny, and the last of these stands cost him his life.

Cicero had accepted the Greek idea, now current among Roman jurists and other thinkers, of a Natural Law (*ius naturale*) which was a corollary of the admission of noncitizens to Rome's legal system (*ius gentium*). That is to say, he was convinced that right is right and wrong is wrong objectively. And what was most wrong of all, he believed, was for one person to tyrannize others. He accepted the injunction of the Stoic philosophy that men and women should treat one another generously and honestly. According to Stoic doctrine, all individuals share a spark of divinity that makes them akin to one another, irrespective of race or status or sex, in the universal brotherhood of humankind.

That was one of the principal elements upon which Cicero insisted in a series of wonderfully well written treatises on moral themes—a recognition not only of one's own unique personality but of the personalities of others. This was the most civi-

BUST OF CICERO
The numerous portraits of Cicero that remain, which bear great likeness to their subject, are distinguished by the attention paid to precise rendering of his features. In fact, a facial wart can be seen on many of them.

lized ideal, for practical purposes of living, that the world had ever seen; it has deeply influenced Western thought from his time to our own. And Cicero stressed this ideal with all the more fervent conviction because he believed that the man best equipped to teach the good life was the public speaker. As he explains in a number of analyses of that art, every orator must not only be a man of wide and liberal culture, but, if he is to do his job properly, he must also behave decently and well.

Toward the First Triumvirate

Pompey was arrogant, shifty, and aloof. Yet none of the gloomy predictions of his desire to become an autocrat proved correct. Instead, as soon as he landed in Italy, he duly disbanded his troops. By so doing, he indicated clearly that he entertained no ambition to become a dictatorial tyrant. But he had two requests to make of the Senate. The first was an application for land that could be given to his impatient veterans. This must have been foreseen and was reasonable. His second request was that all the actions he had performed in the East should be ratified as decisions of the Roman state. This was equally predictable.

However, a series of obscure metropolitan intrigues now got under way, during which leading conservatives preferred to take a short-term view and oppose his demand. They regarded his failure to consult the government when he was in the East as another in a series of high-handed and illegal acts. In the face of this pressure, the Senate continually delayed its decision about Pompey's requests; few things contributed so greatly to the fall of the Republic, which was shortly to follow, as this refusal to give him what he wanted.

The senators made two further ominous decisions. One of these was in relation to Crassus. At the end of 61 B.C., a company of tax gatherers were claiming a rebate on the purchase price of Asian revenues they had contracted to collect, since these were proving less profitable than expected. They persuaded Crassus to back their request. But Cato persuaded the Senate to kill the proposal.

Pompey and Crassus, then, had both been snubbed. And now Caesar was snubbed as well. It was the practice for the Senate to allocate to the consuls of any given year, even before their election took place and their names were known, the provinces they would be sent to govern at the conclusion of their terms of office. And so now the provinces which would go to the consuls for 59 B.C. were duly allotted, and it was decided that they should be merely "the forests and cattle drifts" of Italy. This was an abnormally trivial assignment and a deliberate affront directed against Caesar.

The Senate had opposed and offended Pompey, Crassus, and Caesar—all three of them at once. Evidently its members no longer possessed the acute judgment that had won Rome the Mediterranean world. What happened next seems by hindsight inevitable. The three men who had received this treatment joined forces against those who had insulted them. Their agreement took the form of a coalition, at first secret and before long publicly known, that historians describe as the First Triumvirate. Later historical writers saw the event as the end of the Roman Republic, or at least as the beginning of its end. The oligarchy never recovered its power.

Masterpieces of Roman art

FUNEREAL RELIEFS
(ca. 50 B.C.) In funereal monuments, couples had themselves portrayed as if they were alive. The man wears the toga appropriate for a Republican citizen; his face is stern, sculpted with realism. Placed along roads, funereal monuments indicated social ranking and reflected a desire for immortality.

VILLA OF THE MYSTERIES
(70–60 B.C.) One of Pompeii's most opulent homes was named after this fresco, which depicts the initiation into the Bacchic cult. It is known for the dimension of its figures and its beautiful composition. On every side, scenes from real life, such as this boy reading the ritual, are coupled with scenes from another world, one filled with gods and satyrs.

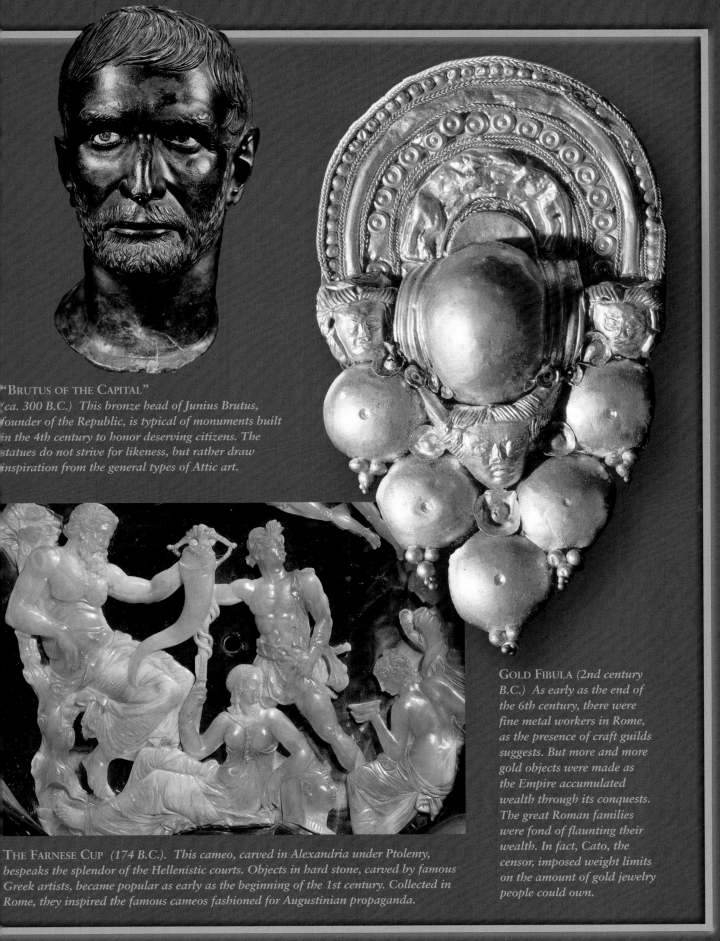

"BRUTUS OF THE CAPITAL"
(ca. 300 B.C.) This bronze head of Junius Brutus, founder of the Republic, is typical of monuments built in the 4th century to honor deserving citizens. The statues do not strive for likeness, but rather draw inspiration from the general types of Attic art.

GOLD FIBULA *(2nd century B.C.) As early as the end of the 6th century, there were fine metal workers in Rome, as the presence of craft guilds suggests. But more and more gold objects were made as the Empire accumulated wealth through its conquests. The great Roman families were fond of flaunting their wealth. In fact, Cato, the censor, imposed weight limits on the amount of gold jewelry people could own.*

THE FARNESE CUP *(174 B.C.). This cameo, carved in Alexandria under Ptolemy, bespeaks the splendor of the Hellenistic courts. Objects in hard stone, carved by famous Greek artists, became popular as early as the beginning of the 1st century. Collected in Rome, they inspired the famous cameos fashioned for Augustinian propaganda.*

FRESCO FROM THE VILLA FARNESINA *(ca. 25 B.C.) These theater masks, painted with light strokes against a light background in the manner of watercolor, are the work of an anonymous artist who decorated the Roman house of Julia and Agrippa, the daughter and son-in-law of Augustus. Sketched on a frieze framing small monochromatic paintings —seascapes, chiaroscuro landscapes—they attest to the variety of painting techniques used in Rome.*

BLUE GLASS DOVE *(first half of 1st century B.C.) When blown glass was discovered in Phoenicia and pieces were imported to Italy, fine objects were made and distributed. This dove, discovered in a tomb, is an exquisite example of the glassblower's craft.*

CUP FROM THE TREASURE OF BOSCOREALE
(end of 1st century B.C.) The great
treasures found in the villas near Pompeii
attest to the Romans' passion for silverwork,
starting in the 2nd century. Owning such objects
of luxury, as well as displaying them, was a way
of identifying social rank. This unusual silver
cup, representing the height of the embossing
technique, serves to frame the bust of a woman
personifying Africa and probably had a
decorative function.

FRESCOES FROM THE HOUSE OF PUBLIUS FANNIUS SYNISTOR
(ca. 40–30 B.C.) Painted in bold red and ochre, with architectural elements creating a kind of
theater set, these frescoes are typical of Second Style Pompeii painting. The trompe-l'oeil columns
divide the space into successive planes that lead to a door.

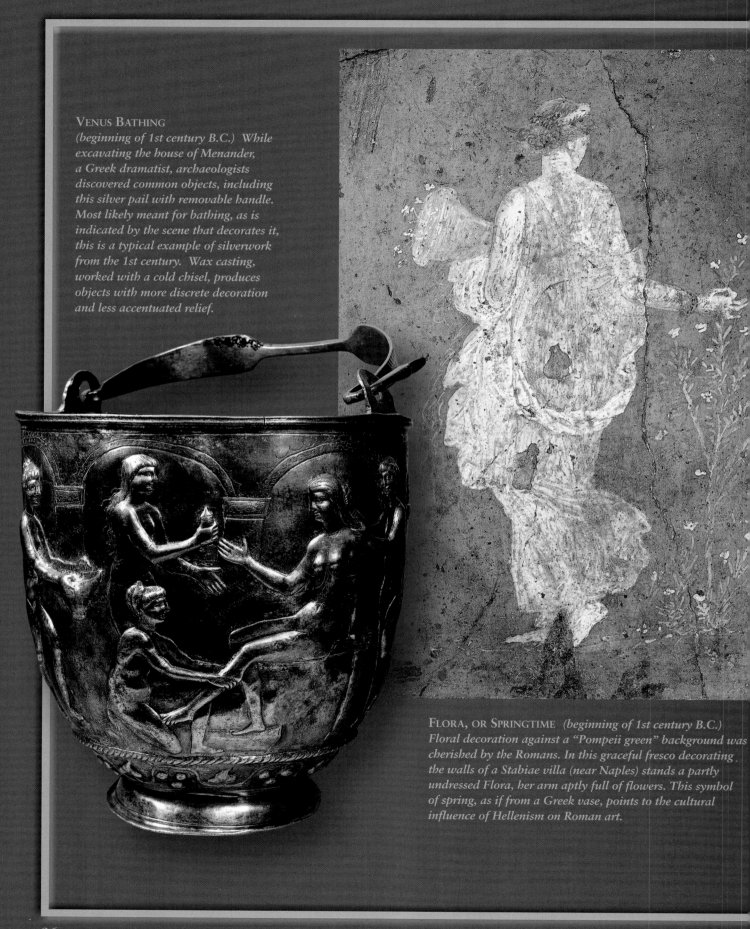

VENUS BATHING
(beginning of 1st century B.C.) While excavating the house of Menander, a Greek dramatist, archaeologists discovered common objects, including this silver pail with removable handle. Most likely meant for bathing, as is indicated by the scene that decorates it, this is a typical example of silverwork from the 1st century. Wax casting, worked with a cold chisel, produces objects with more discrete decoration and less accentuated relief.

FLORA, OR SPRINGTIME *(beginning of 1st century B.C.) Floral decoration against a "Pompeii green" background was cherished by the Romans. In this graceful fresco decorating the walls of a Stabiae villa (near Naples) stands a partly undressed Flora, her arm aptly full of flowers. This symbol of spring, as if from a Greek vase, points to the cultural influence of Hellenism on Roman art.*

PORTRAIT OF AGRIPPINA
(middle of 1st century B.C.)
The women of the emperor's family circle— his wife and daughter— also posed for official images, though their faces were generally more frozen and serious than those of the men. Designed in Rome by an artist hand-picked by the emperor, the model was then reproduced by a local sculptor. As a gesture of loyalty to the emperor, members of the regional elite often imitated the hairstyles of the empresses.

PORTRAIT OF EMPEROR TRAJAN
(beginning of 2nd century B.C.) This bronze head highlights the striking similarity between funeral masks and Roman portraiture. It also reveals that the official portrait, though meant to publicize the image of the emperor throughout the Roman world, did not necessarily idealize his features. Trajan's wrinkled chin and cheeks and his worried expression realistically portray a weary, aging emperor.

AUGUSTUS'S ALTAR OF PEACE
(13–9 B.C.) This monument, standing on a podium and decorated with bas-reliefs, contains the altar Augustus wanted for celebrating his reign. The nourishing earth (Tellus), symbol of peace, is surrounded by the winds that help ensure fertility. In Augustinian art, mythology was used to express the goals of a reign—namely, peace and prosperity.

EQUESTRIAN STATUE OF MARCUS AURELIUS *(c. 166–180) Roman art was, above all, an art of propaganda, one in which likeness was far less critical than function. The emperor was idealized, his dress and attributes all-important. Sporting the beard of a philosopher, Marcus Aurelius presents himself here as the head of the army, so as to remind all that he played a personal role in the military campaigns at the end of his reign.*

THE CELSUS LIBRARY IN EPHESUS *(110 A.D.) Under Trajan, the consul Tiberius Julius Aquila equipped the leading city of the eastern Aegean with a luxurious library in honor of his father, T. Julius Celsus, governor of the province of Asia. Decorated with a façade of columns and covered entirely in marble, in true Hellenistic tradition, this temple to education could hold up to 120,000 manuscripts.*

THEATER MASKS
(118–134 A.D.) This mosaic, from the Villa Hadriana, represents two masks of acting, a courtesan and a slave crowned in ivy. Its artistic quality derives from details made with marble pieces (tesserae), the effect of perspective, and the play of shadow and light obtained through subtle gradations of color.

THE PORTLAND VASE *(end of 1st century B.C.) This elegant vase is an example of the cameo glass technique, developed under the reign of Augustus. Shaped in a mold, the vase is made from a first layer of deep blue glass, then covered with a second layer of white glass, in which the decoration is engraved. In 1786, J. Wedgwood made a highly popular replica in stoneware which earned him his fame.*

EMPEROR COMMODUS AS HERCULES
(ca. 190 A.D.) This astonishing portrait of Emperor Commodus, which represents the prince's victory over the Nemean lion, is a perfect example of the esthetic revolution at the end of the 2nd century A.D. Contrasting the shadow around the emperor's head and the polished aspects of the lit areas, the artist made a Baroque-like sculpture that dramatically mirrors the torments of a troubled time.

CUP OF LYCURGUS

(4th century A.D.) Lycurgus, king of Thrace, suffocated and died in the branches of Ambrosia, who transformed herself into a vine to escape her attackers. This myth decorates one of the most spectacular vases from late antiquity. From a block of modeled glass, the artisan sculpted high-relief motifs, which stand out from the background of the cup.

BLOWN GLASS PHIAL

(3rd–4th century) From the 2nd to the 4th century, glass objects made in the workshops of Cologne were well-known and made available throughout the Empire. Plates, cups, bottles, and amphorae, in clear or colored glass, were blown using a mold. This vase is decorated with the faces of two children.

THE ARCH OF CONSTANTINE

(315 A.D.) Commemorating the first decade of Constantine's reign and his victory over Maxentius in the Battle of Milvian Bridge, this arch points to the permanence of architectural forms, but also to stylistic evolution. Realism is replaced by symbolism. The size of the figures reflects their importance, hence the preeminence of the emperor.

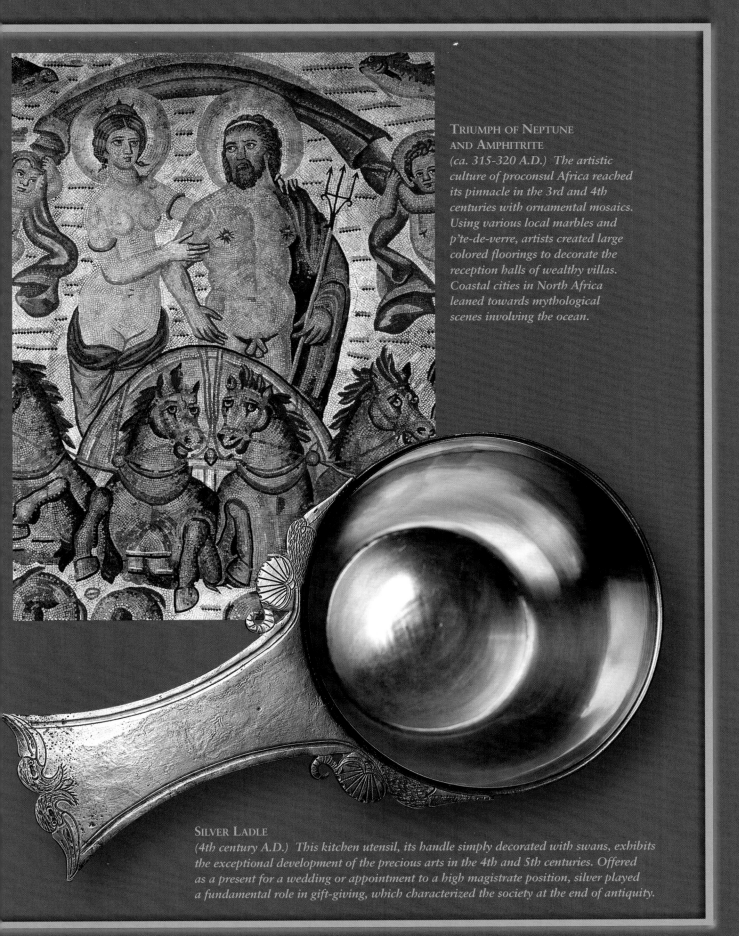

**TRIUMPH OF NEPTUNE
AND AMPHITRITE**
*(ca. 315-320 A.D.) The artistic
culture of proconsul Africa reached
its pinnacle in the 3rd and 4th
centuries with ornamental mosaics.
Using various local marbles and
p'te-de-verre, artists created large
colored floorings to decorate the
reception halls of wealthy villas.
Coastal cities in North Africa
leaned towards mythological
scenes involving the ocean.*

SILVER LADLE
*(4th century A.D.) This kitchen utensil, its handle simply decorated with swans, exhibits
the exceptional development of the precious arts in the 4th and 5th centuries. Offered
as a present for a wedding or appointment to a high magistrate position, silver played
a fundamental role in gift-giving, which characterized the society at the end of antiquity.*

CHAPTER 8

Caesar

The first consulship of Caesar

When Caesar was elected to the consulship for 59 B.C., he at once pointed the way to Rome's autocratic future by pushing through a series of measures in favor of his fellow triumvirs, Pompey and Crassus, and himself.

One of his first actions as consul was to satisfy Pompey's veterans by a land bill. When his archenemy, Cato, blocked the measure in the Senate, Caesar secured its acceptance in the Assembly by forcible methods, which were held against him for the rest of his life. These methods even included beating-up his fellow consul. He was supported, however, by his fellow triumvirs, so that his alliance with them came to be revealed, and Pompey married his daughter Julia. Caesar then went on to ensure the ratification of his new son-in-law's eastern arrangements. Caesar also satisfied Crassus by securing a generous financial concession for his friends the tax-collecting knights.

It was now the turn of the other triumvirs to help Caesar in his own political career. Instead, therefore, of the unimportant province the Senate had assigned to the consuls for this year, he got himself allotted an infinitely more significant province consisting of Cisalpine Gaul (northern Italy) combined with Illyricum (Dalmatia).

At this juncture, however, occurred the death of the governor of Transalpine Gaul (southern France). This was a piece of good fortune for Caesar, who saw that region as a far more promising starting-off point for military conquests and arranged for it to be added to the province already assigned to him. He knew it would be best to assume office as provincial governor as soon as his consulship was over, since, if he became a private citizen, he would be liable to prosecution for the violent acts he had committed as consul. Before leaving Rome, however, he formed an alliance with a young politician named Clodius, a talented mercenary soldier who he hoped would look after his interests in the capital, with the help of numerous clients, urban gangsters, and trade guilds (collegia), whose exploitation Clodius made into a fine art.

BUST OF CAESAR
While there is certainly no dearth of representations of Caesar, from coins to cameos, the originality of this portrayal lies in its medium: green schist.

The Gallic War

Between the River Seine and the Roman province lived two hundred tribes of Celtic race. The most important of them, each surrounded by a ring of lesser dependent peoples, were the Arverni (Auvergne), the Aedui, and the Sequani. While the shifting relationships among these tribes made Gallic unity out of the question, their side-by-side existence created a certain precarious balance and, for considerable periods, a sort of peace.

This, however, was now imperiled by the Helvetii, a Celtic people of Germany who had been driven out of their homes into Switzerland and had decided to migrate westwards to the Atlantic coast. Certain Roman leaders decided that this mass migration must be stopped, since it would threaten the security of the Transalpine province. And once Caesar's consulship had come to an end, he and the army he had gotten together hastened northwards.

We know a great deal about the operations that followed from his own *Gallic War*. It was the best account of warfare that had ever been written by a Roman, and it retained this supremacy for centuries. It was entitled "Commentaries," a term denoting a commander's dispatches. Caesar's formidable intellect and lucid, concise Latin transform these ostensibly modest works into masterpieces.

At Armecy, he wiped out tens and perhaps hundreds of thousands of the Helvetii, while the survivors turned back into Switzerland. Next, in the same year, he dealt with the Sequani. At odds with the Aedui, they had imprudently invited Ariovistus, chief of one of the tribes of west Germany, to come to their aid, and in 61 B.C., he had defeated the Aedui.

Ariovistus secured recognition as king and ally of the Roman people, and at the time, Caesar favored this. But soon afterwards the chief's territorial ambitions began to cause alarm among the Gauls, who appealed to Rome, whereupon Caesar reversed his favorable attitude to Ariovistus. On the plain of Alsace, he engaged the Germans and put them to flight. Ariovistus escaped but died soon afterwards, and Caesar's friends declared him the triumphant successor of his relative Marius as destroyer of menacing barbarians.

In 56 B.C., the three leaders met together at Luca, just inside Cisalpine Gaul (part of Caesar's command), which was chosen because Caesar did not want to leave his province and face prosecution. At their conference the triumvirs decided how to fulfill their future ambitions. Pompey and Crassus were to become consuls together for the second time in 55 B.C. Then Crassus would take up a command against Parthia, an Iranian feudal empire beyond the Euphrates. Pompey was awarded the rich provinces of Spain for five years and Caesar's provincial command was likewise prolonged for a further five years so that he could exploit and extend his new conquests in Transalpine Gaul.

However, it at once became apparent that this country was not yet fully conquered after all, for the Veneti of western Brittany, a people with a powerful fleet, were in rebellion. They learned with anger that Caesar was planning an invasion of Britain, which would seriously upset their control of cross-Channel trade. But Caesar sent a fleet against them, and they were crushed in a battle in Quiberon Bay (56 B.C.). Then early in the next year, Caesar threw back a German migration from the east. He built a bridge over the Rhine and led a force across it for a brief stay

MODEL OF ALESIA
(Saint-Germain-en-Laye Museum) Built for Napoleon III by General Verchère Refflye, this model shows the work Caesar had done in front of the fortress of Alesia. The first obstacles were traps. Then came staggered rows of pits, five rows of stakes, two deep and wide ditches filled with water, the vallum (rise and fencing), and finally the towers.

103

on the other side, where no Roman commander or troops had ever set foot before. The bridge was a display of his army's superb engineering, but it was also a demonstration that there were no bounds to the frontiers of Rome and his own ambitions. This last purpose was once again in his mind when, as the Veneti had foreseen, he launched his first expedition to Britain. A subsidiary motive was his desire to lay hands on the considerable wealth of the country. But his main purpose was to eclipse Pompey as a leader of armies to hitherto unknown lands.

Pompey, not to be outdone, later objected that the English Channel was merely an insignificant mudflat. But Caesar had reason to disagree. When he had landed on the southeast coast of England and had put two legions ashore, many of his eighty ships were heavily damaged on the beach by high tides that he had not foreseen. The ambush that this encouraged the British to attempt was duly beaten off. The entire Roman force sailed back to Gaul only eighteen days after its arrival.

The following year, Caesar led a second and larger expedition to Britain. This time he took five legions and two thousand cavalry on eight hundred ships—by far the largest fleet the Channel had ever seen, and larger than any it was to see again until 1944. Embarking at the same point as before, he landed near Sandwich and at once marched into the hinterland. But history repeated itself, for a storm in the night destroyed forty of his ships and disabled most of the rest. So he had to return to the coast to organize repairs and protective measures. Meanwhile, the British tribes, dropping their habitual feuds for the moment, had appointed King Cassivellaunus as commander in chief of their united forces. But Caesar, beating off guerrillas as he went, forced his way across the Thames—the British tribes in his rear failing to provide a diversion—and stormed the king's capital near St. Albans. Then, after a stay of three months on the island, he and his army were transported back to Gaul.

Caesar hoped that he had established a network of client and states beyond the imperial frontiers. Time showed, however, that this had not been achieved; Rome did not succeed in annexing any portion of Britain for nearly a hundred years to come.

When Caesar returned to the mainland, it had become clear that the conquest of the country was far from complete. In the northern part of the country, outbreaks of rebellion indicated the possibility that detachments of Caesar's army might be isolated and cut to pieces; one tribe revolted, another massacred a garrison of one and a half legions. In 53 B.C., he summoned three conferences of Gallic chieftains in the north in an endeavor to stamp out disaffection.

Nevertheless, in the following year the Gauls rose in general revolt. They conferred the supreme command on the only talented leader they produced in these wars, Vercingetorix of the tribe of the Arverni in central Gaul.

That winter, Caesar had returned to the Cisalpine part of his command. But now, on hearing the news of the rebellion, he hastened back across the Alps with unexpected speed. Caesar directed his attack against the chief fortress of the Arverni, Gergovia. But there he received his first serious setback of the war and was compelled to break off the siege. Caesar had sent his deputy Labienus to the north, but now he summoned him back. Together they besieged Vercingetorix who, by an unwise decision following a defeat, had retired behind the walls of the fortress of Alesia (Alise Sainte Reine). Huge reinforcements came to relieve him, and for four

BARBARIAN FIGHTING
A ROMAN LEGIONARY
(2nd century B.C.)
The conflict between the wild and shaggy barbarian, with unrefined features and fervid expression, and the Roman legionary, stone-faced and stalwart, is a recurring theme in Roman art.

days Caesar's army had to resist an attack from both directions. But then the Gallic relief forces were routed, and the Great Revolt was at an end.

The Gauls had, on the whole, failed to unite with any effectiveness. And the losses they had suffered were appalling: At least a third of all their men of military age were killed, and another third were sold into slavery. And now their large territory, reduced to subject status, was assessed for Roman tribute as three separate new provinces. By the annexation of this land which forms a bridge between the Inner and the Outer Seas, the whole character of the Roman Empire had been transformed. It was no longer a purely Mediterranean dominion.

Caesar had shown himself to be one of the supreme military commanders of all time. His powers of endurance were phenomenal. A first-class horseman, he also thought nothing of covering a hundred miles a day in a light carriage on terrible roads—while all the time dictating official letters or literary works to relays of secretaries. But his outstanding personal qualities as a commander were speed, timing, and adaptability. His generalship was breathtakingly quick in mind as well as in movement—far too quick for his enemies.

In Rome, however, the political situation had gradually fallen to pieces. Julia, Caesar's daughter and Pompey's wife, died in 54 B.C., so that the links between the two leaders were seriously weakened. And then the triumvirate ceased to exist because their third partner, Crassus, in his attempt to overcome the Parthians, met with disaster and was killed. This meant that Pompey and Caesar, with their rival aims and ambitions, now stood alone in direct confrontation.

Early in the following year, Clodius was murdered, and in the resulting emergency Pompey assumed his third consulship, holding the office for some months

GLANUM
The site of Glanum, in Saint-Rémy de Provence, has two interesting monuments. The first is the Julii (left), a three-tiered mausoleum built in 40 B.C. by a distinguished local family. The other is the arch with a single opening, built under Augustus. It commemorates Rome's victory over the barbarians.

105

without a colleague. He married Cornelia, daughter of the aristocratic Metellus Scipio, whom he elevated to become his fellow consul. He was moving away from Caesar and soon afterwards allowed himself to be pushed by his advisers into even less friendly measures towards him. These culminated in a decision that the appointment of a new provincial commander to replace him should come up for discussion in the Senate in March 50 B.C.

But Caesar had the backing of a young tribune, Curio, who persistently vetoed demands that any such successor should be appointed. Curio produced an alternative suggestion, but a small group of diehards ensured its rejection. The deadlock was complete, and one of the consuls called on Pompey to take up the command of all the forces of the Republic. Pompey accepted the commission and took over two legions which had been about to depart for Syria.

When a message from Caesar arrived in Rome, the young tribune Antony (Marcus Antonius), who had succeeded Curio as his representative, could scarcely induce the senators to allow it to be read. They proceeded instead to pass their emergency decree with Caesar as its target, and Antony and a colleague hastily left Rome for the north. Then, on the night of January 10, 49 B.C., Caesar crossed the small river Rubicon, which formed the border between Cisalpine Gaul and eastern Italy. When he moved across this bridge, taking a single legion with him, he was breaking Rome's law of treason which forbade a governor to lead his troops outside his province.

And so, as Caesar himself declared, the die was cast, and the crossing of this little stream was one of the formal turning points in Roman history. It meant that the nation was plunged into an empire-wide civil war for which neither side was ready.

THE BARBARIAN
VERCINGETORIX
*After being captured
by the Romans (50 B.C.),
the Gallic chief appeared
on coins like this silver
Denarius (48 B.C.). With
his unkempt hair and
beard, he represented
how the Romans viewed
the barbarians.*

Catullus and Lucretius

But the fifties B.C. had not all been war and politics. For example, this was also the time when two of the world's outstanding poets completed much of their work. The formal mastery of Catullus is fully displayed in his jewel-like miniature epics, yet it was not by these longer poems that he impressed the world of the future, but by his shorter pieces. Some of these give expression to a heartbroken intensity—inspired by his love for the hopelessly unfaithful "Lesbia," who was really called Clodia and may have been a fashionable, immoral sister of the politician Clodius. Catullus is the product of agonizing tension between a powerful mind and tormented emotions. He responds to the demands of love with an unprecedented seriousness. And although his verses fully reflect the lively, immoral, and precarious social scene of his day, the service of the community is no part of his aim and the service of its leaders even less: Caesar and Pompey he mentions briefly and contemptuously as irrelevancies.

His older contemporary Lucretius (b. ca. 94–d. 55 B.C.) does not mention these great men by name at all. Lucretius was an adherent of the philosophy of the Athenian Epicurus (341–270 B.C.), who had sought to prove that the universe was completely material. But Lucretius, with startling incongruity, transformed the philosopher's undistinguished Greek prose into an impassioned Latin poem on the nature of the universe, *How Things Are (De Rerum Natura)*—the only philosophical poem of antiquity that has come down to us in complete form.

The scientific doctrine he presents is of no more than historical interest today. Yet its presentation displays Lucretius as the most original thinker of his day. Our

CITHARA PLAYER
*Though men were often
seen reading in Roman art,
the depiction of a woman
playing music or being read
to symbolized her education,
as in this fresco from Stabiae,
Gulf of Naples.*

purpose in life, Lucretius and his master declare, should be happiness. This assertion has damned the Epicureans in the eyes of posterity on the grounds that they are advocating sensual pleasures—a mistaken conclusion, since they equated happiness with freedom from disturbance (*ataraxia*), only procurable by the acquisition of the right kind of knowledge.

Caesar and Pompey, the poet must have thought, did not possess this kind of knowledge at all, and it was therefore predictable that he should not refer to them. But he expresses, in forthright terms, the poorest possible view of the politicians dragging the Roman Republic down to extinction:

> *"Men lost,*
> *Confused, in hectic search for the right road,*
> *The strife of wits, the wars for precedence,*
> *The everlasting struggle, night and day,*
> *To win towards heights of wealth and power."*

The civil war

After crossing the Rubicon, Caesar moved rapidly into the center of Italy. He was joined in Ariminum (Rimini) by the friendly tribunes from Rome, Curio and Antony; then they pressed on, and one town after another opened its gates to them. His enemies included most of the senior senators, and this made them too confident. They were also too jealous of Pompey and would not allow him the powers a commander needed. So, in the face of Caesar's advance, Pompey retreated southwards through the Italian peninsula, while his uneasy allies, the consuls, fled from

Rome. Then the consuls set out across the Adriatic, followed by Pompey himself. He was probably justified in making for the eastern provinces, for in the East he had huge resources to draw upon.

Caesar could not pursue his opponents yet, for the command of the sea was in their hands and threatened the grain supply of Italy. So Curio, acting on his behalf, seized the wheat-producing island of Sicily, though he was then defeated and killed in north Africa. Caesar himself, after convening Senate and Assembly meetings at Rome, set off by land to attack Spain.

Meanwhile, in southern Gaul, the Greek city-state of Massilia was forced to surrender to Caesar, who allowed the place to remain autonomous but brought its long career of independent statehood to an end. He then paid his second visit of the year to the capital, where he assumed for a brief period his first tenure in the post of dictator. This enabled him to fulfill his ambition of arranging to become consul in the following year. And his brief dictatorship also gave him a chance to make a start with some of his gravest administrative problems.

Finally, he moved against his opponents in the Balkans. He endeavored to blockade Pompey's key base in Albania, but the attempt was a failure, and he recoiled inland into the Thessalian plain. There, in the largest battle ever fought between Romans, his superior generalship won the day near Pharsalus (48 B.C.). Pompey himself escaped and decided to proceed to Egypt; he chose it because the government of the boy king Ptolemy XIII had backed him against Caesar in the civil war. But as Pompey landed on the Egyptian coast, he was struck down and assassinated, for the Egyptian politicians intended to be on the winning side.

QUEEN CLEOPATRA
(Limestone relief from Idfu) Cleopatra's legendary beauty and keen political sense earned the queen fame in the Roman world. She was defeated by Antony's rival, Octavian, in 31 B.C.

They also wanted to leave Caesar no excuse for staying in Egypt, for he was known to be on his way in hot pursuit of Pompey, and very soon afterwards he arrived. His intention was to estort an enormous sum from this wealthy and still ostensibly independent country. But the official reason for the visit was to arbitrate between the monarch and his half-sister Cleopatra VII, who had been driven into exile. When, however, Cleopatra, a highly intelligent twenty-one-year-old charmer, secretly came to see him in Alexandria, Caesar, over thirty years her senior, took her into the palace and lived with her as her lover. Thereupon he found himself perilously besieged by the royal army, which favored the king.

It was not until March of the following year that a relief force enabled Caesar to bring his Egyptian enemies to battle. Ptolemy XIII was killed, and Caesar confirmed Cleopatra as queen of Egypt and a client of Rome and of himself. Then Caesar at last returned to Italy and the capital.

He had been away for much too long. Antony, his deputy at Rome, had not been able to stop some of his fellow nobles from getting out of hand. Pompey's death had not meant the death of his cause, and his sons Cnaeus and Sextus, supported by many prominent Romans in north Africa and Spain, were now ready for battle. At the height of winter, Caesar crossed over to north Africa, and after a campaign involving many hardships fought a totally successful battle on the isthmus at Thapsus. The enemy commander Metellus Scipio, Pompey's father-in-law, killed himself, followed shortly afterwards by Cato, whose suicide at Utica provided the Republicans with a martyr and a saint.

The following spring, he won a hard and horrifying soldier's battle in southern Spain. Pompey's son Cnaeus was caught and killed soon afterwards. The gigantic convulsion of the civil war was over. Henceforward Caesar employed the title *Imperator*, not with the meaning of "emperor," but to show that he was the military commander who totally surpassed all others.

The dictatorship of Caesar

The first need, when these campaigns were over, was to reward his ex-soldiers. So Caesar settled these retired legionaries in thousands, establishing colonies for them in Italy and in the provinces. But the most original feature of his foundations was the inclusion of civilians as well—including eighty thousand of the capital's penniless unemployed. This meant that Caesar, like no one else before him, had seriously begun to tackle the obstinate problem of the impoverished workless population of the city.

Caesar had all the appetite of great potentates for erecting magnificent buildings. A great new hall for public business, the Basilica Julia, was under construction in the Roman Forum, and close by, another forum named after Caesar himself began to take shape. Its precinct flanked a shrine of Venus the Mother (Genetrix), since it was from this goddess, through the mythical Aeneas, that the Julian family claimed to be descended.

He placed a statue of Venus in the temple and beside it a gilt bronze statue of Queen Cleopatra VII. She could see it for herself, because in 46 B.C. she arrived in the city with her surviving thirteen-year-old half-brother (with whom she shared the throne) and her infant son, Caesarion, whose paternity she ascribed to Caesar. She stayed on at

THE ROMAN CALENDAR

The first calendar—legend has it that it was introduced by Tarquinius the Elder—is based on the phases of the moon. It included 12 months and 355 days, to which the Great Pontiff inserted days into February every year so that the year would correspond to the Sun. March was the first month of the year until 153 B.C., which explains why the names of the months from September to December mean, in Latin, the 7th, 8th, 9th, and 10th.

But this system had time-lag problems, which Julius Caesar corrected by borrowing the Egyptian 365-day calendar. He also added one day every four years. This Julian calendar, including these "leap years," is what we use today. Quintilis and Sextilis were renamed Julius and Augustus (July and August) in honor of Julius Caesar and Augustus.

Sometimes counted from the time of Rome's founding, years were named after the consuls in power. Weeks did not exist, but three celebrations punctuated the month: the *calends* (1st day of the month), the *nones* (5th or 7th day, depending on the month), and the *ides* (13th or 15th day, depending on the month).

The day was divided into 12 hours, from sunrise to sunset. Hours were therefore shorter in the winter and longer in the summer.

the capital for the rest of Caesar's life, and it is possible to identify certain of his actions that show her influence. For one thing, his plan to establish magnificent public libraries at Rome was based on the world-famous library at Alexandria. And Caesar's revision of the gravely dislocated Roman calendar, a reform that with minor adjustments has survived until the present day, was directed by an Alexandrian astronomer.

Caesar's rising personality cult was stressed by the large number of his portrait busts, which were made and distributed around Italy and the provinces. This marked an important stage in the development of one of Rome's outstanding art forms. It had first developed among the Greeks of recent centuries. Like biographers, the Greek sculptors desired to stress the unique, private pattern of the personage they were depicting. The Romans showed themselves extremely receptive to these same aims, which coincided with their own interest in family history and moral character. From the third century B.C. onwards, the sculptural portrayals of individuals had received increasing attention in the city, and after 100 B. C., Roman portraiture began to become a major art. Portraits also started to appear on the national coinage. The designers of these coins first selected early Roman heroes for portrayal, then the recently dead, including Sulla. It marked a decisive stage when heads of the living Caesar appeared on his coins, in January or February 44 B.C.

They imitated sculptural portraits—some of which still survive today. It was Caesar himself who gave these sculptors their first really important opportunity. His fine, sensitive features brought out the best in them—and skillful artists could even capture the piercing gaze of his dark eyes. His position in the state demanded an interpretation of his personality in all its aspects. In this way, then, was launched the great series of portraits of the rulers of the Empire, which are among its principal artistic gifts to Europe.

The few examples of his surviving busts which can be dated to his lifetime cunningly blend realism with grandeur—for Caesar was as grand as any king. Yet he had no intention of reviving the ancient Roman kingship. Instead, the constitutional status he chose for himself was the dictatorship. In February 44 B.C., he was appointed dictator for the rest of his life—PERPETVO, as his coins unequivocally assert. It meant that the other nobles, however many consulships and other offices they might hold, would never be able to get their hands on the real controls and profits of public life.

But their resentment evidently did not weigh with Caesar, who was forming plans to leave the intrigues of the capital and get back among his admiring, incomparable army. He was consumed by a desire for further military glory, and it had to come soon, since he was fifty-six and suffered from precarious health.

CAESAR'S FORUM
(46 B.C.) In addition to restoring several monuments, Caesar also built an entirely new Forum that housed a temple to Venus, the divine ancestor of the Julian family.

AVNORVM SAITXORVM ETSILENORVMDELECI AVNORVM SAITX

COINS OF THE REALM

Until they issued their first coin—the As, in the third century B.C.—the Romans simply traded cattle herds (the word *pecunia*, meaning money, comes from *pecus*, meaning herd), then bronze ingots marked with a symbol (animal, trident, spear, and so on). The As was coined in the Temple of Juno Moneta (Councilor), from which our word *money* comes.

During their relationship with Greater Greece, the Romans adopted the silver coin, first giving it the same value as the Athenian coin, the Drachma, before creating their own currency units, the Sestertius (2.5 As) and the Denarius (10 As). From that point on, the value of the coin was indicated.

The magistrates who issued the coins gradually replaced the national symbols (the she-wolf, the bow of a ship, a quadriga, a victory) with scenes that depicted the accomplishments of ancestors, or even their own endeavors (buildings they had built or restored, victories, and the like).

Julius Caesar preferred gold coins (Aureus), which until then were uncommon. But, in the name of propaganda, he was the first to have his own portrait engraved.

Continuous coin reforms were then carried out, all resulting in progressive devaluation. Emperors followed in Caesar's footsteps and used their own portraits or those of their families. The names of the magistrates were removed and replaced by the names and titles of the emperor. These official portraits are indispensable to numismatists, who date coins, and to historians, who follow the evolution of imperial ideology. In addition to their esthetic value, the coins, quite remarkably, point not only to how the Empire expanded and unified but also to Rome's political history.

The East was Caesar's first objective, and its provinces witnessed the marshaling of the great Roman army to await his arrival. He was to leave the city on March 18, 44 B.C. When this became known, the news brought the growing hostility of the nobles to a head. It was distasteful enough to be governed by a perpetual dictator on the spot, but the prospect of government by his aides or secretaries in his absence was intolerable. There had been suggestions of conspiracies against his life before. But now planning began in earnest. Its chief instigator was Cassius, a proud man who had come over to Caesar in the civil war but did not feel he had been sufficiently rewarded. And Cassius won over his less dynamic and more philosophically minded brother-in-law, Marcus Brutus. Another leading conspirator was Brutus's distant relation Decimus Brutus Albinus, one of Caesar's principal commanders in the Gallic War. With these and others to lead them, the various groups of malcontents coalesced into a body of sixty determined plotters.

Caesar was aware that many noblemen detested him. But a mixture of fatalism and contemptuous pride caused him to ignore the threat. Indeed, so little was he concerned with the evident danger to his life that he even disbanded his personal bodyguard of Spaniards. Then, three days before he was due to depart for the east, the Senate gathered for a meeting in Pompey's theater; there the conspirators surrounded Caesar and stabbed him to death. Not long before, all senators had sworn an oath of allegiance to the father of their country, as Caesar had now come to be called; they were clients bound to protect their patron. But at the moment of reckoning they rushed out of the building, and Caesar lay where he had fallen.

For all his immeasurable abilities as a general and administrator, he had failed—and would probably have continued to fail—to rescue Rome from its major dilemma. The Republic had become impotent, and there was no practical alternative to one-man rule. Yet one-man rule was just what the nobles refused to accept, and so they put Caesar to death. It seemed an insoluble problem. Yet there now came another sort of man altogether, who performed the seemingly impossible task of finding a solution after all; he was the nineteen-year-old Octavian, grand-nephew of Julius Caesar, who had adopted him in his will as his son.

BRUTUS'S DENARIUS
This coin was issued by Brutus during the civil war period that followed Caesar's murder. The freedman's cap alludes to the Republic's renewed liberty after the assassination, which is symbolized by daggers. In this manner, Brutus sought to justify himself and guarantee the loyalty of his troops.

From the baths to the banquet

〜∽〜

A day in the life of a Roman citizen had two distinct halves. From sunrise to the beginning of the afternoon was the *negotium*. This was a time to take care of business: relationships with customers, political or legal activities—all the transactions that happened around the Forum. Then came the *otium*. This was a time to rest, a period to relax both the body and soul.

In general, a Roman would start the day by going to the baths. If he were very rich, he might have private baths in his home. But for the most part, he went to one of the many public baths in the city, where he would clean and take care of his body and meet contemporaries. Then he would go home for dinner with his family or friends, or perhaps be invited out.

The banquet (*cena*), which combined the pleasures of abundant, fine food with cultivated conversation, played an essential role in Roman social life. In a dining room decorated with frescoes and ornamental mosaics, opening onto an interior garden, the guests would sit on table beds arranged in a U-shape; the seating arrangement would strictly adhere to social order. The different dishes on the menu were set up nearby on console tables. The wine, diluted with water and sometimes honey, was passed from cup to cup. Slaves did the serving. Often, poetry or musical interludes would enliven the evening. The guests would exchange poems, essentially love poems. The conversation, which was greatly influenced by Greek culture, roamed freely from mythology to philosophy.

Always on the lookout for rarer and more expensive dishes and more original entertainment—the lavish banquet hosted by Trimalchion, the rich and vulgar freedman from Petronius's *Satiricon*, is just one example of the excesses of the Empire—the Romans often incurred criticism from moralists and forced the censor to enact sumptuary laws. Mecenus, Augustus's friend, who always seemed to be going to a banquet, and who presented himself without even a belt, was the archetype of debauchery for Seneca the Younger, a philosopher and dramatist.

The emperors, especially the Julio-Claudians, also organized sumptuous celebrations, which have nurtured the image of Rome as a civilization of epicureanism and hedonism in literature and countless motion pictures.

ROMAN SLAVES
Except for the Saturnalia (December 7–14), during which masters reversed roles with their slaves and served them, rich Romans were accustomed to having a servile household staff.

GETTING READY
The guests, seated on the three beds of the triclinium, were served by young slaves who would see to their comfort throughout the banquet.

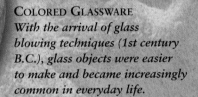

THE LUXURY OF SILVER
To display his wealth, the host of the banquet used, or sometimes simply exhibited, silverware and silver plates.

COLORED GLASSWARE
With the arrival of glass blowing techniques (1st century B.C.), glass objects were easier to make and became increasingly common in everyday life.

THE ROLE OF POETRY
Poetry, the erotic sort in particular, played a major role in the banquet and led to a new literary genre, the elegy.

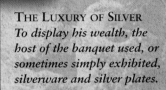

THE BATHS AS CULTURAL CENTERS

The baths, first and foremost, met the demand for public hygiene. But they also displayed the opulence of a city or the individual who built them. The baths were a special meeting place. In 25 B.C, Agrippa had the first public baths built on the military esplanade. But it was only after Nero that the typical blueprint for large baths emerged, reaching throughout the Empire, from Titus to Diocletian. Hot baths (*calarium*), warm baths (*tepidarium*), and cold baths (*frigidarium*) made up the main axis, while annexes housed the changing room, pool, palestra, and massage rooms. Surrounded by porticos, the baths were made for the purpose of exercising the body, but they also often included meeting rooms, art galleries, and libraries, which turned them into genuine cultural centers. In this way, they reflected the dynamism of the imperial cities.

OUTSIDE DINING ROOM IN HERCULANEUM
From stone benches decorated with cushions, the guests could admire the décor: stone and shell fountains and mosaics depicting Neptune and Amphitrite. The table was set in the center.

CHAPTER 9

Augustus

The Second Triumvirate

After Caesar's murder, his right-hand man Antony, consul in 44 B.C., used a variety of methods to gain control of events; he took steps at the same time to arouse the people against the assassins, Brutus and Cassius, who before long retreated to the east. Cicero attacked Antony fiercely in a series of brilliant speeches, the *Philippics*. And with Cicero's encouragement the young Octavian, exploiting his adoption by his murdered great-uncle Caesar emerged as a rival to Antony.

In April 43 B.C., a senatorial coalition including Octavian defeated Antony at Mutina (Modena) in Cisalpine Gaul and compelled him to withdraw into the Transalpine (Narbonese) province. There, however, he was joined by a number of commanders, including Lepidus (son of the consul of 78 B.C.), a henchman of Caesar. In November, Octavian became reconciled with Antony and Lepidus at a conference in Bononia (Bologna), and the three men were granted a five-year autocratic appointment—the Second Triumvirate.

VICTORY AT ACTIUM
This cameo made of sard, celebrating Octavian's naval victory against his rival Antony (31 B.C.), is one of the many engraved gemstones that served as Augustinian propaganda.

After a holocaust of their political enemies, in which three hundred senators and two thousand knights were hounded to death, Antony and Octavian crossed the Adriatic and won two battles at Philippi in Macedonia against Brutus and Cassius, both of whom committed suicide (42 B.C.).

But their relations with each other showed increasing signs of strain. This was partly because of Antony's liaison with the queen of Egypt, Cleopatra VII. In 40 B.C., Antony married Octavian's sister, Octavia, and in these circumstances his simultaneous association with Cleopatra was unacceptable not only to Octavian, whose family was insulted, but also to conservative Roman opinion in general.

In 37 B.C., a partial reconciliation between the two men provided for a five-year renewal of the triumvirate. But the understanding proved short-lived, since henceforward Antony, abandoning Octavia, lived openly with Cleopatra, who built up under his overlordship an extensive imperial system of her own including many client states. At this point, too, the third triumvir, Lepidus, seeking to contest Octavian's western supremacy by force, failed to command the support of his own legions and was disarmed and forced into retirement.

Octavian's rivalry with Antony was becoming increasingly apparent, and having raised as much money as he could, Octavian declared war—not against his compatriot Antony, but against Cleopatra. With her as his companion—and she provided a substantial proportion of his ships and supplies—Antony had brought up his navy and army to guard strongholds along the coast of western Greece. But at the beginning of 31 B.C., Octavian's fleet, under his former schoolmate Agrippa, succeeded in sailing from Italy across the Ionian Sea and capturing decisive strongpoints along the Greek coast. After Octavian arrived, Antony was finally cornered in the Gulf of Ambracia (Arta). At the battle of Actium, just outside the gulf, he tried to extricate his ships in the hope of continuing the fight elsewhere. But although Cleopatra and Antony succeeded in breaking out, only a quarter of their fleet was able to follow them.

Both fled to Egypt. When the country fell to Octavian (30 B.C.), they committed suicide at Alexandria. Their conqueror declared the country a Roman possession, thus eliminating the last survivor of the three Greek monarchies that had succeeded to the heritage of Alexander, and he made it a unique sort of province, under his own direct control. His seizure of Cleopatra's treasure made him wealthier than the Roman state itself.

The battle of Actium was hailed by subsequent writers as one of the most decisive battles ever fought because it established Octavian's position as master of the entire Greco-Roman world.

The principate of Augustus

From now on, by a long series of patient measures, Octavian established the Roman principate, a system of government that, while not dispensing with republican forms, depended on him as the first man of the state (*princeps*) and enabled him to maintain control over its affairs. Remembering that Caesar had been murdered because of his recourse to naked power, he understood that the nobles would only tolerate his autocracy if he concealed it behind republican traditions. For the first eight years after his victory at Actium, the constitutional basis of his power remained a succession of consulships.

But in the middle of this period, in 27 B.C., he pronounced "the transfer of the state to the Senate and people," thereby earning the misleading, though outwardly plausible, reputation as the restorer of the *res publica*, or ancestral system. At the same time he was granted, for ten years, an area of government comprising not only Egypt, which was his personal domain, but also Gaul, Spain, and Syria. He ruled this huge collection of "imperial" provinces through governors who were his own subordinates (*legati*).

Augustus's new Senate was reduced in numbers from Caesar's nine hundred to the earlier figure of six hundred. He was elected its president and overshadowed it by his grandeur. The Senate's strength was no longer political but administrative; the achievement of the new order was to take politics out of administration for the first time in Roman history. This was only one of the many acts of transformation that Augustus performed, veiling them always under the guise of traditionalism.

Four days after the new political arrangements were announced in 27 B.C., the ruler's name "Caesar" was supplemented by the novel designation "Augustus." The adoption of this term to define his new status indicated his superiority over the rest of humankind and yet avoided dictatorial or divine appellations that would cause conservatives offense.

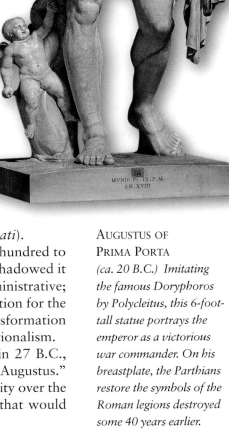

AUGUSTUS OF PRIMA PORTA (*ca. 20 B.C.*) *Imitating the famous Doryphoros by Polycleitus, this 6-foot-tall statue portrays the emperor as a victorious war commander. On his breastplate, the Parthians restore the symbols of the Roman legions destroyed some 40 years earlier.*

AVNORVM SATYRORVM ETSILENORVM DELECT AVNORVM SATYR

THE EMPEROR AND HIS ADMINISTRATION

The expansion of the Roman world gradually rendered republican institutions ineffective, and the civil wars of the 1st century B.C. helped institute a single ruler. But the Romans, who were traumatized by the memory of the monarchy, detested the title of king. Therefore Octavian, who was invested with civil and military powers after 31 B.C., retained the semblance of the republican regime— the magistracy, the Senate, and for a time, the Assembly—without real power. He himself was the prince *(princeps)* of the Senate, before receiving the title "sacred" *(Augustus)*.

He also added Caesar to his name, in memory of his adoptive father, and Imperator, which was the title held by triumphant generals (from which comes the word "emperor").

The emperor held proconsular power— that is, he was responsible for the armies and the provinces. He also held tribunician power, which made him inviolable. As Pontifex Maximus (Great Pontiff), he assumed the highest of all religious positions. As prefect, he carried out the duties of a censor and therefore chose the senators. He had the right to judge, and his edicts became law. He diminished the powers of the magistrates by appointing senior officials accountable to him alone: prefect of the praetorium (imperial guard), prefect of the harvest tax (provisions for Rome), prefect of night surveillance (protection against fires), and prefect of the city (administration of Rome).

Alongside the public treasury, he created the imperial treasury. Finally, four ministries were established, charged with communications with the provinces and foreign affairs, finances, justice, and requests sought from the emperor. As the years went by, the republican fiction died and imperial power grew into absolutism.

Military operations continued in numerous areas, and the eastern frontier was pushed a large distance forward by the annexation of a huge area of central Asia Minor under the name of Galatia (25 B.C.). Augustus himself visited Gaul and directed part of a campaign in Spain until his health gave out. In 23 B.C., he fell ill and was thought to be on the point of death.

The next to die, however, was not Augustus, but his young nephew Marcellus (23 B.C.), who had been married to his daughter Julia. After his death, Julia became the wife of Agrippa, who continued to travel and fight as the deputy of the *princeps* and even shared his tribunician power (18 B.C.).

THE GEMMA AUGUSTEA
This cameo was made by a famous Greek engraver in honor of the emperor. As soldiers raise a trophy before the barbarians, Augustus reigns over them like a god.

Agrippa must have seemed a likely candidate for succession and his powers continued to be renewed together with his master's. But the nobles would never have accepted this "new man," and Augustus appeared to be indicating his own alternative views regarding likely successors when he adopted, as his own children, Gaius and Lucius, the sons of Agrippa and Julia. Yet they were only three and one year old respectively, and Augustus hedged his bets by giving important military employment to his grown stepsons, Tiberius and Nero Drusus.

In 12 B.C., Agrippa died, and Augustus compelled his widow Julia to marry Tiberius, against the wishes of both of them. During the next three years, Tiberius returned to military life, moving northwards the limits of the province of Illyricum (Yugoslavia) and creating a new middle Danubian province of Pannonia (Austria and Hungary). At the same time his brother, Nero Drusus, crossed the Rhine and invaded Germany as far as the Elbe. This was the first step towards the annexation of the country.

Tiberius, who replaced Nero Drusus in Germany on the latter's death (9 B.C.), was elevated three years later to a share in his stepfather's tribunician power. But shortly afterwards, he threw up all his responsibilities and withdrew into retirement on the island of Rhodes. This dramatic step was ascribed to jealousy of his stepson

Gaius, who was introduced to public life in the following year, as was his brother, Lucius, three years later. But only a very short time afterwards, by an extraordinary chance, both of these young men were dead (4, 2 A.D.). Now there was no other possible successor but Tiberius. So Augustus adopted him as his son.

Tiberius's next task was taking over Bohemia, at that time the nucleus of an unprecedentedly well organized German empire. In 6 A.D., a two-pronged Roman invasion of Bohemian territory was under way. But then, disaster struck across the Rhine; a talented German, Arminius, a chieftain of the Cherusci, led his people against the unwary Roman commander Varus, and killed him and destroyed his three legions in Teutoburg Forest near Detmold. The result was that the annexation both of west Germany and of Bohemia had to be postponed indefinitely—and, as it turned out, forevermore—with incalculable results for the future of Europe, since these millions of Germans remained outside the Roman world.

Earlier Roman commanders had maintained personal guards, and Augustus developed these precedents by the creation of a standing praetorian guard. He also established a city police at Rome, and a watch or fire brigade.

In 6 A.D., he founded a new military treasury to defray legionaries' retirement pensions from the proceeds of indirect taxes. This was one of a number of administrative innovations which the aging and tiring ruler introduced during the last decade of his life, with the help and perhaps the guiding initiative of Tiberius. In 13 A.D., Augustus deposited his will at the House of the Vestals at Rome. Then, in the following year, he died, and Tiberius became emperor.

Augustus had proved himself one of the most gifted administrators the world has ever seen and the most influential single figure in the entire history of Rome. The gigantic work of reform that he carried out not only transformed the decaying Republic but also created a durable, efficient Roman peace. This Pax Romana insured the survival and eventual transmission of the classical heritage,

RELIEF OF VESTAL VIRGINS *(13–9 B.C.) This relief, situated within the Altar of Peace of Augustus, could only be seen by the priests in charge of the public cult.*

Greek and Roman alike, and made possible the diffusion of Christianity, of which the founder, Jesus, was born during this reign.

Although in every respect that mattered, he was scarcely less of an autocrat than Caesar had been, Augustus contrived to cloak his absolutism in guises which looked old-fashioned enough to pass muster. The people who approved of his republican façade were the nobles. But above all others, he gained the loyalty of the knights and the middle class, whom this new regime notably benefited. Many of the satisfied beneficiaries were not Roman but Italian, for Augustus felt and encouraged

TROPHY OF TURBIA
(6 B.C.) Rising above Cimiez (Alpes-Maritimes), this trophy (a memorial raised on the field of victory) commemorates the triumphs of Augustus over the people of the Alps. The columns on the rotunda are Doric.

AVNORVM SAIYRORVM ETSILENORVMDELECIAVNORVM SAIYR

THE ORGANIZATION OF THE PROVINCES

The territories occupied after the First Punic War were entrusted to the magistrates in power. But because they were too few in number, each province was granted for a year to a magistrate who had left his office (proconsul or propraetor). He was given military, judicial, and administrative attributions, and almost unlimited powers. The function was not paid, but it was profitable: Aside from the credits voted upon and often misappropriated by the Senate, the governor could impose taxes or exploit people freely. The inhabitants of the provinces (except for those living in free cities) were taxed. The taxes were collected by syndicates of publicans from the equestrian class, who also loaned money at very high rates. In this way, the Republic systematically impoverished the provinces.

Under the Empire, however, senatorial provinces were distinguished from imperial ones. Peaceful provinces, which did not see any need for troops, were answerable to the Senate. They were administered by a praetor or a consul who had left office less than five years prior, and who held the position for a single year. When there was one or more legions, the emperor took charge of the province and delegated his powers for several years to a former magistrate or a procurator. In all the provinces, the governor was responsible for administration and justice.

Another difference under the Empire was that governors were appointed, and therefore committed fewer abuses. Furthermore, tax collection was entrusted to a treasury or imperial tax official, who was not quite so greedy as the equestrian syndicate members. Except for Egypt, which was the emperor's private property— even senators could not visit there—the provinces were well administered and enjoyed a period of peace and prosperity.

a new patriotic feeling for Italy, very different from the Greco-Roman concepts of Antony and Cleopatra. He summed up this pro-Italian, pro-Roman trend of his policy by the title that he chose to have conferred upon himself in 2 B.C.: *pater patriae*, father of his country. His proclaimed fatherhood of Romans and Italians went back to the most ancient roots of the community, in which the *pater familias*, or head of household, had been the revered key figure.

The conventional view of his character, in ancient times, differentiated between his cruelty in his youthful years and his mildness when he was older. But there was not so much need for cruelty in his later career as there had been earlier, though when even towards the end of his days harsh measures were needed, he remained ready to apply them. His domestic life, too, though simple and homespun, was conducted on ruthless lines. When his daughter Julia and granddaughter of the same name moved in immoral smart circles suspected of subversion, he exiled them without compunction, and his third grandson, too, suffered banishment and perhaps death.

Augustus was short of stature, but his fine countenance with its calm and mild expression proved a godsend to the best sculptors of the time, Greeks and Hellenized easterners who devoted to his features a remarkable series of sympathetic, moving interpretations. These portrayals, displaying a blend of idealism and realism, were reduplicated throughout the empire in thousands of busts and statues and portraits on coins.

Augustus was also the greatest of all the adorners of Rome. Something of the classic grandeur of his buildings can still be seen today in the Theater of Marcellus and the remains of the massive Augustan Forum. Flanked by huge colonnades and side apses, the new precinct culminated in the Temple of Mars the Avenger—the avenger of his adoptive father, the god Caesar, who had himself started this precedent of con-

TREASURE OF BOSCOREALE
(end of 1st century B.C.)
This silver cup illustrates Augustus receiving the surrender of the barbarians —a classic scene of imperial propaganda.

FRESCO FROM LIVIA'S VILLA *(20–10 B.C.) When their property lacked a garden, Romans would often decorate their dining rooms with trompe l'oeil décor.*

structing new Forums. Outside Rome, too, there were innumerable arches, trophies, and other memorials of the Augustan age. And from his wife Livia's mansion on the outskirts of Rome, at Prima Porta, comes a reminder that not all the art of the period was formal and grandiose. One of the rooms is adorned with wall paintings that create the illusion of an enchanted garden; beyond a trellis are orchards and flowerbeds in which birds and insects perch among the foliage.

The economic basis

This elegance, and the whole way of living for which it stood, was the product of a new solidity in the finances of the Empire. The principal direct taxes paid by the population of the Empire, other by than Rome and Italy, which enjoyed exemption, were a levy on all occupiers of land and a poll tax. The most important of the indirect levies—the only dues to which Roman citizens were liable—were customs dues. But their rates, at two percent, were low enough not to hamper commerce.

Its free operation was ensured by a system of fleets which, for the first time, were organized to police the Mediterranean, so that maritime interchanges gained in speed and security alike. But the most important means of communication and organization was provided by the comprehensive network of roads extending throughout Italy and the provinces. By the second century A.D., there were more than fifty thousand miles of first-class roads in the Empire and over two hundred thousand miles of lesser roads. These roads were systematically and resourcefully designed, constructed and drained. They were made to span rivers by the creation of soaring bridges; they penetrated mountains by tunnels that aroused admiration for centuries.

In the favorable circumstances created by Augustus, interregional trade became solidly established as a significant economic factor. Metalworking flourished at Rome and Capua, and glassblowing became a prosperous activity in Campania and north Italy alike. And Italy in return bought a large range of provincial wares, including slaves, grain, metals, marble, linen, papyrus, furs, and ivory.

Nevertheless, trading never became the economic basis of the Roman world. There were practical problems. Fuel was scarce, and transportation, while risky and erratic by sea, was slow and expensive on land—it did not pay, for example to cart grain for more than fifty miles. For these reasons, commerce and industry probably never amounted to more than ten percent of the Empire's total revenue. The rest came from agriculture: principally wheat, with barley second.

The great bulk of the "free" population of the Roman world, comprising the inhabitants of the villages and rural areas, remained extremely poor, living at subsistence level. But for the citizens of the towns, the Pax Augusta was a splendid thing. It meant the triumph of the bourgeoisie—the businessmen and traders and all the people who had a share in the city-state system and participated in its profits.

And so, from a considerably wider section of the population than had ever flourished in the previous history of Rome, Augustus deserved the compliment that was paid to him in the last days of his life. As the ship on which he was traveling sailed beside the busy Campanian port of Puteoli, it passed a merchant vessel that had just arrived from Alexandria. Thereupon its crew and passengers, wearing white robes and garlands, burned incense and offered a salute to the father of their country, crying out that it was to him that they owed their lives, freedom, and prosperity.

BUST OF AUGUSTUS
Made by Greeks during the Augustan period, this bronze bust of Emperor Augustus bears the characteristic draping of Hellenistic art.

Augustan literature

Alongside Agrippa, the most important of Augustus's advisers had been the Etruscan Maecenas (d. 8 B.C.). Through him, the ruler was able to win the goodwill of some of the greatest writers the world has ever known.

The Roman Forum under the Empire

THE HEART OF ROME
The Roman Forum was first conceived around 600 B.C. as a large space for a public market. Traversed by the Via Sacra ("Sacred Way"), the oldest Roman road, it was occupied by political and administrative buildings during the Republican era. Although damaged several times by fire, and completed in large part by the imperial forum, it continued to be the center of Roman civic life under the Empire.

1. Basilica of Maxentius and Constantine
2. Temple of Peace
3. Temple of Antoninus and Faustina
4. Temple of Venus and of Rome
5. Temple of Romulus
6. Arch of Titus
7. Temple of Vesta
8. Regia
9. Arch of Augustus
10. Temple of Caesar
11. House of the Vestal Virgins
12. Temple of the Dioscuri
13. Basilica Julia
14. Temple of Saturn
15. Temple of Vespasian
16. Temple of Concord
17. Gold milestone column
18. Rostrums
19. Ombilic of Rome
20. Arch of Septimius Severus
21. Curia
22. Aemilia Basilica
23. Sacred Way

Virgil first astonished literary circles in Rome by the novelty of his *Eclogues (Bucolics)* (45–37 B.C.). These ten short poems transmuted into a melodious, evocative Latin the pastoral themes introduced to Greek literature more than two centuries earlier. The four longer *Georgics* that followed (36–29 B.C.), celebrated the beauties of the rustic life. The *Georgics* are the supreme literary expression of that emotional love for Roman Italy which became the center point of Augustus's policy and peace.

VIRGIL BETWEEN
TWO MUSES

(4th century A.D.) In this mosaic from Carthage, the poet Virgil sits between Clio, the muse of history, and Melpomene, the muse of tragedy. It illustrates the respect Virgil enjoyed until the end of antiquity. On the poet's knees, a scroll shows the first words of the eighth verse of the Aeneid.

Next Virgil turned to heroic epic, in the tradition that went back to Homer. But the subtleties of his *Aeneid* are far from Homer's balladlike extroversion. The Trojan Aeneas, escaping from the Greek sack of Troy, is destined for many wanderings and adventures. In north Africa, he encounters the mythical Queen Dido of Carthage, and the sadness of their doomed romance owes less to Homer than to the more recent Greek poetry of Alexandria, magically transformed. Finally Aeneas reaches Italy. As he lands on its shores, he is taken down into the underworld, a scene in which the poet discloses his deepest reflections upon the nature of the universe. Then Aeneas is compelled to join battle with the peoples of Italy. The wars end in peace, he marries a Latin bride, and Rome's foundation will follow—for this is what the poem is really about.

Its theme is largely war. War leads to peace, and it is the Augustan peace of which Virgil is thinking. His age, following upon the prolonged nightmare of civil strife, was one of those times in the history of the world when order looked more important than liberty, and Augustus's feat in bringing peace seemed to Virgil the greatest of all possible national gifts.

Yet Aeneas wins his war only after he has suffered bitterly. In the end, Virgil reckoned military conquest lower than the conquest by human beings of their own souls and hearts. He was a man deeply divided within himself. The benefits Augustus had brought to a war-torn world inspired him with deep gratitude. Yet he also knew that such triumphs are built on pain.

The second of the outstanding Augustan poets, Horace, was born in 65 B.C. at Venusia in Apulia, in southeast Italy. At the battle of Philippi (42 B.C.) Horace served on the side of Brutus and Cassius, but after their defeat he returned to Italy. He obtained a job at Rome and got to know Maecenas.

His *Satires* (35 and 30 B.C.) advocate wisdom through serenity, in the manner of a Greek philosopher. Then, after Maecenas had given him a farm in the Sabine hills, Horace published his famous *Odes* (23 and 13 B.C.), treating of love, wine, nature, friends, and state affairs. Meanwhile, he was also composing his *Epistles* (ca. 20–15 B.C.), which were more profound and mature versions of the *Satires*. The man who emerges from these later works is kindly, humane and mild, but also a gentle but persistent mocker of others and himself.

Augustus, against whom he had formerly fought at Philippi, became his friend, through Maecenas. Indeed, later he became virtually the court poet. Nevertheless, when the ruler offered him the post of private secretary, he declined. Horace had no eye for whatever hardness the new regime might possess. He always remained his own master and kept the core of his quiet but distinct personality intact.

The blend of myth and patriotic antiquarianism which had so profoundly attracted Virgil was the inspiration of Livy of Patavium (b. ca. 59 B.C.–d. 17 A.D.) throughout his entire life. His *History of Rome* took forty years to complete. It consisted of one hundred and forty-two "Books" (one hundred and seven of them are lost), which would have filled twenty or thirty modern volumes. Writing in fluent, lush prose, he offers highly colored evocations of the foundation and early epic age of Rome and provides many rousing narratives, including a superb account of Hannibal's invasion. Rome receives its supreme glorification from Livy, and so does the Roman character, for it is to Livy more than any other writer that we owe our idea of what this was. Rome's traditional heroes and their actions, as he so vividly depicted them, were handed down to later Europe as revelations of what the human

THE PONT DU GARD
(2nd half of 1st century B.C.)
This aqueduct, spanning 825 feet, crosses the gorges of the Gardon valley, where it provided water for the colony of Nîmes. With its three tiers of arcades, it is admired as a masterful work of engineering as well as art.

THE SITE OF BAALBECK
(Lebanon) Having become
a colony under Augustus,
Baalbeck (or Heliopolis)
was home to the largest
temple in the Roman
Orient, the temple of
Heliopolitan Jupiter.
Here, Greco-Roman
architecture is combined
with oriental traditions.
On top of a high podium
built of carved stone, six
columns—with Corinthian
capitals and topped with
the remains of an entab-
lature—still stand out
in the landscape.

spirit can achieve. And the most favored of these heroes was Augustus, restorer of peace and republican moral standards.

Yet at the same time, Livy, like Virgil and Horace, still retains a degree of detachment from the Augustan order. He always felt deep sympathy with humble individuals caught up in the great warlike crises. And his work shows notable caution about the feasibility of any real return to the glorious past. "Our defects are unendurable to us," he declares, "and so are their cures."

The poet Ovid (b. 43 B.C.–d. 17 A.D.) was the only one of these writers whose aloofness veered over into catastrophe. Ovid's genius for vivid description and narrative has been one of the greatest influences Rome has exerted upon the culture of the Western world. This gift finds its fullest expression in the *Metamorphoses*, a vast Arabian Nights of every sort of myth, folk tale, and anecdote, written in a lighter version of Virgil's epic meter. The sort of poetry Ovid was writing did not appeal to the *princeps*, and so in A.D. 8 the blow fell, and the poet was exiled to far-distant Tomi (Constanta in Rumania). He himself describes the charges that had led to this disastrous result as "a poem and a mistake." The poem to which he refers was perhaps *The Art of Love*, far too immoral for the tastes of Augustus. The "mistake" may have had to do with the banishment for adultery of Augustus's granddaughter Julia, her lover being executed at the same time for alleged plotting. Perhaps Ovid, the emperor suspected, had known more than he should—and ought not to have remained silent about it.

CHAPTER 10

The inheritors of empire

The successors of Augustus

Tiberius (14-37 A.D.) had a splendid record of military and administrative achievement. But he was also grim and suspicious and lacked Augustus's talent for public relations. In particular, he found it difficult to get on with senators.

During the first years of his reign, he employed as his principal generals his nephew Germanicus and his own son, Drusus the Younger. Germanicus fought three unproductive campaigns against the Germans beyond the Rhine frontier, then was transferred to the East. This terminated in his death (19 A.D.). Four years later Drusus the Younger also died, so that Tiberius had already lost his two principal heirs.

Meanwhile, a strong personal position was built up by Sejanus, prefect of the praetorian guard. The government displayed continual fear of conspiracies, which existing treason laws were employed to suppress. Sejanus took the lead in initiating such accusations and became more powerful still after Tiberius, in 26, retired from Rome to the Campanian island of Capreae (Capri), never to set foot in the city again for the rest of his life. Sejanus encouraged the emperor to detect seditious intentions in Germanicus's widow, Agrippina, the daughter of Agrippa. She and her two elder sons were arrested in 29–30 A.D. and put to death during the following years, leaving a third son, Gaius Caesar, as the successor to the throne. He was known as Caligula—"Little Boots"—because of the miniature military uniform he had worn as a child.

Meanwhile, Tiberius was told that Sejanus was plotting against Caligula, whose succession would mean an end of his ascendancy. Tiberius secretly transferred the praetorian command to his own confidant Macro, who arranged for Sejanus to be arrested in Rome during a meeting of the Senate. This was done, and its members immediately ordered his execution.

When in 37 A.D., at the age of seventy-nine, the emperor died, it was Caligula who became the next emperor. The transition was arranged by the officers of the praetorian guard, who thus launched their career as emperor makers.

Caligula was the first emperor to show aversion to the long hours of laborious duty needed to keep matters under control, preferring instead to delegate work to the Greek or Hellenized ex-slaves who were his secretaries, so that he could concentrate on amusements instead. The turning point of his reign came in 39 A.D., when he formed a powerful dislike for the Senate, an attitude that became strongly accentuated when one of their number was detected in a plot. Although honors were

THE TRIUMPH OF TIBERIUS *(1st century A.D.) On this embossed silver cup from the treasure of Boscoreale, a procession leads the crowned emperor, standing on his chariot, to victory.*

AVNORVM SATYRORVM ETSILENORVMDELECI AVNORVM SATYR

THE JULIO-CLAUDIANS: A FAMILY OF MADMEN

Under the Empire, there were no rules of imperial succession, which led to some unfortunate results. To wit, Augustus sought to found a dynasty, but had no biologicial sons. Just as Julius Caesar had adopted him, Augustus adopted his grandsons, Gaius and Lucius; when they died, he adopted his wife's son, Tiberius. Power was then handed down to Gaius Caligula, grandson of Tiberius's brother and great-grandson of Augustus. Tiberius was succeeded by his nephew, Claudius. The throne then went to Nero. (Claudius had married Nero's mother, even though she was his niece.)

Suspicious, dishonest, and perverse, Tiberius ended his days as a recluse in Capri. Caligula, on the other hand, was a bloodthirsty madman: Without reason or provocation, he had senators, horsemen, freemen, and slaves executed. Before being assassinated by the praetorians, he appointed his horse consul, married his sister Drusilla, and ordered an army to collect seashells. Claudius was considered a simpleton. He was a fearful emperor—finicky, fickle, and impassioned only by scholarship. His last wife, Agrippina, poisoned him so that her son, Nero, could ascend the throne.

Not to be outdone, Nero had his half brother (Britannicus), his mother (Agrippina), and his wife (Octavia) executed. While he participated in the Olympic Games as a chariot driver, he considered himself an artist, writing and producing theater. Nero expanded his palace by taking advantage of the great fire that burned through Rome. He was accused of arson, but in turn accused the Christians. In the end, he committed suicide to escape a rebellion.

The abuses committed by the Julio-Claudians discredited imperial power, and the court became accustomed to a servility from which it would never recover.

THE CLAUDIA GEM
(1st century A.D.) This sard cameo, resembling those of the Augustinian period, depicts Emperor Claudius and Germaniucs, accom-panied by their respective wives, who were both named Agrippina.

showered on him, conspiracies and rumors of conspiracies continued to abound, and security precautions were sharply intensified. Before long, however, the praetorian high command decided that he was a bad risk, and early in 41 A.D., a group of its officers murdered him.

After his death, his fifty-one-year-old uncle, Claudius, was hailed emperor by the guardsmen. The Senate, however, included many members unwilling to accept Claudius, and they supported a rebellion planned by the governor of Upper Illyricum (Dalmatia). This terrified Claudius just as a similar seditious move had upset Caligula, and the suppression of the plot was followed by further measures against senators of dubious loyalty.

At the same time, however, the government of Claudius was impressively active in provincial and foreign affairs. Just a century after the reconnaissances of Julius Caesar on the island of Britain, the southern and central regions of England were now occupied, in what was perhaps the best planned of all Roman conquests, and their annexation as the province of Britannia immediately followed.

Claudius devoted unremitting absorption to the judicial duties which were one of the most important functions of an emperor. His predecessor's employment of Greek freedmen as advisers was continued, and certain of these men, especially Narcissus and Pallas, rose to great power.

His young wife Messalina, who had borne him a daughter, Octavia, and a son, Britannicus, seemed more interested in indulging herself than in exerting power. In 48 A.D., however, she was charged, perhaps rightly, with conniving in an attempt by one of her lovers to seize the throne, and both she and her lover were put to death. The next year Claudius married again, selecting his niece Agrippina the Younger. For the rest of his reign the aging emperor, worried about plots and weakened by infirmity and drink, increasingly lost his command of what was going on. The government

was in the hands of Agrippina and of Pallas and another of her protégés, the new praetorian prefect Burrus. Agrippina arranged in 50 A.D. that her own thirteen-year-old boy by a former marriage should be adopted by Claudius as his son, taking the name of Nero, so that he—rather than Britannicus, who was four years younger—would succeed to the throne.

And then Claudius suddenly died (54 A.D.). It is believed that Agrippina fed him poisonous mushrooms. With the help of the praetorian commander and of his tutor, the leading writer Seneca, Nero succeeded peacefully to the imperial throne. In view of his youth, it was Agrippina herself who became the effective ruler of the Empire. Her preeminence, however, was brief, since already in the following year, Nero started to assume his imperial duties. Yet when certain liberal ideas he initially proposed proved impracticable, he lost interest in public affairs and felt that chariot racing, music, drama, and sex seemed more rewarding activities. In consequence, the Empire was largely governed by Seneca and Burrus.

Meanwhile, Nero, fearing that his mother might encourage a conspiracy, enticed her to the Campanian coast, where he caused her to be assassinated (59 A.D.). In 62 A.D., Burrus died, and Seneca went into voluntary retirement.

Nero, long since estranged from his young wife Octavia, divorced her and put her to death, marrying a famous beauty, Poppaea—formerly his friend Otho's wife—who bore him a daughter (63 A.D.). In the next year Rome was ravaged by

THE CLAUDIAN TABLET *(48 A.D.) This beautiful inscription in bronze, from the Museum of Gallo-Roman Civilization in Lyons, France, records the speech made by Claudius before the Roman Senate in 48 A.D., in which he allowed the Gauls to be admitted into the Senate. This decision was an important stage in the political assimilation of inhabitants of the provinces.*

a fire, for which the government penalized the small Christian movement as scapegoats. Suspicions that Nero himself had been responsible for the fire gained strength when work was started on his new palace, the Golden House, designed to extend, with its parklands, over a wide area of the city and situated partly on the sites of houses that had been gutted by the fire.

Furthermore, in 65 A.D., the emperor's reputation deteriorated further when he carried out a long-cherished ambition by appearing in his first public performance on the stage. Senators were profoundly shocked, and soon afterwards the first of a series of plots against his life was detected and betrayed.

In the following years, Nero's position became seriously undermined. Provincial governors and army commanders felt tempted to rebel. Vindex, the governor of Gallia Lugdunensis (central Gaul), broke into open revolt (68 A.D.). His insurrection was defeated. But then Galba, governor of Nearer Spain, was hailed emperor by the soldiers of the single legion he commanded, and this was confirmed by the Senate at Rome. Nero found himself abandoned even by the praetorian guard, and in June he committed suicide.

The year of the four emperors

When he learned that Nero was dead, Galba, who was about seventy-one years of age, marched slowly on Rome. But when the new emperor arrived outside the city in October, he caused a bad impression by killing a number of marines who had come to meet him. The bad news traveled, and on New Year's Day, 69 A.D., the army in Upper Germany overthrew his statues and called on the Senate and the Roman people to choose a successor. On the following day, the Lower German forces saluted an emperor on their own account, their governor Vitellius.

Galba decided that lacking a son of his own, he must adopt an heir. This was an important precedent for future emperors but of no avail to himself because the selection he made earned the fatal displeasure of Otho. Otho had been a close friend of Nero until Nero had taken his wife Poppaea. He had been the principal supporter of Galba's revolt and expected the succession to the throne for himself. On January 15, therefore, he had Galba put to death, thus earning notoriety as the first emperor to arrange his predecessor's murder.

Otho must have known that Vitellius had been hailed as emperor in Germany. And now Vitellius's legionaries moved rapidly southwards in the direction of Rome. In early March, they had reached the banks of the Po before Otho's advance guard was ready to hold them up. In the ensuing engagement near Cremona, Otho's commanders were resoundingly defeated, and he committed suicide. It was April 16, and he had reigned for three months. The Senate immediately recognized Vitellius as emperor, and he followed his generals down towards Rome. However, on arrival in the capital, he learned that the eastern legions had transferred their allegiance to Vespasian, the governor of Judaea; the Danube armies did the same, thus for the first time assuming their historic emperor-making role of the future.

EMPEROR NERO
This much-maligned emperor was also a man of taste and an art enthusiast. He dreamed of turning Rome into a cultural city built around the imperial palace, the splendid Domus Aurea (Golden House).

A Danubian legionary commander named Primus, who had joined Vespasian's cause, made a sudden dash for Italy, apparently without awaiting orders from his new chief. Vitellius planned to hold the line of the River Po against him, but in late October, his army, superior in numbers but tired, was overwhelmed by Primus, and as the victors advanced on the capital, Vitellius's remaining forces melted away. Primus's troops forced their way within the walls, and Vitellius, who had gone into hiding, was discovered by the invading army and lynched.

Vespasian and his sons

The Senate promptly declared Vespasian his successor, and a week or two afterwards, his main force arrived in the city under the command of Mucianus, who put an end to the ambitions of Primus by superseding him. With the help of Mucianus (until his death some five years later), Vespasian addressed himself to

THE ARCH OF TITUS *(ca. 81 A.D.) This arch celebrates Titus and Vespasian's victory over the Jews. On the vault, reliefs illustrate two episodes from this campaign: the procession bringing precious spoils from Jerusalem and the triumphant emperor advancing on his chariot, accompanied by the personifications of Rome and Victory.*

DOMITIAN'S PALACE
*(end of 1st century A.D.)
Under the Empire, Palatine
Hill became the emperor's
place of residence. The huge
and luxurious palace of
Domitian occupied the entire
southeast part of the hill.*

the reconstruction of the Empire and its defenses, gravely damaged by the civil wars. He was a man of plain tastes and was proud of them. He worked without stopping; and he decided things by prosaic, common sense methods that made him one of the most effective of all the emperors. It was no coincidence that his three immediate forerunners had survived for only a few months each, after which they all perished violently, whereas his own reign lasted for ten years.

He revived the ancient censorship (73–74 A.D.), utilizing the office not only to purge the Senate of men who had sided against him but also to augment it by many new members, provincials as well as Italians. His fellow censor was his son Titus, whom, although no one had ever made such use of a member of his family before,

AVNORVM SATYRORVM ETSILENORVM DELECTA

JUDAISM UNDER THE EMPIRE

When Alexander died, the country of the Hebrews was dominated by the Ptolemy kings of Egypt, then the Seleucids of Syria, before gaining independence in 142 B.C. Then came a period of utter turmoil, which led Pompey to intervene in 63 B.C. and take Jerusalem. In 4 B.C., when Herod died, the country was divided up and the province of Judea entrusted to a procurator.

The procurators (including Pontius Pilate, from 26 to 36 A.D.) sought to impose the imperial cult, which triggered a revolt in 66 A.D. Vespasian and Titus then took over Jerusalem and destroyed the Temple. In 132 A.D., a new uprising, caused by Hadrian's uncompromising atti-

tude, was crushed; a number of Jews were deported; and a Pagan city in which Jews were forbidden was established in Jerusalem.

Yet the Diaspora, which since the 3rd century B.C. was sizable, was well received by Rome. Caesar and Augustus had protected the freedom of the Jewish cult, respecting the Sabbath and condemning popular reactions against Jews and desecration of synagogues.

In Rome, where the Jewish community had been settled since the 2nd century B.C., Jewish converts were influential. Still, although protected under the Empire, they felt somewhat threatened by the growing power of Christianity.

he also employed as his praetorian prefect. Moreover, as the first emperor to have a son whose maturity and distinction already fitted him to succeed to the throne, he openly declared his intention of founding a new dynasty with Titus as his heir. During the summer, he succumbed to a stomach chill and died.

Titus's tenure of the throne (79–81 A.D.) was so short that it is impossible to say whether his charm, for which he was famous, would have carried him through a longer period of rule. Titus made himself popular by lavish expenditure. Yet at the very outset of his reign, Italy had been struck by disaster when an eruption of Vesuvius, dormant since before the beginning of history, buried Pompeii, Herculaneum, and other centers, thus providing excavators from the eighteenth century onwards with the richest of all collections of evidence about the ancient world.

Titus died prematurely at the age of only forty-two. Yet rumors that he was poisoned by his younger brother and successor, Domitian, were probably unjustified.

When Domitian became emperor, he showed little sympathy with the old republican forms but instead followed a meticulous policy of systematic absolutism. As time went on,

FIXED IN LAVA
(Garden of the Fugitives, Pompeii) The bodies of 13 people who left cavities in the ashes of Mount Vesuvius were immortalized by archaeologists, who poured in plaster to make casts.

and particularly after his adoption of the unprecedented title "perpetual censor" (84–85 A.D.), this tendency caused consternation among the senators.

In 89 A.D., the seditious pattern of the previous dynasty began to repeat itself, and the Roman commander in Upper Germany rose in rebellion. Domitian swooped down and mercilessly crushed the revolt. But his suspicions of the senators were greatly increased by this traumatic event. As Domitian became increasingly afraid of retaliation, terror began to spread among the rest of the senatorial class. Among those alienated and frightened were the commanders of the praetorian guard. And they, without the knowledge of their own soldiers, joined his wife Domitia in a conspiracy which struck the emperor down in 96 A.D.

Trajan, Hadrian, and Antoninus

The sixty-six-year-old former consul Nerva, who was declared his successor on the very same day, must have been privy to the plot. But it caused such great anger among the rank and file of the praetorian guard that after a short interlude, he was compelled to hand over Domitian's assassins and allow them to be executed. Immediately afterwards, he adopted a son and heir from outside his own family. Nerva was acting like Galba before him, but his choice was a great deal more successful. It fell on Trajan, aged forty-four, the governor of Upper Germany; his adoption inaugurated a period of over sixty years in which successions to the throne were determined by adoption rather than by birth.

Trajan's father was descended from Roman settlers in Further Spain and his mother was a Spaniard. His origin was symptomatic of the rise of the provincial element within the ruling class. Attractive and affable, Trajan possessed the rare qualification of popularity among Senate and army alike. His governmental policies were progressive. In Italy, one of his achievements was the foundation of the *alimenta*, a system of financial provision for poor children.

An impressive public works program was also carried out on Trajan's orders. The spiral reliefs on Trajan's Column at Rome indicate the source of the vast expenditure on such projects: They were paid for by the wealth of conquered Dacia (Rumania). Trajan enlarged the Roman army to thirty legions, and with this great army, overran Dacia in two large-scale wars (101–106 A.D.). Its capital was captured and the kingdom became a Roman province. Gigantic sums of gold and silver were seized and brought to Rome, the last really large profits its treasury ever derived from a war.

Trajan had decided that the peace concluded half a century earlier with Parthia must be brought to an end because it had not provided a satisfactory imperial boundary. But when Armenia fell to him with ease (114 A.D.), he decided to go onwards and annex the whole of Mesopotamia as well. The end of the following year saw Trajan at the Persian Gulf. Never before had a Roman commander marched so far, and it would never happen again.

However, it was a transient success. The Parthians rallied their forces, and attacked Trajan's extended lines of communication. He suppressed the rebellions where he could and even proclaimed the conversion of the kingdom of Parthia into a Roman client state. But this was little more than an empty gesture, and almost immediately he turned back towards home. His weakened health made him unable to carry on. He was ill, suffering from high blood pressure, followed, it would appear, by a paralytic stroke in 116 A.D. In the following year, in the southeastern. corner of Asia Minor, he died.

Trajan's talent for civil government, the popular aggressiveness of his military policies, and his agreeable personality had earned him the title of the Best Ruler (*Optimus Princeps*). Yet, by and large, Trajan remains a classic example of a good man carried away by the exciting Roman tradition that conquest was glorious. His successor Hadrian, a distant relative from the same part of Spain, had served him

EMPEROR IN STONE
This bust, sculpted in a feldstone-flecked column, most likely represents the Emperor Nerva.

in many important posts. On Trajan's deathbed, it was given out that the emperor had adopted him as his heir.

Hadrian now assumed the imperial powers. Without delay, he decided—as his predecessor may well have decided already—that the newly occupied eastern territories were untenable, and he withdrew the Roman frontiers to the Euphrates again. While he was away from the capital, however, four of the most eminent senators

TRAJAN'S FORUM
(107–113 A.D.) Celebrating Trajan's victory over Dacia, this is the last and most grandiose of Rome's forums.

AVNORVM SATYRORVM ETSILENORVM DELECT

HADRIAN'S VILLA

A writer, musician, painter, and sculptor, Hadrian also left a record of his talents as an architect: his mausoleum (Saint Angelo Castle) and the Pantheon in Rome, and Villa Hadriana in Tivoli. The latter, built over 16 years, was a huge property covered with gardens in which everything—statues, waterfalls, animals roaming free—was meant to surprise. Underground passages for service workers meant that strollers above could walk peacefully. Buildings were seemingly placed unsymmetrically and at random, which was against tradition.

For a long time, it was thought that Hadrian had patterned his villa after the exotic places he had visited in his travels—among them the Poecile (a colonnaded courtyard in Athens), the Vale of Tempe in Greece (famous for its coolness), and Canopus, an Egyptian port. Today, the property seems more of a manifestation of deified imperial power. For example, a small building traditionally named the Maritime Theater is in fact a representation of the heavens in a planetarium, reproducing the movement of the constellations.

When Hadrian died, the villa was abandoned—and in time, collectors stripped it of its artworks. But not all may be lost, since the site has been only partially excavated.

VILLA HADRIANA
(Tivoli) Greek architectural forms elegantly outline this basin at Hadiran's Villa. It is called Canopus, after the ancient Egyptian port, a sought-after residential area because of the canal that went to Alexandria. Several of the sculptures point to the emperor's fondness for the art of countries he visited, including Egypt and Greece.

found themselves accused of plotting against his life and were put to death, probably by the independent initiative of his praetorian prefect (118 A.D.). This treatment permanently damaged his relations with the Senate.

The remarkable feature of Hadrian's twenty-one-year-long principate was the fact that he spent more than half of it outside Italy, traveling widely throughout the provinces of the Empire. His motives for all these journeys were varied. One was pure curiosity; he was the most fanatical of all the many Roman sightseers. In addition, he had formed a novel conception of what the imperial territories meant. He saw the imperial territories no longer as a collection of conquered provinces but as a commonwealth in which each province and nation possessed its own identity. Yet probably the foremost aim of his travels was to keep the army, in which he maintained a constant and expert interest, in a state of skilled readiness. One of the first fruits of this active military policy, following upon a minor reverse on the British frontier, was the best preserved of all the fortifications of the Empire, Hadrian's Wall from the Tyne to the Solway, manned by fifteen thousand auxiliaries watching over the bare brown hills that rolled away to the still unconquered north.

Following up the governmental policies of Trajan, Hadrian aimed at enlightened centralization—and he pursued it with particular skill. Yet he continued to be dogged by the unhappy relations with the senators which had marred his early years. Then, in 136 A.D., a dangerous plot resulted in further executions, whereupon Hadrian, who had no son and was sick, decided that he must proceed with

the adoption of an heir. His first choice died almost at once and was replaced by the fifty-one-year-old Antoninus, who soon afterwards, on Hadrian's death, succeeded peacefully to the throne (138 A.D.).

Antoninus, like his two predecessors, was of western provincial origin. His reign was aptly summed up by the conferment of the title Pius, indicating devotion to his duty, the gods, his country, and his adoptive father. The greater part of the Empire enjoyed peace during the twenty-three years of his reign.

137

CHAPTER 11

The imperial society

Imperial art and architecture

The sculptural portraiture of private persons flourished throughout the imperial period. But above all, it is the emperors of the age and their relations who are depicted in a series of extraordinarily skillful portrait busts, designed to acquaint the peoples of the Empire with their rulers. Augustus had been shown in many guises, but Claudius's knobbly countenance seemed to defy accurate representation. Some sculptors compromised, others idealized. When his stepson Nero succeeded to the throne, they had to think once again how to depict the rapidly increasing grossness of the imperial features. Far from minimizing the idiosyncrasy of Nero's appearance, they endowed his peculiarities with just that touch of elevation which made the emperor seem, if still a fat lout, at least a lout of slightly superhuman dimensions.

EROTICISM IN POMPEII
Until as recently as the 1960s, only men were allowed to see Pompeii's erotic frescoes on tours.

The portraits of this age aim at a new smooth, fluent surface texture, enhanced by the subtle use of flesh and hair tints, of which only traces survive today. The sculptors are fond of deep incisions, appropriate to the strong sun and shadow in which their busts and statues originally stood. The outstanding example of this relief sculpture is the continuous series of spiral designs on the Column of Trajan. Towering over the massive new Forum, the reliefs, more than a hundred in number, offer a bird's-eye view of numerous events in the emperor's Dacian wars. This panorama includes no fewer than twenty-five hundred human figures, and a wide variety of incidents is selected for illustration—battles and sieges, visits by envoys, buildings and fortifications, and above all, events relating to the emperor himself.

Among other great arts of the early Empire was the painting of walls and ceilings. The bulk of the pictures that have come down to us are of an earlier date than the great reliefs. They appeared in town houses at Pompeii and Herculaneum and elsewhere. The eruption of Vesuvius which overwhelmed the region in 79 A.D.

preserved a great many of these paintings. Figure paintings were greatly in favor; very often they were devoted to the mythological and theatrical themes dear to Nero. There are also paintings of romantic landscapes, fantastic Nile scenes, and studies of still life. Floors were covered with vivid mosaics, sometimes, like the paintings, reproducing Greek masterpieces of the past. This was one of the most enjoyable and picturesque of Roman arts.

These paintings and mosaics adorned large terraced villas opening out upon the sea and town houses which still retained their traditional grouping round the atrium. There were other forms of housing for the middle class and poor, and on this subject Pompeii has yielded a good deal of information, revealing domestic arrangements of considerable variety and a general standard of living (not only for the richest elite) never achieved again until the nineteenth century.

In another respect, too, Pompeii is a uniquely informative source of evidence for the lives of its ordinary citizens. At the moment when the eruption buried the town, the walls of its buildings were covered by thousands of graffiti. Very often, there are references to the annual civic elections, and one such election was imminent at the time when the eruption took place. The graffiti also recorded many curious aspects of the loves and erotic fantasies of a great number of individuals.

A STREET IN HERCULANEUM
Herculaneum was heavily populated by Romans, but when Vesuvius erupted in 79 A.D., the city, unlike Pompeii, was able to be evacuated before being covered in a thick layer of lava. The site was discovered in 1688 and open-air excavation began in 1823, when a number of multi-storied buildings were found. Not only have walls and décor survived, but also beams, doors, and furniture.

ARCHAEOLOGY'S CONTRIBUTION

Until the 18th century, important sites of antiquity were excavated by "antique dealers" who were in search of works of art for private collections and of architectural elements to use as models. In the 19th century, Schliemann's discoveries in Troy and Mycenae and Fiorellio's in Pompeii piqued the interest of scientific archaeologists who wanted to unveil the everyday realities of ancient civilizations, which were generally rarely touched upon in books.

In certain regions, aerial archaeology revealed building plans that had disappeared. From this point on, archaeologists worked meticulously. They took stratigraphic samples to date the layers of ruins and drew from the analyses made of the materials contained in the layers (pottery, coins, and so on).

These scientists also drew upon other disciplines such as numismatics (the study of coins) and epigraphy (the study of inscriptions, especially on stone and bronze, including official texts, epitaphs, and graffiti). Comparing these seemingly simple documents, of which there are many in Roman civilization, informs us about the evolution of social classes and the organization of cities, armies, and cults, not to mention family life, careers, living conditions, the evolution of language, and the economy.

**THE IMPERIAL
CULT IN POMPEII**
*Between the columns of
the forum portico and the
macellum (right)—the public
market where meat and fish
were sold—is a statue gallery
that attests to membership
in the imperial cult.*

The lives of the inhabitants of Pompeii are also illustrated by the remains of about twenty inns and one hundred and twenty bars. At the ancient colony of Ostia, on the other hand, which was the port of Rome, only two inns and fourteen bars have come to light, since these people preferred to drink in the social clubs of their trade corporations (*collegia*). In these prosperous years, the population of this great business center grew to approximately one hundred thousand. This expansion dictated a revolution in housing for the not particularly wealthy, in the course of which the Pompeii-type dwelling was replaced by tall apartment blocks that accommodated greater numbers of people. The interiors of the apartments, adorned with mosaics and wall paintings, often contained seven rooms or more.

And at Rome, too, increasing signs of the same sort of apartment blocks have come to light. It is true that, up to the second century A.D., we still have complaints

AVNORVM SATYRORVM ETSILENORVM DELECTA

THE BURIAL OF POMPEII

Pompeii, situated on the Bay of Naples, has been inhabited since the earliest days of antiquity. Until the 1st century B.C., residents still spoke the Oscus language. The city's prosperity was built largely on agriculture and commerce, and it continued to grow and to be gloriously embellished in a Hellenistic vein.

During the Social War, Pompeii allied with the rebel Italians and was besieged by Sulla. It received a colony of veterans, adopted Latin, and became a vacation spot. In 79 A.D., while the city was still recovering from an earlier earthquake, Mount Vesuvius violently erupted and buried Pompeii beneath 30 feet of ashes.

Two thousand of Pompeii's residents suffocated to death. The city was forgotten until the 18th century, when treasure looters, digging at random and without regard for the destruction they caused, recovered a few beautiful pieces.

It was only in 1860 that Fiorelli, an archaeologist, began leading his excavations. Buildings were unearthed and objects were catalogued. Plaster casts were made from the cadavers of residents surprised by the eruption.

Eighty percent of Pompeii was unburied; public buildings and houses— some of whose roofs were removed, constitute an example of an ancient city that appears to live on.

of rickety, ill-constructed, high-rise tenements in the capital. Some of the worst abuses, however, had been eliminated by Nero, who made efforts to impose a more spacious plan and scale.

He was given this opportunity by the Great Fire of Rome (64 A.D.) which he was unfairly accused of having started himself to make room for his Golden House (*Domus Aurea*), for this and its parklands took over nearly four hundred acres of what had been the most thickly inhabited zone of the city—the largest piece of land that any European monarch has ever carved out of his capital to make a residence for himself. The Golden House consisted of a number of separate pavilions set among elegantly designed formal landscapes. The central porticoed building contained an octagonal hall that can still be seen today.

Electoral Inscription
(Pompeii) Among the numerous mural inscriptions in the ruins are electoral notices that praise one local candidate or the other.

Nero's successors abandoned the Golden House. Domitian built a magnificent villa looking down onto the Alban Lake. It has not survived, but much can still be seen of a considerably more elaborate country palace erected by Hadrian near Tibur (Tivoli). Extending for a mile across the slopes beneath the city, this complex virtually forms a town in itself. The architect exploits the gently undulating site by ringing every change on the theme of curve and countercurve, and his impressive mastery of concrete achieves ingenious, romantic effects. Another building that owes its design to Hadrian was Rome's Pantheon. His recon-

LIVING IN POMPEII:
THE SPLENDOR OF THE HOUSE

North of the Street of the Baths, in the direction of Vesuvius, was residential Pompeii. The forum and public buildings occupied the southern part of the city. First came the most famous homes, because of their size and their good condition and especially the splendor of their décor. The House of the Faun attests to the evolution of domestic architecture. The front of the home, centered around the atrium, was reserved for utility rooms only (kitchen, bedrooms). The tablinum, the office in which the master of the house received his "clients," led to the second part of the house, which was influenced by Hellenistic culture. There was a garden of leisure decorated with statues, a summer dining room that looked outside, and a covered colonnade, or peristyle, which allowed the family and its visitors to delight in fine Greek pleasures.

Pompeii before the eruption of Vesuvius

struction of Agrippa's original temple is the best preserved today of all the ancient Roman edifices. The huge colonnaded portico leads into a rotunda one hundred and forty-two feet high and wide. Its concrete interior wall contains vaulted niches and recesses which show that the Romans had full trust in their mastery of this material so that they could boldly lighten it by inserting such cavities. The great space is tranquil and sublime. But unlike an earth-bound Greek temple, it dwarfs with its hugeness. This cavernous grandeur warns humans that they are in the presence of all the gods—for that is what "pantheon" means.

Such was the greatest among the innumerable shrines devoted to the religious needs of the Roman population. But ample provision was also made for their pleasures. There were enormous bathing establishments, and there were theaters everywhere. But there was also another sort of entertainment altogether, provided by the Flavian Amphitheater. Begun by Vespasian and completed by Titus, it was designed for gladiatorial combats and the slaughter of wild animals, and it could also be flooded to stage imitation sea fights. Known much later as the Colosseum, after the colossal statue of Nero that had stood nearby, this amphitheater remains one of the most marvelous buildings in the world.

THE PANTHEON
(118–125 A.D.)
The dome of Hadrian's new pantheon is higher than that at Saint Peter's in Rome. Its sophisticated décor contrasts with the simple coffered ceiling lit by a circular window.

Greek theaters had normally displayed two stories of arcades, and Rome had a theater with three. But the Colosseum was extended up to four of these stories. It provided seats for about forty-five thousand spectators and standing room for five thousand more. The entertainments provided in these arenas remained extraordinarily popular, and rulers found it advisable to arrange such displays on a munificent scale. The gladiators' legal and moral status was utterly degraded, but many graffiti bear witness to the admiration that they nonetheless provoked in the hearts of the public.

The pattern of the Colosseum was duplicated throughout the Roman world in other amphitheaters of widely varying dimensions. And indeed, it was these first and second centuries A.D., when the Pax Romana gained such remarkable strength, that provided the greater number of the amphitheaters and other kinds of buildings that are still to be seen in Rome and its provinces.

Economic and social imbalance

The cities of these regions were entering upon the climactic period of their development. In industry and commerce the provinces had begun to eclipse Rome itself. For example, the glass and bronze wares of Italian Capua were superseded by products made in Gaul. In the second century A.D., the main output of pottery was from the Rhineland, which became before long the principal industrial area of Europe; the Danube area, too, was developing an east-west commercial axis of great importance for the future.

Yet the basis of the imperial economy was still not commerce but agriculture. In this sphere there were certain encouraging signs. For example, many fruit trees were brought as far as the shores of the Rhine, and olives were introduced into southern Tunisia and southeast Spain. Spain also produced a great deal of wine: The Monte Testaccio on the outskirts of Rome is a mound consisting of fragments of forty million jars that had once been full of cheap wine imported from Spanish vineyards.

The rich farmer-landowners possessed huge agricultural complexes. Among many hundreds of such "rustic villas" may be named Cheragan (on the Garonne, in Gaul), covering forty acres and housing four or five hundred dependents; and Anthée (near Philippeville in Belgium); and Chedworth in Britain, which was a luxurious administrative center for a group of farms. The owners of such palaces were very wealthy men, although on the whole, this was an age not so much of a few millionaires as of many affluent bourgeois. Nevertheless, in spite of all this development, the basic facts of the agricultural economy were still much as they had been

PASTORAL SCENE
(sarcophagus, 2nd century A.D.)
The Romans eased the sorrow of death by depicting pastoral scenes on their sarcophaguses.

AVNORVM SATYRORVM ET SILENORVM DELECT AVNORVM SATYR

THE VILLA: FROM FARM TO LUXURY HOME

At first, the villa was simply a farm in Italy belonging to a rich landowner who resided in Rome. Around a large courtyard stood residential buildings, cowsheds, and barns. Also present were wine and oil presses, food supplies (stored in large jars that were buried in the ground), workshops used for maintaining equipment, a vegetable garden, and an orchard. Depending on the wealth of the owner, there were many servant laborers who worked under a steward, known as the *vilicus.*

In the 2nd century B.C., affluent Romans customarily left the city during the hot summer months. They therefore built a modest master house (*pars urbana*) next to their farm (*pars rustica*). The riches from the conquests of the eastern provinces and contact with the Hellenistic world soon brought about the display of new luxuries and extravagances. These included guest rooms around a

colonnaded courtyard and several works of art imported from Greece or copied in Italian workshops.

By the end of the Republic, the villa was transformed from a farm to a full-scale luxury home built in a region celebrated for its climate and charm. Near Rome, the town of Tibur (Tivoli) was particularly cherished, since one could stay in close touch with business. The region of Campania, around Naples, was a genuine resort center that included the town of Pompeii and the Isle of Capri.

A few privileged individuals spent the winter at the southern tip of the peninsula, around Taranto. Often graced with extravagant architecture, equipped with every comfort (including baths), and filled with works of art, these magnificent villas were maintained by veritable armies of slaves. It was not unusual for an important figure, such as Cicero, to have no fewer than nine villas.

THE SITE OF TIMGAD
(Algeria) Founded by
Trajan for veterans of the
third legion of Augustus,
Timgad is a typical
example of urbanism.
The streets are laid at
right angles, following the
model of Roman camps.
Too crowded after the
3rd century, the city was
expanded under Severus.
The arch marks the border
between the old and new cities.

in earlier years. For one thing, the placid rhythm of the Antonine world still depended upon slaves, and they were still wholly excluded from political and social privilege. But excluded also were the "free" agricultural workers, who formed an even larger proportion of the population. It was not the depressed rural poor of the countryside but the prosperous people of the cities who felt loyalty to the imperial regime in gratitude for services rendered.

Even if the poor did not secure many material blessings, at least Roman law as it entered under the initiative of Hadrian, upon its Golden Age, was now doing a good deal to protect them from the worst illegalities of exploitation. Yet, *equality* had come no nearer than it had been before. The community was divided into two main groups to which the law gave entirely separate treatment. The superior class (*honestiores*) included senators, knights, landowners, soldiers, and civil servants. Everyone else belonged to the lower category (*humiliores*), who possessed inferior legal rights. Roman law had always favored the upper echelon of society; now, from the time of Hadrian onwards, such preferential treatment became crystallized

146

in legal forms. This was ominous, for beneath the tranquil surface of second-century life, it confirmed the depressed status of the underprivileged and thus deepened the basic rift which in the following centuries would bring the Empire down.

From Seneca to Apuleius

In the imperial age the most eloquent exponent of the Stoic philosophy was Nero's minister Seneca (b. ca. 4 B.C.—d. 65 A.D.). We have nine tragedies attributed to Seneca. These plays, to which Shakespeare and other European dramatists owe a great debt, breathe the enlightened tolerance and humanity of Stoicism, including its sympathy for slaves. This same spirit pervades Seneca's letters and ethical treatises, which the Renaissance came to value for the moral guidance they provided.

TOWING SCENE
This Gallo-Roman bas-relief, found near Avignon, shows how important river transportation was for carrying merchandise —in this case, wine stored in amphorae, or urns.

He also set the tone for a new phase of Roman literature by his use of scintillating verbal tricks and vivid pointed epigrams to which the lapidary, or jewel-like, Latin language so readily lends itself. This same sparkling, oratorical, "Silver Latin" style, combined with a similar Stoic viewpoint, was adopted by Seneca's nephew Lucan in his poem, the *Civil War* or *Pharsalia*. Its subject was the struggle between Pompey and Caesar. This mordant, powerful poem won great fame in the Middle Ages and earned its author a place as one of Dante's four Lords of Highest Song.

Nero's fatal displeasure eventually fell on both Seneca and on Lucan, and it descended also on his "arbiter" of court fashions, Petronius, who wrote a lively, scandalous picaresque novel known to us as the *Satyricon*, a highly entertaining Latin narrative of three disreputable but elaborately educated young homosexuals on the move around the Greek towns of south Italy. This work, of which a large por-

AVNORVM SATYRORVM ETSILENORVMDELECI AVNORVM SATYR

THE WESTERN PROVINCES: A SOURCE OF WEALTH

Starting in the 3rd century B.C., Rome gradually took over several western provinces. The wars against Carthage gave it control over Sardinia, Corsica, Sicily, and Spain. In order to defend Italian territory and roads, Rome intervened in Illyria, Dalmatia, and Narbonne Gaul. Then, under the Empire, it headed south of the Danube (Rhaetia, Noricum, and Pannonia) and into Germania. Caesar's conquest of "tufted" Gaul (named for its dense forests) was personally motivated. The Romans ventured into Brittany (Great Britain) for commercial reasons.

The provinces offered Rome various resources. Sicily, Sardinia, and Spain provided cereals and Gaul, wine; Corsica, Spain, and Portugal raised livestock. Wood for building came from Spain and Portugal and granite from Corsica; pottery from Gaul was celebrated. Mines were thriving: silver and iron in Sardinia; silver, gold,

iron, and pewter in Spain; silver-bearing lead and pewter in Brittany. Auxiliary troops were recruited in Gaul (cavalry) and in Spain (cavalry and sling bearers from Baleares).

Under the Republic, farming for resources was to the detriment of the provinces. But there were compensations: The Empire granted provincial residents beneficial political status and, in doing so, brought about progress and prosperity.

Sardinia, Corsica, Sicily, Gaul, and the Iberian Peninsula became so romanized that even a Roman would feel at home in these places. The use of Latin in these regions gave birth to the family of Roman languages, despite invasions. Just as prosperous, but not as romanized, were Brittany and those provinces in contact with tribes above the Rhine and Danube, which were the first to be invaded. Today they speak Germanic languages.

tion survives, includes poems and prose discussions. It also contains set pieces or short stories, of which the longest and most famous is the *Dinner of Trimalchio*, a self-made, vulgar industrialist of slave origin living in Campania, who emerges as the most entertaining comic figure of all ancient literature. His banquet and reminiscences, as well as the coarse, colloquial remarks of his guests and hangers-on, reflect needle-sharp observation and keen sensual gusto.

In the generation that followed him, the most original talent was that of Martial (b. ca. 40 A.D.–d. ca. 104). Although Spanish, Martial caught the authentic Italian note of riotous, mordant satire and has imprinted his definition of this term on subsequent European letters. Juvenal, born in about 50 A.D., strikes a grander and harsher note, and his sixteen long poems reveal him to be the foremost of all Roman satirists, who did more even than Martial to establish satire as a tradition of the Western world. Juvenal flays the evils of the contemporary Roman scene with ironical, savagely pessimistic invective. Although Juvenal wrote during the time of Trajan, in a Rome much more relaxed than it had been under the hated Domitian, the Empire seemed to him a sick, maladjusted organism, overflowing with deplorable men and vicious women.

THE ELEUSINIAN MYSTERIES
(Marble burial urn) These famous mysteries—rituals associated with the agrarian goddesses, Demeter and Persephone—attracted many followers to Eleusis as early as the Hellenistic period.

An equally damaging view of Roman society, once again despite the current Trajanic improvements, was implicit in the work of Tacitus (b. ca. 55 A.D. –d. ca. 116?), the greatest of Roman historians. His supreme achievement was the narration of Rome's history from the death of Augustus to the death of Domitian (14–96 A.D.). This survey is divided into the *Histories* and the *Annals*. Of the former work, dealing with the last twenty-eight of those years, only the first part, describing the convulsed Year of the Four Emperors, is still extant. But the greater portion of the subsequently published *Annals*, dealing with the earlier period from Tiberius to Nero, has survived. His haunting, penetrating, moralistic analyses of the men holding such monstrous power in their hands comprise our earliest account of the imperial phenomenon. Tacitus was unique for the meticulous care with which he collected and sought to verify his facts, far exceeding in this respect the biographers who were his contemporaries, Suetonius and Plutarch.

Under the Antonines, a very different sort of commentary on the life of the Empire was provided by the Greek author Lucian of Samosata (Samsat in eastern Turkey), who wrote a series of essays ridiculing such targets as religious charlatans and travelers who told exaggerated tales.

His capacity for storytelling was shared by a contemporary Latin writer of unique gifts, Apuleius. Apuleius was the archmanipulator of an unfamiliar sort of Latin prose artfully combining the florid with the archaic, for which there was a current vogue. This fantastic, luscious style, incorporating a wealth of Roman and Greek literary echoes, appears in his *Metamorphoses* or *Golden Ass*, the only Latin novel which has survived in its entirety. The writer tells of a certain Lucius, who is accidentally turned into a donkey and undergoes many other fantastic experiences. The numerous stories this long narrative incorporates include the worldwide Cinderella folk tale of the fairy bridegroom, which Apuleius combines with the Greek myth of Cupid and Psyche; his account of their weird, romantic adventures attracted endless admiration and allegorical interpretation in later antiquity and medieval and Renaissance Europe as well.

The mystery religions

When Apuleius describes how his hero is initiated into the mysteries of the Egyptian goddess whose merciful hand raises up and saves the fallen souls (*psychai*) of human beings, he seems to be recording a profoundly felt experience of his own. And this is based on an ecstatic empathy with the Mystery faiths and Savior cults which marked, in a sense, the transition between decaying state paganism and rising Christianity. The gods and goddesses of the old national religion of Rome still provided a great stimulus to patriotism, yet they were too sterile to fill the spiritual vacuum during this era when men and women became increasingly preoccupied with the needs of their own souls.

What they turned to, above all, was a passionate belief in certain saviors who would endow their chosen devotees with a life of blessedness after they were dead. These Mystery Savior faiths went back to the elaborate secret rituals of Demeter in early Greece and to the disturbing, frenzied worship of Dionysus. Among the kingdoms of Alexander the Great's heirs, this Dionysiac cult became particularly widespread, and in Italy, where the god was known as Bacchus, the religion attained enormous popularity. The ecstatic element tended to be toned down into mere hedonism, the afterlife being often depicted as just a jolly party with facilities for alcoholic and sexual gratification.

More profound excitement, however, was inspired by the Mystery cult of Cybele, the ancient divine earth-mother of Asia Minor. The worship of Cybele, accompanied by stirring ritual dramas, raised hopes of immortality to a fever heat of excitement, and innumerable people throughout the Roman Empire believed passionately in her. But even more, like Apuleius, believed in the Egyptian Isis. Accompanying her in the liturgical drama was the god of the underworld, Osiris, who stood for the birth and death of the year, and the annual Finding of Osiris was the occasion for unrestrained jubilation.

As the worship of Isis turned into a cosmopolitan Mystery religion, her major festivals provided ceremonies exceeding those of Cybele in their theatrical, emotional appeals to ear and eye. Her penitents roamed the streets of the cities intoning hymns or competed with one another in acts of piety and self-mortification. From the first century B.C. until the final decline of paganism hundreds of years later, her faith remained the most widespread of all the religions of the Roman Empire.

CULT OF BACCHUS
This Pompeian fresco, in which a maenad *(a priest of Bacchus) makes an offering, shows how popular religions from Greece and the Orient became in Rome. Once initiated, the follower could contemplate the divinity.*

Chapter 12

Collapse and recovery

Marcus Aurelius and his son

When Antoninus Pius died in 161 A.D., he bequeathed the Empire to Marcus Aurelius, his adopted son and the husband of his daughter. Marcus Aurelius promptly appointed a co-emperor, Verus, who had likewise been an adoptive son of Antoninus. This regime of an imperial pair was an important innovation that would be seen again during the centuries to come. Marcus Aurelius, whose inmost thoughts have come down to us in his *Meditations*, was hard-working and a man of the highest ideals. Verus, though attractive, was a lightweight. Nevertheless, when a crisis arose in the East, it was he who was sent to deal with the situation, and in 163–66 A.D. his generals annexed Mesopotamia.

But an event which occurred in another part of the imperial frontier lands heralded the permanent transformation of the world scene. German and other tribesmen, "barbarians," as the Romans called them, began to pour across the upper, middle, and lower reaches of the Danube in a series of wide, collusive thrusts. The fighting which now resulted was more serious than anything of the kind that had been seen before, and it continued to engage Marcus Aurelius for the remaining fourteen years of his fife. Breaking through into the provinces of central and eastern Europe, the land-hungry Germans even crossed the Alps into Italy itself, where they destroyed cities and laid siege to the Adriatic port of Aquileia.

AVNORVM SATYRORVM ETSILENORVM DELECI AVNORVM SATYR

THE EMPEROR: A LIVING GOD

Making gods of their heroes and establishing a cult in their honor was a traditional practice in ancient societies. In Roman legend, Romulus entered the company of the gods after his death. As early as the 1st century B.C., ambitious men sought inspiration from Hellenistic monarchies that worshiped their sovereign as a god.

Julius Caesar recalled that his family was descended from Venus, and after his death he was proclaimed a god and awarded a temple in the Forum. Augustus, insisting that he was the son of a god, assumed the priestly functions of the Great Pontiff *(Pontifex Maximus)* and the power of the tribunes. Rome worshiped his "spirit"—the godhead linked to every individual—and his image was revered. In Italy and the provinces, Augustus was also honored with temples, altars, sacrifices, and games. This cult was inaugurated in the eastern provinces before spreading to the West.

During his lifetime, Augustus assumed a certain number of divine attributes that were often included in his portraits. His death made him a god, and his priests were charged with fostering his cult. This was apotheosis: the mortal Emperor made god.

After Augustus, emperor-worship became a general rule. Apotheosis (acquisition of divine status after death) was resorted to by most of Augustus's successors. Increasingly, however, the emperor came to be considered a god in his own lifetime—and some emperors did their utmost to bring this about: Caligula claimed to converse with Jupiter; Nero liked to be depicted as the Sun god; Domitian insisted on rites of adoration worthy of the East; Hadrian designed his villa at Tivoli as the home of a god; Marcus Antoninus took the name of Elagabalus (avatar of the solar god Baal, who was worshiped in Syria) and decreed that he be revered in Rome.

The Roman armies, though incapacitated by an epidemic brought back from the East—perhaps the novel scourge of smallpox—gradually and painfully regained control of the situation, and Marcus Aurelius formed two ideas for dealing with this German pressure. One was to admit large numbers of tribesmen into the Empire as settlers and potential auxiliary soldiers. This had been done by Augustus and Nero; and Marcus Aurelius now adopted the policy on a more systematic scale.

His second solution involved the annexation of Marcomannia (Bohemia) and a further province of Sarmatia to its east, providing the Empire with shorter frontier defenses. But Marcus Aurelius never succeeded in carrying out his plan. It was put off, first because of a rebellion by his principal eastern general (175 A.D.), and then because he himself died. After his death, the proposed annexations were abandoned.

Because Marcus Aurelius had a son of his own, Commodus, he elevated him to be his heir. Commodus's excessive addiction to emotional religions and gladiatorial sports made him one of the most eccentric of Rome's emperors. While eagerly developing his own personality cult, he showed no desire to govern the Empire himself, and the effective power remained in the hands of successive praetorian prefects. Finally one of them, Laetus, became convinced that Commodus's growing megalomania had become too hazardous, decided that he must die, and then commissioned a professional athlete to murder him.

The dynasty of Severus

The city prefect Pertinax was elevated to the throne, but he was killed after a three-month reign. From now on, a period of civil war ensued. The chaotic events of these months served to emphasize, once again, the insuperable flaw in the arrangements governing Rome's imperial successions.

THE TRIUMPH OF MARCUS AURELIUS *(170–180 A.D.) This relief comes from an arch of triumph that no longer exists. The spare decoration and small number of characters help focus attention on the figure of the emperor.*

The successor to Pertinax, a rich senator, Didius Julianus, set an unedifying precedent by purchasing the throne at an auction held by the praetorians; soon afterwards, however, news came from the provinces that two governors had been declared emperor by their legions. They were Severus, a forty-eight-year-old north African, proclaimed on the Danube, and Niger, whose troops saluted him in Syria. Obeying a command from Severus, the Senate put Didius Julianus to death, after a reign of nine weeks. Severus marched south and entered Rome. Then he set out for the East and overwhelmed Niger at Issus (194 A.D.). Encouraged by that success, he declared his elder son, Caracalla, his heir.

Since the Parthians had given aid to his enemy Niger and had made inroads into Roman territory, it was against them that Severus next turned (197–99 A.D.). Parthia was dealt an unprecedentedly severe blow, which proved to weaken it permanently—as Rome would later have reason to regret.

LEPTIS MAGNA
(Libya) First a Punic trading post, Leptis Magna became a Roman colony under Trajan. It was at its peak under the reign of Septimius Severus, who was born there in 146 A.D. Ruins from the early Empire stand beside structures from the 3rd century: the new forum with its porticos and basilica, and the colonnaded street, 60 feet wide, leading to the port.

On returning from the East, he stationed a new legion just outside the capital at Albanum (Albano Laziale). Augustus had fixed the number of Roman legions at twenty-eight. Trajan had maintained thirty legions, and Severus now raised this total to thirty-three, including a larger proportion of provincials than hitherto. Severus elevated the army to these unprecedented dimensions because he knew that a big and permanent change had taken place: Ever since the frontier crisis of Marcus Aurelius, imperial defense had become a far graver problem than ever before.

Three years later, Severus took his new army into action, setting out with his wife and two sons for Britain, where tribal attacks had breached Hadrian's Wall. The large-scale invasions of Caledonia (Scotland) that he now proceeded to undertake yielded, as usual in this area, no permanent results, but Hadrian's Wall was rebuilt and restored as an effective frontier. Soon afterwards, however, at Eboracum (York), the emperor died (211 A.D.). He was reported to have given a last piece of advice to his sons: "Be on good terms with one another."

However, his two sons hated each other, and Caracalla, a temperamental and violent young man, almost at once had his brother, Geta, murdered. Then, in 213 A.D., he set out for Germany, where he defeated some of its tribes and bought off others with a subsidy. Next he set off for the East, identifying himself with Alexander the Great, whose conquests he was eager to rival. But near Carrhae (Haran) he succumbed to an assassin (217 A.D.). This was his Mauretanian praetorian prefect Macrinus. Macrinus's reign was brief and undistinguished. His conclusion of the Parthian war on not very favorable terms was followed by retrenchments in military pay, and Severus's Syrian sister-in-law, Julia Maesa, was able to organize a rebellion in which Macrinus was defeated and lost his life.

The disintegration of the Empire

Between 218 and 268 A.D., the main internal difficulty was the proliferation of military usurpers. Throughout the whole of this period, about fifty usurpers assumed the imperial title, and out of the twenty-seven "regular" emperors of the third century, seventeen were killed at the hands of their own people, and two of the others were forced to commit suicide.

Therein lay one of Rome's most grievous and costly problems. The old custom by which its rulers were appointed by the Senate had become a farce. In reality, they were placed on the throne by one or other of the armies, after which the Senate was ostensibly asked for its approval. The armies' motive for changing emperors was greed; they felt eager for the lavish gifts which their protégés were always compelled to distribute. In consequence, the soldiers acclaimed new imperators with ludicrous frequency, and the previous incumbent was nearly always killed.

The Danubian armies were by far the largest in the Empire, and during the recurrent civil wars of this epoch it was their candidate, more often than not, who gained the throne. The Rhine armies felt neglected by Rome in favor of the Danubian legions, and they put forward Postumus (259–268 A.D.) as an emperor of their own. He set up independent consuls and Senate at Augusta Trevirorum (now Trier) on the Moselle. Not only Gaul but also Britain and Spain rallied to his cause, and for fourteen years western Europe was a separatist state, confronting Rome in a cold war which at intervals broke into open hostilities.

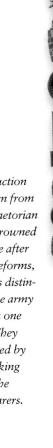

MILITARY ENSIGN *(Reconstruction of an ensign from the 3rd praetorian cohort) Crowned by an eagle after Marius's reforms, these poles distinguished the army units from one another. They were carried by lower-ranking soldiers, the ensign bearers.*

THE EASTERN PROVINCES

Other than establishing a governor, the Romans brought about little change to the political and administrative organization of the Hellenistic kingdoms in the Orient, which had been conquered by Alexander the Great and Hellenized. They expanded or improved existing cities, in which the elite continued to speak Greek.

Greece, which had become a province of Achaea, and its neighbors (Macedonia, Epirus, and Thrace) thrived under Pax Romana (Roman peace). The great intellectual and artistic centers such as Athens, Rhodes, and Corinth were blooming. Asia Minor, which was divided into many provinces—Asia (handed down to Rome by Attalus II, Pergamum king), Lycia, Pamphylia, Cilicia, Galatia, Bithynia—was prosperous under the Empire due to the export of cloth, marble, wood, wine, olives, and wheat. The fact that the ports were expanded is proof that the merchants were wealthy.

Syria was annexed by Pompey, after which the conquest spread to Palestine and the kingdom of the Nabataeans. Mesopotamia and Assyria were periodically occupied. The splendor of coastal cities can be explained by local production (purple dye from Tyre, wine, dates, and Damascus prunes) and by caravans arriving from the Orient filled with silks, perfumes, and spices.

Egypt, which was the Roman emperor's private property, was relentlessly exploited. Its wheat fed Rome. But the Valley of the Nile sometimes suffered from famine and, although Alexandria was one of the main centers of Greek culture, the conditions of Egyptian peasants did not change after the pharaohs. There was one exception in this Hellenized Orient: Dacia. It was conquered by Trajan, and a Roman language is spoken there even today. Its present name, Romania, is a souvenir from the Roman Empire.

The eastern garrisons, too, second only to those of the Danube in size and strength, were equally ready to put forward rulers of their own choice. The most vigorous, durable, and menacing of the oriental dissidents came from the oasis city of Palmyra (Tadmor), upon the borders between Syria and Mesopotamia. Annexed by Rome in the early first century A.D., Palmyra was located at an important desert crossroads. When Parthia succumbed to the more dangerous Persians, Palmyra became even more important, indeed indispensable, as a bastion of the Empire. Its chieftain, Odenathus, was made the commander of Rome's entire defensive system in the East. But when he fell to assassins (266–267 A.D.) his gifted and learned widow, Zenobia, declared her independence and expanded the dominions she already held in Syria and Mesopotamia by annexing Egypt and the greater part of Asia Minor as well. Then she declared herself Augusta, Empress of Rome, and her son was hailed as Augustus (ca. 270 A.D.).

ROMANS AGAINST BARBARIANS
(Marble sarcophagus, Capitoline Museums)
Starting at the end of the 2nd century A.D., combat scenes pitting Romans against barbarians multiplied on sarcophaguses, replacing traditional epic models. The theme was rendered with intentional confusion. Gestures and faces barely emerge from the tangle of horses and bodies.

The dismemberment of the Empire, from which both Zenobia and Postumus had torn enormous territories, could scarcely go further. Moreover, it came at a time when Rome's external enemies had never been stronger and more menacing. In the East, Prince Ardashir (Artaxerxes) of the Sassanian dynasty, ruler of a large area extending from the Persian Gulf to Isfahan, invaded Parthia and overthrew the last of its monarchs. The new Sassanian state was far more formidable and centralized than Parthia. It was also intensely nationalistic, claiming the right to all the Roman Empire's eastern territories. The Persian army was the most up-to-date attacking force of the age. And the Romans failed to reduce this new foe to manageable proportions or bring it to a workable agreement. Their eastern military operations, hitherto something of an imperialistic luxury, now became a direly urgent and hugely expensive necessity.

Shapur (Sapor) I (ca. 234–270 A.D.) adopted, at his coronation, the provocative title of "King of Kings of Iran and non-Iran." He was the most dangerous single enemy the Roman emperors had ever had to confront, and during the first two decades of his reign, he launched three major invasions. Mesopotamia and Armenia were overrun, and Antioch, the capital of Syria, was temporarily lost to Rome as well. Then, in 260 A.D., the Roman emperor Valerian himself fell into Shapur's hands. This event, the most inglorious in all Roman history, continued to be emphasized in Persian propaganda, and Valerian remained a captive for the rest of his life. His son Gallienus did not succeed in rescuing him.

During these same disastrous years, the Romans' position on the Rhine and Danube boundaries, too, deteriorated gravely. But new German peoples appeared who were far more dangerous than any that had ever been seen there before. They were the Goths.

In the 230s—when the eastern frontier was the scene of perilous new threats—these Goths surged across the lower Danube and penetrated far into the Balkans

(248 A.D.). The commander of the Danubian armies, Decius, defeated this invasion. But his attempt to reinforce the Danube defenses proved inadequate, for in their monarch Kniva the Goths had a leader capable of grandiose strategies, threatening Rome almost as perilously as Shapur at the opposite extremity of the Empire.

These two menacing foes at either end of the Empire, the Germans and Persians, took collusive advantage of each other's attacks on the forces of Rome, which were consequently faced with prolonged, gigantically costly warfare on two fronts. Since one man could not face both ways at once, the imperial armies were now divided between two commands, anticipating the later division between the Eastern and Western Empires. Valerian took the East and Gallienus the West, and after Valerian's capture by the Persians, Gallienus fought on. In the last year of his life (268 A.D.), the Goths mustered unparalleled numbers of warriors and ships at the mouth of the river Dniester, and Greece and Asia Minor were ravaged yet again. The invaders, laden with plunder, began to return northwards by the Balkan land route, and the Roman Empire had reached the lowest depths of disarray.

THE OASIS OF PALMYRA
At the beginning of the 3rd century A.D., impressive monuments were built in Palmyra, like this arch of triumph on the Via Principalis. This street, 30 feet wide, crossed the city and was bordered by Corinthian columns that marked the way to the temple of Bel, built under Tiberius.

155

The military recovery

But in fact, an extraordinary recovery was about to begin, preceded by Gallienus's reorganization of the army. He had made the military system more professional. And he had set up a new, mobile strategic force, based on cavalry, that had now for the first time become an element of primary importance in the previously infantry-dominated army. The headquarters of the new formation was at Mediolanum (Milan), which was now virtually the advance capital of the Empire. This troop concentration in Italy was an important extension of the ideas of Severus, who had located a legion on Italian soil. It was also a step that created a powerful reserve. Yet such a force, for all its strategic benefits, was a grave security risk, as was confirmed when its very first commander tried to make himself emperor, and then its second, the future emperor Aurelian, led a successful plot which put Gallienus to death.

AVNORVM SAITRORVM ETSILENORVM DELECI

THE CITY OF SOLDIERS: THE CAMP

Every night, the mobilized army built a temporary fort, referred to as the camp. A military tribune and centurions sent as scouts chose a site on high ground and near a water source, pastures, and trees to use for wood, fire, and fencing. First, a sacrifice was offered to assure the gods' favor. Next, surveyors marked out the main streets and camp boundaries, indicating where everyone was to stay.

The soldiers would dig a ditch around the camp, throwing the earth towards the inside in order to build a *talus*, or fortifying sloping wall, supported by a chain of posts (when the army was far from any forest, each solider carried several posts with him for this purpose). At the intersection of the two main roads (the *cardo* and the *decumanus*) stood the general's tent, located near the forum. At the forum were an altar and a tribunal, a platform from the top of which the general addressed the troops. The soldiers slept in eight-person tents that were lined up in order of battle.

Along the frontiers, the permanent camps had barracks, stables, and wooden or even stone sheds that would keep soliders warm in the winter. The communities that often arose on the sites or around their edges became the origins of a number of modern cities.

And yet Gallienus's new army, at the very end of his life, had won a major military triumph against his foreign foes. As the Goths returned northwards through the Balkans, he succeeded in cutting them off, winning the bloodiest battle of the century at Naïssus (Nis in Yugoslavia), in which fifty thousand enemy soldiers met their deaths (268 A.D.). The expulsion of the Goths was completed by Aurelian, known as "hand on hilt" (*manu ad ferrum*).

Then Aurelian turned on Queen Zenobia of Palmyra. Asia Minor and Egypt were recaptured and brought back under Roman rule, and he twice defeated her principal general in Syria (271 A.D.). Palmyra itself fell to him, then revolted, and then fell again, and the queen walked in golden chains at Aurelian's triumph. And with her walked Tetricus, the last monarch of Postumus's splinter state in the West. Following upon the suppression of Zenobia, Aurelian had immediately moved across the Empire to Gaul and defeated the rebel army on the Catalaunian Plains (near Châlons-sur-Marne).

Aurelian built a new defensive wall round Rome, enclosing all the regions that had been added to the city since the last wall had been built six hundred years earlier. Moreover, he decided that the defenses beyond the lower Danube were no longer tenable, and in consequence Dacia, a province since the time of Trajan, was abandoned and the frontier brought back to the river, which provided a shorter and stronger boundary. The entire military picture had been transformed within the space of only fifteen years. Rome had seemed in a state of such advanced disintegration that recovery could scarcely be imagined. Yet by the exceptional talents of successive Danubian generals, commanding troops as good as any that Rome ever produced, the seemingly impossible had come to pass, and the Empire was restored.

The stoicism of Marcus Aurelius

This tumultuous epoch was also an age of extraordinary intellectual and spiritual achievement—in several respects the culmination of the pagan world.

The keynote had been set at the outset of the period by the emperor Marcus Aurelius. He was one of those rulers, rare in human history, whose practical achievements have been eclipsed by what he wrote. His intimate disclosure of his deepest thoughts, known as the *Meditations*, is the most famous book ever written by a monarch. The notes were meant to be private, and their author did not intend this highly personal masterpiece of self-admonition to be published.

Marcus Aurelius's doctrine was an austere one. Life is desperately short and transient, a temporary visit to an alien land. And all we have the power to do, as long as it lasts, is to act as responsibly and unselfishly and kindly as we can to those who are our fellow travelers on this transitory enterprise. Much of this is the old Stoicism, but none of its previous devotees had ever communicated the urgency and hardness of self-reliant moral effort in phrases that strike home so poignantly.

Marcus Aurelius sought to reinforce these ideals with a rigorously ascetic attitude typical of the age that was now beginning. Nowhere can one find more relentless attacks on the "twitchings of appetite," which were all that the pleasures of eye, ear, food, and sex appeared to him to amount to. Moreover, as one hard year suc-

PRAETORIUM
OF LAMBESSA
(Algeria) In 125 A.D., the headquarters of the north African army (3rd legion of Augustus) were moved from Timgad to Lambessa. Under the Severus emperors, this camp for legionaries was promoted to capital of the new province of Numidia. The praetorium, *a square building that housed the offices of the military administration, stood at the intersection of the* cardo *and* decumanus, *the primary roads of the camp.*

ceeded another, his spirit was tortured by ever more serious doubts about his own personal adequacy. All he could do was struggle on, fighting off moods of depression. Left far behind are the bright classical incentives to material achievement, the sunny sense of unlimited power. But in terms of humanly decent principles, translated scrupulously into a consistent way of living, Marcus Aurelius's creed was the culmination of ancient paganism and of Rome.

A great age of lawyers

He had also done much to carry onwards the Golden Age of Roman Law ushered in earlier in the century by Hadrian. Marcus Aurelius's legal adviser, Quintus Cervidius Scaevola, left extensive written works behind him. Cervidius was also the teacher of the emperor Severus. In his reign, this legal Golden Age developed a second phase that produced the most far-reaching of all Rome's contributions to posterity, comprising the working out and writing down of existing principles over the entire field. Moreover, Severus chose the greatest jurists of the day as his praetorian prefects.

One of them, Papinian, who became praetorian prefect from 203 until 212 A.D., is the most famous name in all Roman jurisprudence. He never wrote a comprehensive treatise but compiled extensive collections and summaries of legal decisions. Master of terse and exact Latin, he produced solutions which are closely reasoned and give the fullest weight to considerations of equity and humaneness. And then Ulpian, who came from Tyre in Phoenicia, was joint prefect from 222 to 223 A.D. His massive works, designed to cover the whole range of the law, are businesslike and superlatively clear. Another praetorian prefect of the time was Paulus. While falling short of Ulpian's lucid precision, Paulus excelled him in breadth and powers of argument.

When, three centuries later, Justinian's jurists summed up the achievements of Roman law, more than half the contents of this *Digest* came from these three writers—Papinian, Ulpian, and Paulus.

AVNORVM SATYRORVM ETSILENORVM DELECT

JUSTICE AND ROMAN RIGHTS

Justice was first rendered under the authority of two praetors: an urban praetor for citizens and an "immigrant" for cases involving foreigners. By the end of the Republic, there were 16. In civil cases, the praetor would organize the trial and go before one or two judges, who were individuals chosen by the parties or randomly chosen from a group of senators and horsemen. Under the Empire, judgment was most often entrusted to a professional jury, from the centumvir court. The emperor could choose to judge any case and disputed decision. Under the Republic, criminal trials were taken before permanent juries (senators or horsemen) and were presided over by a praetor. The accusation was supported by an individual, and the defendant had the right to a lawyer. Under the Empire, juries were professional, but they eventually lost power, since more and more cases were judged by the emperor.

Legal advisors helped individuals draft deeds and counseled the parties in a trial. They also inspired the praetor edicts. These edicts eventually formed Roman law. In the 1st century B.C., Scaevola published a civil law. In 533 A.D., Justinian published the *Digest*, which summarized 2,000 prior law books and could be considered the source of modern law.

New buildings and portraits

The stupendous baths which were inaugurated by Severus bear the name of his son Caracalla, who completed them. There were finally eleven such public baths in the pampered capital and smaller replicas and variants in almost every town of the Empire. They displayed much ingenious multiplicity of function, being designed not only for luxurious bathing at various temperatures but also for all the diverse social activities of an elaborate community center, in which many people spent a substantial part of each day.

Surrounded by an enclosure containing gardens and open-air gymnasiums, the main building was provided with vast unseen services of heating, water supply, and drainage, designed to deal with the needs of sixteen hundred bathers. The central feature of the complex was a great cross-vaulted central hall containing a swimming pool. This hall, measuring one hundred eighty-five by seventy-nine feet, is so large that men and women almost vanish inside its immensity; this is the architecture not of humanism but of a new age in which the individual is one of a mass.

Nor was third-century architecture the only art to move away from the traditional classicism; marked changes were apparent in portrait sculpture as well. Contrary to what is often believed, these developments started as early as the reign of Marcus Aurelius. His best-known busts, it is true, are as emptily classicizing as any of the products of the immediately preceding age. But a few of Marcus Aurelius's surviving heads give us an almost violent impression of what the author of the harrowing *Meditations* was really like. And, by the same token, the reliefs on the Column of Aurelius at Rome show a different world from the Column of Trajan: a world in which wars are no longer military parades and triumphs but, as Virgil had known long ago, scenes of horror and tragedy.

In the years of turbulence that followed Commodus and Caracalla, the artists' search for the inner man and woman had astonishing results. As in earlier times, it was the portraiture of the emperors themselves that directed the most original trends, since the propaganda of these rulers demanded that their features should be known to the world. But in the mid-third century, the emperors were of a new type, tough soldiers, rugged and careworn. And each successive ruler was very willing for his subjects to see him laden with these cares and anxieties, which were endured on their behalf and enhanced by his artists almost to the point of caricature.

So these men provide a startling series of portraits, particularly during the ruinous years 235–268 A.D. Their faces are made to reflect, quite deliberately, the almost unbearable strain to which their vigilance to stave off disaster was subjecting them. Some portraits emit an aura of intense feeling, almost as though they are representing the tormented visage of a medieval mystic. And tremendous play was made with the eyes, their irises and upward-rolling pupils deeply incised with the sculptor's drill: They were seen as the mirrors of the soul. This was an age in which the torments of practical life were counterbalanced by an intense concentration on spirituality.

We are reminded of the greatest of these pagan spiritual revivals when we see the portrait busts of Gallienus, which display him in the guise of a Hellenic philosopher. For he was the friend and patron of Plotinus, the greatest philosopher the Roman Empire ever produced.

Plotinus, Mithras, and Mani

Born in 205 A.D. in Upper Egypt, Plotinus studied philosophy for eleven years at Alexandria. After joining an imperial expedition against the Persians, he settled in Rome as a teacher, remaining there, in touch with the cultivated court of Gallienus, until he retired to Campania, where soon afterwards he died (ca. 269–270 A.D.). His instruction took the form of seminars that he recorded in a series of essays written in Greek. One of his students, Porphyry of Tyre, collected and pub-

COLUMN OF MARCUS AURELIUS
Built by Commodus to celebrate the victories of his father against the Quadi and the Marcomanni, this column borrows the spiral motif that wraps around the shaft of Trajan's Column. It is used to recount episodes from the military campaign.

lished them in six books known as the *Enneads*, from *ennea*, "nine," because this was the number of treatises in each book.

Plotinus saw the universe as a complex, orderly structure that continuously and perpetually descends from its transcendent First Principle. The One, as Plotinus conceived it, is beyond thought or definition or language. It is superabundant reality and goodness, absolute and pure. Plotinus's One has been said to be nearer than any other Greco-Roman philosopher's concept to the God of the Christians. Yet this One is not, like the Christian God, a power that intervenes in earthly things since, although it is their creator, it remains wholly external to them and outside all the orders of being.

The structure of the One is repeated in the structure of human beings, and they all contain within themselves the potentiality of union with the One: Their life is an upward yearning, an impulse to reunite themselves with the One. The whole philosophy of Plotinus seeks to animate our dulled sense of the supernatural. Lowly and degraded though our mortal bodies are, the soul and mind of every man and woman provide steps by which they can rise to the heights.

Indeed, by so doing they can, on the rarest occasions, catch a glimpse of the One and even reunite with it. They can achieve this by looking within themselves. Many earlier philosophers had spoken in praise of such contemplation. But Plotinus saw it as the dynamic device for thinking away the limitations of body and space and time into nothingness, until we merge with the supreme reality itself.

CONSUL TAKING OFFICE
(Acilia's sarcophagus, ca. 260 A.D.) A procession of men in togas accompanies the deceased as he takes office at the consulate. The movement of the cloth and the large, ample folds, as well as the portrayal of hair and beards, betray the use of the trepan, a tool characteristic of the art at the end of the Empire.

FROM *VOLUMEN* TO *CODEX*

A major evolution in books took place in the 3rd century A.D, when the *codex*, a book of bound parchment pages, gradually replaced the *volumen*, made from strips of papyrus.

This historic change can easily be explained by the high cost of papyrus. Imported from Egypt, papyrus was fabricated from the stem of a Nile plant, which was split lengthwise and then arranged in perpendicular layers to form pages. Once they were glued together, these pages made long, carefully finished strips that were then rolled onto a stick called an *umbilic*.

These rolls were heavy and bulky. Some books, up to 30 feet in length, were difficult to handle and even harder to read. For this reason, the poet Martial sang the praises of the convenience of the *codex*, which could be carried much more easily. Its use was facilitated by the import of parchment, made from scraped and polished sheepskin; it originated in Pergamum. Inexpensive and able to be inscribed on both sides—and even scratched into—parchment helped widen the spread of literature.

Book lovers of the time, who generally had slaves and thus leisure time, could borrow books from other readers and have them copied. They could also visit booksellers, some of whom had teams of copyists who fulfilled special orders.

Plotonius is the Western world's pioneer of those who have believed they can achieve such ineffable joyous reunion by intellectual discipline alone, without the need for religion or drugs. In this successful search for intimacy in a bottomless universe, he presents paganism at its noblest. But he offers no likelihood that it could maintain itself, as Christianity was about to do, as a faith for all classes, since his words were manifestly directed to an intellectual and spiritual elite.

Yet there was another

AVNORVM SATYRORVM ET SILENORVM DELECI

DEATH AND AFTERLIFE

After being displayed in his house, feet facing the door, the deceased was carried away by a procession. Rich Romans enlisted musicians, and their slaves carried wax busts of great ancestors. Burials and cremations were both practiced, the latter disappearing under the Empire. Necropolises, or cemeteries, were situated outside the cities along the roads.

Superstitious in all things, the Romans feared the dead, who were called *manes*. These were living beings who dwelled underground and needed to be fed and surrounded by everyday objects. Flowers and various foods were offered to them on the family's altar—

for example, for their birthdays. Several times a year, and over the course of a few days, public celebrations devoted to the dead were held to ward off their evil spells. During these times, political and economic activities were suspended and temples were closed.

Roman religion did not develop lofty theories or images of the afterlife. All references to the world of the dead (including Hell, Styx, and Acheron) were borrowed from Greek mythology and stayed within the limits of literature. It was not until eastern cults, and especially Christianity, became widespread that the idea of another life after death developed.

pagan belief, during this same epoch, which much more nearly competed with Christ for the control of the Western world. This was the cult of the Sun. To Rome, the divinity of the Sun came very early on. The cult of this deity offered flattering analogies to the imperial regime and its resplendent, sunlike leaders. Under Severus, whose wife came from Syria, where reverence for the Sun was especially strong, its worship almost took command of the whole state religion. The emperor Aurelian established a massive temple of the Unconquerable Sun as the focal point of the entire religious system of the State (274 A.D.). The birthday of the god was to be on December 25, and this, transformed into Christmas Day, was one of the heritages which Christianity owed to his cult.

The Sun cult could well have become the religion of the Mediterranean area for an indefinite period ahead. But it did not do so, in the end, because such a divinity was too impersonal, too lacking in urgent human appeal.

A branch of the cult came into being in order to respond to such yearnings. It was the worship of an ancient Iranian deity, Mithras, who was god of the Morning Light. Mithraism had no public ceremonies or professional priestly class. It was personal—supplying the intimate element that the Sun faith lacked.

And its popularity increased at great speed, especially among the army, particularly its officers. The Mithras of legend was a hero figure, unconquerable like the Sun himself, a superman for critical times—and he was also an ethical, austere model of conduct. Moreover, all the excitement inherent in initiations of an elect was offered by the melodramatic form and staging of his rites.

The worship of Mithras, then, possessed ideas, moral urgency, and intimate emotional force. Yet it was Christianity that won the day. The "biography" that was Mithras's holy book was unconvincing and failed to persuade its readers that he had ever really appeared on this earth to provide help for human beings.

The Dualists believed in the conflict between good and evil powers contending with each other for the control of the universe. This belief goes back to very ancient times. Evil manifestly exists. But how can this be so, if a benevolent and all-powerful God (or gods) created and controls the world?

EMPEROR GALLIENUS
The last emperor from the aristocracy, Gallienus favored culture and the arts during his reign (253–268 A.D.). The emperor and his wife, Salonina, were surrounded by a splendid court, which included the philosopher Plotinus.

161

THE PALMYRA TRIAD
*(1st century A.D.) This
limestone relief depicts
the three most important
divinities of Palmyra—
Baalshamin, master
of the skies (center),
flanked by the Moon
god and the Sun god.*

Many have felt that there must be *two* opposing forces, a good and an evil power, locked in a struggle. An enormous variety of dualistic beliefs gradually arose, but through them all ran the conviction that the world, created by the evil power, has to be condemned and thrown off, and that men and women escape the body by purging what is nonspiritual. And to teach how such liberation was to be achieved was the business of the Dualists, known as Gnostics (from gnosis, "knowledge"). This was the secret enlightenment they were able to impart to their initiates.

The culminating period of this Dualist movement started in about 240 A.D., when a young Persian named Mani began to preach at the national capital Ctesiphon, and the large Greek city of Seleucia, which lay on the opposite bank of the Tigris. A contemporary of Plotinus, Mani taught for thirty years. In the remote past of the Universe, he declared, the Dark had encroached on the Light, and Primal Man failed to repel it. His failure and fall were what created our own flawed world.

Yet as life still pursues its dirty path, pronounced Mani, there is hope, for the darkness is slowly being blotted out by Light; once this process is completed, a Savior will return (whom he identified with Jesus Christ, though this was not a Christian religion), and all will be Light once again. Mani's aim was to found a religious community of his Manichaeans that would embrace the entire earth. He proved too radical for the Persians, whose kings, bowing to the traditional national religion, put him to death (ca. 274–277 A.D.). Yet by then his doctrine had permeated huge regions of the Roman world. The Roman government hated these Manichaeans because it regarded their Persian origin as potentially seditious. And later, when the Christians made their bid to become the national religion of Rome, Manichaeanism found itself unable to stand up to them. It was too passive to offer really effective rivalry and too antisocial to form a powerful, cohesive church.

162

CHAPTER 13

The supreme state and church

The new state of Diocletian

While these last manifestations of paganism were reaching their climax, the Roman Empire had become a very different place. The first of the two great agents of change was Diocletian. After rising to become commander of the imperial body-guard, he successfully asserted his claim to the throne (284 A.D.), and two years later appointed an old Danubian comrade, Maximian, as joint Augustus. Then he converted this dual regime into a system based on four rulers, the tetrarchy, by nom-inating two further Danubians as secondary emperors or Caesars: Galerius, who was to preside over parts of the East, and Constantius I, who was to rule over west-ern areas under Maximian.

There had been partitions of the Empire before, but this arrangement was more thoroughgoing and intended to be permanent. Although the tetrarchy multiplied authority, it did not split it; the Empire was still an undivided unit and legislation was in the name of all four men.

Constantius and Diocletian put down rebel-lions in Britain (ca. 287–296 A.D.) and Egypt (293–294 and 297–298 A.D.) respectively, and from 302 A.D. they campaigned successfully across the Rhine and the Danube. In 305 A.D., Diocletian, whose health had become precarious, took the unprecedented step of abdicating and induced Maximian to do the same. They retired into private life at Salonae (Split, in Yugoslavia) and Lucania (southwest Italy) respectively, and Con-stantius I and Galerius became Augusti in their places.

Diocletian was the greatest imperial organizer since Augustus. One of his reforms was to raise the number of provinces from fifty to a hundred; since their areas were now relatively small, it was hoped that provincial governors would have little opportunity to revolt. Another of Diocletian's tasks was to overhaul the structure of the Roman army. Pursuing his predecessors' interest in mobile formations, he cre-ated a new mounted guard which consisted mainly of Germans. This guard was incorporated into one of the two major branches into which the entire army was now divided, the mobile field force. The second division was the frontier force, stationed along the much-strengthened border fortifications.

The total military strength of the Empire was now half a million or more. These massive dimensions made it all the more necessary that the taxes needed to pay the soldiers should be duly gathered in. Throughout the previous half-century, these exactions had caused the peoples of the Empire immeasurable hardship. Diocletian

PAYING TRIBUTE
(ca. 200 A.D.) This detail from the frieze of the Igel mausoleum, near Treviri, shows the lower peasantry paying taxes with crops to the master of the house.

did not lessen the burden, but he tried to ensure that the levies were distributed fairly. He issued an edict fixing maximum prices for all goods and maximum wages for all workers (301 A.D.). However, the tetrarchs neither owned nor controlled the means of production and consumption and proved unable to enforce their orders. The result was that goods disappeared from the market, and inflation resumed its inexorable course.

What had afflicted taxpayers particularly gravely was the irregularity and suddenness of the demands that had descended on them. To eliminate this element, Diocletian placed the whole tax-collecting process on a systematic and regular basis. Henceforward, the sums and supplies required were announced every year. Individual Greek communities in the past had experimented with annual budgets, but this was the first time the idea had been applied on this massive, Empire-wide scale.

These measures were directed towards a more efficient mobilization of resources against internal rivals and foreign foes. Imperial publicity does not refer to the former peril. But there was continual, increasing emphasis on the tetrarchs' role as triumphant defenders against their external enemies. Imperial coin propaganda concentrates remorselessly on the victorious leadership and prowess of its rulers. And this aggrandizement was reflected in imperial ceremonial that developed into a pattern far removed from the early principate.

Thus the mighty palace-fortress at Salonae (Split), to which Diocletian withdrew after his abdication, centered upon a grandiose Hall of Audience. The retired, revered emperor made his public appearances as if framed by the vault of heaven; as he paused, bejeweled and haloed, before taking his throne, the assembled multitude accorded him homage as if he were the image of divinity itself.

Such, it was now felt, must be the treatment accorded to the men who represented the ancient, renowned, and now revived Roman state. To describe them officially as gods, in these spiritually minded times, did not always seem suitable. But there was long precedent for describing the rulers as companions of a god, and in pursuance of this formula, Diocletian and Maximian pronounced Jupiter and Hercules to be their special personal companions and the patrons of their respective houses. In this monotheistic epoch that allowed most of the Olympians to fade, national propaganda concentrated upon deities, such as Jupiter and Hercules, who fulfilled the roles of protectors of the Roman leaders and people.

PORTRAIT OF ORFITUS AND CONSTANTIA
(4th century A.D.) Most medallions of this type (a layer of clear glass covering a gold leaf to be placed at the bottom of a cup or vase) are engraved with Christian motifs. This one, however, which depicts a small figure of Hercules, signifies the survival of paganism.

The growth of Christianity

This revival of paganism, on an even more emphatically national basis than before, was accompanied by violent persecutions of the faith which had become its principal competitor—Christianity. Since the composition of the Gospels two hundred years earlier, the Christian community had grown steadily. It was basically an urban institution, for the main strength of the Christian community lay in the lower and middle classes of the cities. And it was in the ancient city-states of Asia Minor, in particular, that the church most rapidly established vigorous nuclei. But

Christian missionary activities had also, at a very early date, extended to the West as well, and at Rome itself the numbers of Christians probably rose from about ten thousand in 200 A.D. to three or four times that total a century later.

As time went on, the local communities of the church had come under the autocratic control of bishops. This growing importance of the episcopacy took power away from the local elders, but it also made for much more efficient organization. The first of the important bishops in north Africa, Cyprian (d. 258 A.D.), boasted of the solidarity of Christians of every status and grade. And his praise was justified; the church possessed a solidarity, a tightness of organization that was unrivaled in any contemporary religion.

Yet the Christians, from an early date, had encountered opposition. The Greek population of the east had never liked them, because of their deliberate self-separation from the rest of the community, in which the followers of Jesus declared themselves to be mere strangers and sojourners. And this same unfriendly attitude spread to the Roman imperial administration as well. Already in 64 A.D., under Nero, they were blamed for the Great Fire of Rome, but that was a feeble charge.

Severus subjected them to the first coordinated, Empire-wide sanctions, forbidding them to conduct missionary activities and imposing stringent penalties on converts. As the imperial authorities became more desperately harassed by all their problems, the competent organization of the Christians seemed more and more provoking, and Decius declared himself unable to countenance their refusal to join in communal pagan observances. He therefore demanded of every Christian a single performance of the traditional religious rites.

DEVOURED BY THE LIONS
(2nd century) This floor mosaic, found in El Djem, in Tunisia, illustrates the cruelty of combat that pitted condemned men against wild animals.

The members of the Church, being mainly city people, found it hard to escape notice and were dangerously vulnerable. Many succeeded in evading the tests. But others lapsed from their faith, at least for the time being. Some, however, who were called upon to sacrifice refused and were put to death. Shrines of martyrs were established and revered, on the analogy of pagan heroes, and provided great encouragement to the faithful.

But Gallienus called a halt to this persecution, launching a policy of toler-

THE PERSECUTION OF THE CHRISTIANS

After the death of Christ, Christianity spread through the Roman world. Thirty years later, Nero condemned the Christians by burning down Rome, which brought about the kind of persecution that likely caused the death of Saint Peter.

Gradually, Christianity became popular and was no longer considered a Jewish sect. Its strict monotheism, however, posed a political problem: By refusing to sacrifice to the imperial cult, the Christians became enemies of Rome. Furthermore, their isolation made them vulnerable to the hostility of the people, who accused them of incest and the ritual murder of children. There was repression in Asia at the end of the 1st century, under Domitian. But, in the 2nd century, all major cities had churches.

The persecution increased the zeal of the Christian converts, who believed in martyrdom. But many pagans had doubts. It was in the 3rd century, under the reigns of Septimius Severus, Maximan, Decius, Valerian, and especially Diocletian, that persecution intensified. After the Edict of Caracalla (212 A.D.), all free men who were citizens had to sacrifice to the imperial cult. But this persecution was so cruel that it was ineffective. The religious tolerance ushered in by the Edict of Milan (313 A.D.) only confirmed the dominance of Christianity in the Empire.

ance that lasted for forty years, during which the Church established itself on an increasingly firm basis. This caused alarm to pagans such as Plotinus's pupil Porphyry, whose work *Against the Christians* attacked them with unprecedented ferocity. And Porphyry's friends were among the instigators of the Great Persecution, launched by Diocletian and Caesar Galerius. Bureaucracy and army joined forces to maintain anti-Christian measures over a period of ten years, not so much in

HYPOGEUM OF
VIA LATINA
*The Christian paintings
that decorated the cata-
combs as early as the 3rd
and 4th centuries are not
very different from pagan
paintings from the same
period. Favoring dark
lines on light backgrounds,
the decors are often framed,
organized in a space
structured on three levels.
Garlands of flowers under-
line the scenes depicted.*

western Europe, where few casualties occurred, but throughout the eastern provinces and in Africa. Resistance was on the whole resolute and defiant, and there were per- haps three thousand martyrs altogether.

Constantine the Great

As soon as Diocletian had abdicated in 305 A.D., the regular, planned succession to the tetrarchy broke down in hopeless confusion, revealing that the system had no power to survive at all when no longer supported by his personality. Amid a welter of joint, competing occupants of the various palaces, Constantine I, son of Constantius I, emerged to defeat Maxentius (the son of Maximian) in 312 A.D. at Rome's Milvian Bridge, thereby becoming sole emperor of the West. In the following year, Licinius gained control of the East. Then, in 323–324 A.D., Constantine won three great battles against Licinius and became the only ruler of the Roman Empire until his death in 337 A.D.

Constantine the Great was a man of impetuous and wide-ranging energy who felt utterly convinced of his duty to govern and change the world. He carried on the reforming activity of Diocletian over a very wide field. Whereas Diocletian's plans had been conceived to meet a series of emergencies, Constantine's were intended for a stable monarchy that would last for all time. In particular, he continued to reorganize the army, which received ever-increasing commemoration on his coins. He greatly enlarged the proportion of Germans among the troops, and the praetorian guard, which had fought against Constantine on Maxentius's side, found itself abolished altogether, replaced by the largely German mounted guard created by Diocletian.

With the same military needs in mind, Constantine confirmed that Rome was no longer a suitable capital for the Empire. An emperor who lived there was poorly placed to maintain control over the two vital imperial boundaries, the Rhine-Danube line in the north and the Euphrates in the east. He decided that the ideal site was the city of Byzantium on the strategic Bosphorus strait, and there he founded Constantinople (324–330 A.D.), where Istanbul is today. The new city was given a Forum and a Senate of its own, and its people received free distributions from the grain fleet that had served the ancient capital. Rome lost none of its privileges, but Constantine intended to make his new foundation the future metropolis of the Empire.

Constantine also carried through a second and even more far-reaching revolution, the conversion of the Empire from paganism to Christianity. The persecutions initiated by Diocletian and Galerius had not achieved their aim; Galerius, during his terminal illness, had issued, in conjunction with Constantine and Licinius, the Edict of Serdica, granting freedom of worship to all members of the Christian faith (311 A.D.).

Constantine's victory at the Milvian Bridge was won, he later asserted, under the auspices of the Cross, and in the following year he and Licinius echoed Galerius's pronouncement of tolerance in the Edict of Mediolanum (Milan). Constantine always felt a strong need for a divine sponsor. For a time the Sun god had been his choice. But although this deity continued to be depicted on the coins until 318–319 A.D., Constantine had already disclosed, at the time of the Edict of Mediolanum, his own personal adherence to Christianity.

And so Constantine initiated over a period of years a series of measures openly favoring its adherents. Christian priests, other than those of dissident sects, were exempted from municipal obligations. At Rome, the bishop, or pope, was lodged in the Lateran palace, and the church was granted its own jurisdiction. Church and state were to be run in double harness.

The elevation of the church was one of the most surprising phenomena in Roman history. The emperor's motives have been endlessly analyzed and discussed, but it appears that he and his advisers experienced a growing conviction that, however uninfluential the Christians might be, the course of events was working in the Christians' favor—since they alone possessed the universal aims and coherent organization that could unite the various conflicting peoples and classes of the Empire in a single, all-embracing harmony which was "catholic," that is to say, universal.

EMPEROR CONSTANTINE
A certain number of elements helped identify this colossal bronze head, which is more than 9 feet high and dates from the last years of Constantine's reign: the shape of the chin, the hair forming a kind of cap, and the deep pupils that seem to gaze into the distance.

CHRISTIAN TOMB *(Tomb mosaic, Tunisia, 5th century A.D.) In the name of the deceased,* Valentia in pace *(Valentia in peace), is inscribed in a basilica with three naves. The words* Ecclesia mater *(mother Church) are added, an allusion to the communal aspect of Christianity.*

Constantine himself was baptized at the very end of his life, postponing this step until his deathbed, when he could sin no more. By that time, the Christian revolution throughout the Empire was well advanced. His conversion was seen by Petrarch in the fourteenth century as the great dividing line between antiquity and the ages that lay ahead, and, indeed, he had brought a whole new world into being. Constantine himself was profoundly aware of the vastness and holiness of this task: He saw himself as the thirteenth apostle of Jesus and as God's regent upon earth.

It is in this guise that he is displayed in a colossal marble head which stands in the courtyard of the Palazzo dei Conservatori on Rome's Capitoline Hill. The head is nine feet high and weighs nine tons. It formed part of a huge seated statue, of which the wooden body and glittering robe of gilded bronze have not survived.

This vast figure stood in one of the apses of the Basilica Nova. This was a secular building, yet it was a basilica with a difference. Constructed mainly by Maxentius, after whom it is often named, it was altered by Constantine, who changed the principal orientation from the long to the short axis. The lofty nave and aisles, lit by huge half-circular windows anticipating the Romanesque cathedrals of the future, were surmounted by great curving, intersecting barrel vaults. The Basilica Nova, of which three lofty spans remain today, represented the climax of Rome's greatest architectural achievement: its discovery of how to exploit the significance of interior space.

CONSTANTINE'S PALACE *(Treviri) This detail from the coffered ceiling is believed to depict Constantia, the emperor's sister-in-law, or St. Fausta, his wife.*

But the future lay with another sort of basilica, not secular but ecclesiastical. Constantine's religious transformation stimulated the greatest architects of the day to serve the requirements of the new national faith, and these magnificent successors of the humble house-churches of the past were their major creations. Like the Basilica Nova, they were rectangular and longitudinal. But they contained side aisles separated from the loftier nave by long rows of columns. The great colonnades flowed towards the cross on the altar and the apse that rose skywards beyond. This culminating point of the Christian basilica was glimpsed by those who entered the building from the west and saw the rays of the rising sun pouring through the windows of the apse upon the celebrant who stood facing his congregation.

Little can be seen of Constantine's basilica churches today, since they were demolished by later generations in favor of the monuments they themselves were eager to erect upon the same sacred sites. Yet his grandiose basilicas added up to the greatest architectural accomplishment of any single man in Roman history.

The successors of Constantine

Constantine was determined to achieve hereditary succession to his throne, but his endeavors were less successful than anything else he attempted. In 326 A.D., on reports of a plot, he ordered the execution of his wife and his eldest son. Then he groomed for the succession the three boys who remained to him, together with the two sons of a half-brother. Within thirteen years after his death, however, all had been eliminated except one, who was Constantius II.

While prodigious monetary inflation and taxation continued within the empire, Constantius fought against Persia and then turned to the West to put down usurpers. Meanwhile, he was converting Constantine's establishment of Christianity into a lasting reality. He appointed his cousin Constantius Gallus to be his Caesar and presumptive heir, but in 354 A.D., on suspicions of disloyalty, he put him to death. Then he appointed a new Caesar, this time in the West, namely the dead man's half brother Julian, who won an important series of campaigns against the Germans and restored the Rhine frontier. Thereupon his troops proclaimed him emperor, but before the inevitable clash came, the emperor died (361 A.D.), and Julian succeeded in his place.

He had reacted strongly against his Christian background and is known as the Apostate because he abandoned the faith altogether. When he came to the throne, he openly professed adherence to the beliefs of the pagans and reinstituted their cults. He proclaimed general toleration of all religions. However, not only was the Christian church deprived of its financial privileges, but in the religious disorders that followed, its members were penalized severely.

But his anti-Christian campaign came to nothing. The attempt to roll back the Christian tide was too anachronistic to prevail.

In other directions he succeeded better, for he was a hard-working and conscientious administrator. He temporarily cured the raging monetary inflation by placing an extensive gold coinage in circulation. And he made a courageous attempt to cut down the ever-growing imperial bureaucracy.

But his major ambition was to deal drastically with the Persians, who had become menacing once again. After elaborate preparations, Julian marched eastwards and won a victory (365 A.D.). But his column was constantly harassed by the enemy, and in one of these skirmishes he received a wound from which he died. His successor, a Danubian officer named Jovian (363–364 A.D.), reversed both his principal policies, negotiating an unpopular peace with the Persians and restoring Christianity—of which he was a pious adherent—as the religion of the Empire.

JULIAN, THE APOSTATE
An avid defender of paganism, the emperor Julian reigned from 361 to 363 A.D. Here he is represented as a philosopher, suggested by the cloak, beard, and Greek sandals.

169

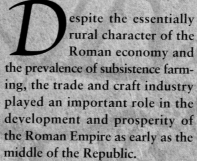

CUTLERY SHOP
This relief from the 1st century A.D. shows how tools improved and how professions became more specialized.

Merchants and artisans

THE WINE BUSINESS
On his burial monument (below), this wine merchant had two scenes from his profession depicted: the retail sale of wine in a tavern and the transport of barrels by cattle-pulled cart.

Despite the essentially rural character of the Roman economy and the prevalence of subsistence farming, the trade and craft industry played an important role in the development and prosperity of the Roman Empire as early as the middle of the Republic.

The growth of the urban population made a market economy indispensable and gave rise to specialized crafts. Every week, large markets provided a wealth of supplies for the population.

Yet merchants and artisans selling in booths or working in workshops maintained a fairly modest life. Only the lucky few who received orders from the state could hire numbers of workers and afford burial monuments. Merchants often formed syndicates or guilds (*collegia*) that gave them the power to defend themselves collectively. Servants, who hoped to be recognized and freed by their masters through their work, also played a part in helping commerce develop.

Furthermore, the Romans took advantage of the resources from each conquered province and organized their economy according to regional divisions. Because their products could be made available throughout the Empire, genuine industrial centers arose. The range of products included pottery from areas with clay-rich soils (especially Gaul) and glassware from regions with an abundance of quartz. Moreover, agricultural products were often collected as a tax in the richest regions of the Empire (wheat from Egypt, Sicily, or Africa; wine from Spain and Gaul; olive oil from Greece and Spain) and supplied to the capital's population and the legions at the frontiers. There was an entire specialized administration—a service of provisions—that made sure these supplies were properly redistributed.

As early as the end of the 4th century B.C., trade in all sorts of goods was facilitated by the construction of a network of roads between Rome and the other parts of Italy. However, because transportation by road was slow and expensive, it was usually reserved for local commerce.

For long distances, water transport on river or sea was both faster and less costly for the Romans. Heavy loads were brought by sailboats in the merchant fleet, and at the beginning of the Empire, larger ports like the one in Ostia made this kind of navigation more efficient.

PORT OF POZZUOLI
At the beginning of the Empire, Pozzuoli was the most active of Italy's ports. Its famous pier is built on 15 huge piles connected by arches.

BUTCHER'S COMMISSION
This relief shows the setting and tools of a butcher, who had himself represented with his wife; she holds the accounting book.

SHOP IN HERCULANEUM
Most of the houses in Herculaneum, Pompeii, or Ostia had a store front. Oil and wine were kept in amphorae, tall jars with narrow necks and two handles.

THE PORT OF OSTIA

As the first Roman colony founded at the end of the 4th century B.C., the city of Ostia owes its economic strength to its geographical location. At the mouth of the Tiber, it gave Rome access to the sea. In 42 A.D., to provide more supplies to the capital, Claudius began building a new port to the north of the city; it was named Portus and was completed under Trajan. Wheat imported from Africa and Egypt was stored in Ostia's granaries before being transported to Rome by river. Modern excavations have uncovered a good part of the site. Among the best-preserved buildings are the communication houses, which are several stories high; the storehouses from the imperial period; and commercial spaces, stores, and taverns. The Guild Plaza brought together the shipping offices and the port businesses; the floor's mosaic (above) illustrates busy commercial trading and the importance of maritime transport.

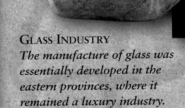

GLASS INDUSTRY
The manufacture of glass was essentially developed in the eastern provinces, where it remained a luxury industry.

BREAD MERCHANT
City residents, who could not grind wheat or bake bread at home, depended on bakers and street vendors for their subsistence.

CHAPTER 14

The fall of the Western Empire

Valentinian and Theodosius

In 364 A.D., the army acclaimed Valentinian I, another Danubian, as emperor; he was the last impressive ruler the Western Empire had. Concluding that in the interests of national defense there should be a second emperor, Valentinian gave the East to his brother Valens, who took up residence at Constantinople. He himself kept the West, ruling at Mediolanum, though the Senate still remained at Rome. His treasury was impoverished by the division, since revenue from the richer eastern provinces ceased to flow in. Nevertheless, at his death eleven years later, he left the Western Empire stronger than ever.

Valentinian achieved this by dealing with a host of successive emergencies. First, the Germans had burst across the Rhine, seizing the fortress of Moguntiacum (Mainz). But the emperor defeated them and then marched up the Neckar valley and won a major victory in the Black Forest. In 374–75 A.D., Valentinian repelled another great incursion of Germans across the Danube. Not long afterwards, however, while listening to the insolent words of German envoys, he burst a blood vessel and died, leaving his throne to his sixteen-year-old son, Gratian.

OBELISK OF THEODOSIUS *(ca. 390 A.D.) Built in the Constantinople hippodrome, the obelisk is decorated with reliefs showing the emperor in his loggia. On this relief, he is surrounded by his family as he presents the winner of the chariot race with the crown of laurels.*

Three years later, the other Eastern Roman Empire suffered a setback. Beyond its borders, two great German states had taken shape, the Ostrogoths (bright Goths) and the Visigoths (wise Goths). But a non-German people living farther away, the Huns, had burst through into the lands of these two peoples in about 370 A.D. The Ostrogothic state crumbled, and two hundred thousand Visigoths, too, were driven across the Danube into the Eastern Roman Empire, where its authorities permitted them to settle. Incensed, however, by their unjust treatment at the hands of these functionaries, the Visigothic chieftain, Fritigern, broke into revolt and ravaged the Balkans. Valens marched rapidly from Asia to deal with the crisis and passed to the attack at Hadrianopolis in Thrace. But the imperial infantry fell almost to a man and Valens himself perished.

His nephew Gratian, emperor in the West, appointed Theodosius I to succeed Valens at Constantinople. For the next decade, Theodosius ruled the eastern empire and then, putting down two usurpers in the West, momentarily reunited the two imperial thrones before his death in 395 A.D.

The frontiers broken

After Theodosius's death, the Empire was once again divided. The East went to his eighteen-year-old son, Arcadius (395–408 A.D.), and the western throne to his younger son Honorius, aged eleven (395–423 A.D.). Both boys, as they grew older, turned out to be incompetent, and the task of ruling the two empires fell to their regents. The effective ruler of the West was Stilicho, half Roman and half German. Stilicho's career was darkened by two clouds. The first was his hostility to the Eastern Empire, where he arranged that the guardian of its young emperor, Rufinus, should be assassinated. The second was his unwillingness to deal firmly enough with the Visigoths' new ruler, Alaric. Alaric had shown his aggressive intentions by a series of invasions deep into Italy itself (401–403 A.D.)—events which induced the timid Honorius to move his capital to the Adriatic coastal town of Ravenna, protected by marshes. Yet Stilicho, instead of proceeding against Alaric, preferred to keep him as a counterpoise to the eastern state.

Then on December 31, 406 A.D., the gravest of all the German invasions of the West took place. A mixed army of men from a number of different tribal groups crossed the frozen Rhine and plundered Moguntiacum (Mainz) and Treviri (Trier). Next, the invaders fanned out into Gaul, marching on throughout the entire country as far as the Pyrenees.

VANDAL ON HORSE *(Mosaic from Carthage, ca. 500 A.D.) Savage invasions, especially by the Vandals in north Africa, forced cities to build ramparts and villas to put up fortifications, as this mosaic illustrates.*

Stilicho did nothing effective to block the invaders because the shock waves of the German onslaught threw up several usurpers in the Roman armies. One of these men crossed over to the continent from Britain, which passed gradually into the hands of Saxon immigrants who had been allowed to settle in the country. Stilicho was under heavy pressure from the Visigoths, whose leader, Alaric, insisted that he should be given four thousand pounds of gold. Stilicho compelled his reluctant Senate to agree but soon afterwards found himself accused of plotting with Alaric to place his own son on the throne. Honorius had him put to death (408 A.D.).

Alaric went on demanding money and land and, when his demands were rejected, he marched in three successive years to the outskirts of Rome. When he arrived for the third time, the gates were treacherously opened to admit him. His army moved in and occupied the city, which horrified the entire Roman world. Yet although much wealth was plundered and fires were started in various areas, the Visigoths stayed in Rome for only three days.

After that, taking the emperor's half-sister Placidia with him, Alaric departed and moved on towards the south of Italy, where he turned back and died. He was buried deep in the bed of a river so that his body should never be found and subjected to impious treatment.

The Visigoth Ataulf, brother-in-law and successor of Alaric, moved his people out of Italy and settled them in southwest Gaul. To prove his good intentions towards the Empire, he married Placidia. But Honorius withheld his agreement to the marriage, and Constantius III forced Ataulf to withdraw into Spain, where he was killed (415 A.D). After his brother, Wallia, returned Placidia to the Romans, he was permitted to take his Visigoths back to Gaul, where they were granted federate status, with Tolosa as their capital (418 A.D.).

TOMB OF GALLA PLACIDIA
(Ravenna, 5th century A.D.)
Galla Placidia, half-sister of
Emperor Honorius, settled
in Ravenna and reigned
with pomp over the city.
Her tomb, in the shape of
a Latin cross, is adorned
with lavish mosaics.

Constantius married Placidia, who provided him with a son. Early in 421 A.D., Honorius proclaimed him joint emperor of the West. But after a reign of only seven months, he died. A quarrel now broke out between Honorius and Placidia, who sought refuge at the eastern capital, accompanied by her four-year-old son, Valentinian III. But when Honorius died of dropsy in 423 A.D., she returned to Italy, and the child became emperor in the West (425–455 A.D.). During the first years of his titular rule, Placidia exercised autocratic control. But there was also another striking figure to be reckoned with—Aetius, a Danubian. As a young man he had been a hostage in the hands of the Visigoths and of the Huns, experiences that had given him valuable insight into these two foreign peoples. Then, after Honorius's death, he had led a large force of Huns to try to block the return of Placidia. Subsequently, he made his peace with her government and became the commander-in-chief.

His most urgent task was to check the Vandals, a German people who had moved from Gaul into Spain and then into north Africa (429 A.D.). Their king, Gaiseric, was a leader who faced the Romans with the most intractable German problem they had ever experienced. A joint army of the Western and Eastern Empires sent against him failed dismally, and a treaty was drawn up according to which the Vandals were granted federate status.

But four years later, Gaiseric invaded the grain lands of Tunisia and northeastern Algeria, and the ancient capital Carthage itself fell into his hands (439 A.D.). Its loss made the dissolution of the Empire lamentably apparent.

This was also the time when the Huns, who had hitherto supplied Aetius with many of his soldiers, began to be the enemies of the Romans instead, fighting first against the Eastern Empire, then against the West. By the early fifth century, they had built up an empire stretching from the Baltic to the Danube. In 434 A.D., this entire territory was inherited by Attila. Evil-tempered and tireless, this square, flat-nosed little man earned the name "the Scourge of God" during his nineteen-year reign.

At first, during the 440s, he remained on friendly terms with Aetius. But then, in 451 A.D., he marched on Gaul. There, on the Catalaunian Plains near Châlons-sur-Marne, he was confronted by a combined army of Aetius's Roman troops and federated Germans. It was the greatest victory of Aetius's career and was the only battle Attila ever lost in his life.

But Gaul's gain meant terror for Italy, since he and his Huns crossed the Alps in the following year, sacking Mediolanum and other leading cities. This time, Aetius had no imperial army to send against him. However, Pope Leo I arrived on the scene from Rome and persuaded Attila to withdraw. Presumably he convinced the king that owing to famine and pestilence, the Huns would not be able to feed off the land.

Two years later, Attila died, and his empire fell apart. The Huns were never a great power again. But by that time Aetius was dead, for Valentinian III, falsely persuaded that he was treasonable, had murdered him with his own hand (454 A.D.). Aetius had labored to keep the destroyers of the Western world in check. With his assassination, its terminal crisis had begun.

The last emperors of the West

Only six months later, two of Aetius's barbarian retainers struck down Valentinian in revenge. The emperor had no heir, so that his dynasty, which had lasted for nearly a century, expired with him.

The year of his death brought immediate catastrophe. Gaiseric the Vandal landed at Ostia and captured the city of Rome itself. He remained for two weeks, extracting loot far beyond Alaric's briefer plundering.

The Western Empire had just twenty-one more years to live. During that period, as many as nine more or less legitimate rulers could be counted. Within the rapidly dissolving government of Ravenna, the predominant personage was now the supreme commander Ricimer. Ricimer's German origin was felt to disqualify him from wearing the imperial purple itself, so instead, he was the power behind the throne for the next fifteen years.

After his death, a new military commander, Orestes, who had been Attila's secretary, gave the Ravenna throne to his own son, Romulus Augustus. But a German general, Odoacer, who commanded a force of his Danubian compatriots in Italy, now proceeded to intervene.

Seizing Ravenna, Odoacer declared Romulus to be deposed and dismissed him. No attempt was made to appoint a new Augustus. Instead, at Odoacer's bidding, the Roman Senate transferred the imperial insignia to Zeno, who occupied the throne at Constantinople (474–491 A.D.). Odoacer, while politely placing the head of Zeno on his coins, continued to rule Italy as an independent monarch.

Later historians fastened on the year 476 A.D. as the date at which the long-declining Western Empire finally fell. The last remaining country of the West had become just another German kingdom.

The failure of the army

The Western Empire had succumbed to its external enemies. Yet these would not have been too formidable if it had still possessed sufficient internal strength. But when the murderous blows were struck, the government could no longer muster the force to ward them off. Italy and the whole Western world were hopelessly disunited within. The disunities assumed various shapes and forms. Each of them in itself was damaging. In combination, they made resistance to the external onslaughts impossible.

One prime cause of disunity was the failure of the rulers to control their generals. This had been a defect inherent in the imperial system from the very beginning, since the Romans had never devised a workable system for ensuring a peaceful transition from one ruler to the next. This defect was a standing temptation to their own commanders to make a violent bid for power.

And the armies of the Empire were failing to perform the tasks of imperial defense. They collapsed before foreign invaders who were, theoretically, much inferior in numbers and equipment. However, in terms of active, effective strength, the western Romans could scarcely mobilize bigger numbers than their foes. Stilicho, in 405 A.D., led a force of not many more than twenty thousand.

This was largely due to the failure of the imperial authorities to enforce conscription. This had been the principal source of recruitment, and Valentinian I, for example, conscripted strenuously every year. But there was widespread evasion of the draft. Military service was no longer considered a patriotic duty but a servitude to be shunned. By the 440s it had become impossible to attempt any call-ups except in the gravest emergencies. And a decade later, we hear of no more Western citizens being drafted at all.

The result was that the defenders of the frontier posts just melted away. The cities were left unguarded even when invaders were almost in sight. True, a fine general like Stilicho or Aetius could still win his battles. But on many occasions the imperial troops were doomed to defeat before they had even caught a glimpse of a German or Hun soldier.

Social catastrophe

The burden of taxation the people had to bear in order to keep this army in existence was appallingly heavy—so heavy that its impositions alienated the poor from the state forever. Harsh regimentation, for this same purpose of paying the army, had been a fact of Roman life for nearly two hundred years.

The system for levying taxes was inefficient because it was so intolerably oppressive, leaving tax dodging as the only alternative to destitution. And it was unfair,

GRAPE HARVESTING
(4th century A.D.) The plant motifs that curl over the main scene—bringing the grapes to the press—and the medallion portraits are typical of 4th-century mosaics. The famous mosaics from Piazza Armerina, in Sicily, are similarly inspired.

since the worst sufferers were the agricultural poor. The unfairness of the land tax, from which the state drew nine-tenths of its income, meant that they were hit much harder than the rich. The impoverished "free" men and women of the rural countryside and the government were thus oppressed and oppressor, and because of this rift, the taxes needed to support the army were not, could not be, paid in.

This also brought about radical changes in society. When the small farmers and agricultural laborers could no longer make both ends meet, they sought protection where they could find it. Thus whole villages placed themselves under the patronage of local landowners. Since agricultural labor was so scarce, the landowners were content to receive these people, who defrayed their keep either by paying rent or by contributing labor. They could often rely on their new patrons to chase the tax authorities away. But later the landowners did an unholy deal with the Western government, and the refugees found themselves on the tax lists once again. The emperors were glad to prevent these tenants from moving away without their landlord's consent, so they were wholly subjected to his control—and so were their children after them. Such men were not exactly slaves, but they foreshadowed the serfs of the Middle Ages.

Thousands of people despaired of making an honest living at all and went underground to form traveling gangs of robbers and bandits. Gaul, in particular, experienced a succession of large-scale disturbances. Such bands operated almost on the scale of a nationwide uprising and even held their own people's courts, "where capital sentences are posted up on an oak branch or marked on a man's bones."

Far back in the distant past was that not totally imaginary golden age when the various classes of the Roman state, even if never truly united, had at least been able to live together. Now the social structure had crumbled, opening a breach through which the external enemy could batter his way in.

Yet the Western Empire might still have held together, brushing aside the claims of the poor, if only the rich and the government had more frequently seen eye to eye. They colluded, it is true, in ensuring that the tenants on the large estates should be allowed no freedom or rights. But in other respects there was little sympathy between the imperial authorities and the upper class.

The nobles of the later Empire were magnificent personages. But they were not particularly addicted to high living, so the idea that the Western world collapsed because of orgies must be abandoned. There had been more orgies earlier, when the Empire had been doing well, than later, when it was faring badly. More serious is the accusation that the senators of the fourth and fifth centuries stood aloof from public life. Many of them held no office, preferring instead to remain at home and enjoy their properties. In spite of lip service to the romantic concept of Eternal Rome, many noblemen were not prepared to lift a finger to save the reality. On the contrary, they often actively undermined it by rebuffing imperial officials, harboring deserters and brigands, and taking the law into their own hands.

CHRIST TEACHING THE APOSTLES
(Rome, catacombs of Domitilia, 4th century A.D.) In this large underground labyrinth where Christians found a final resting place, it was customary for Romans to gather around tombs to celebrate mass.

In the vain hope, then, of keeping their armies in the field, the imperial authorities ruined the poor and alienated the rich. They also alienated, and then largely destroyed, the middle class. The external invasions and internal rebellions of the third century A.D. had dealt this middle class terrible physical blows, while the accompanying monetary inflation caused their endowment to vanish altogether.

The nucleus of the middle class had been provided by the *curiales*, who comprised the members of the city councils (*curiae*) and their sons and descendants. Once they had been munificent benefactors of their cities, but nowadays their most important function was to carry out the orders they received from the central government—and above all, to collect its revenues. That is to say, they had virtually become imperial agents. This meant that from the third century onwards, wealthy men became increasingly reluctant to serve on the city councils.

Since few new families were willing to be enlisted in such a burdensome cause, these memberships often assumed a hereditary character—a situation encouraged by the imperial government, which insisted, as in many other sections of the community, that the sons should follow in the footsteps of their fathers.

But such insistence did not prevent these *curiales* from deserting wholesale from their posts; indeed, the entire middle class of which they formed such an essential part was almost wiped out of existence. In a society which had always so largely depended on this class, its destruction left a vacuum that nothing could fill.

So, throughout the last two centuries of the Roman West, there was an ever-deepening loss of personal freedom and well-being for all but the very prosperous and powerful. The authorities sought to impose maximum regimentation, to pay for the army and prop up the imperial structure. And yet all that they achieved was to hasten the ruin of what they wanted to preserve.

178

Uncooperative attitudes

Another reason the Western Empire fell was because of a disastrous failure to assimilate the Germans in its midst or achieve a workable arrangement with their leaders. When these Germans had first begun to establish themselves on imperial territory, they felt no ambition to become independent of Rome, desiring only to obtain a share of its benefits and, above all, cultivable soil. Even the Visigoth Alaric, who went down to history as the captor of Rome, had at first aimed at a form of coexistence. And his son, Ataulf (410–415 A.D.), formulated the same ideal with great explicitness, stating that he "aspired to the glory of restoring the fame of Rome in all its integrity and of increasing it by means of the Gothic strength."

But the Roman response to this unprecedented offer of partnership was inadequate. True, there were a few writers who paid lip service to multiracial unity. But lip service was all that it was, because even they could not restrain themselves from expressing a deep repugnance for the barbarians.

Sidonius Apollinaris, the highly literate bishop of Arverna (Clermont-Ferrand), while lavishly flattering Visigothic monarchs and observing that they had a common interest in saving the Empire, nevertheless objected fastidiously to the noisy,

St. Sabina Basilica
(Rome, 5th century A.D.)
Founded by the pontificate
of Celestine I (422–432
A.D.), St. Sabina is typical
of early Christian basilicas
that grew out of pagan ones.
The worshipers entered
through a monumental
door, there were three
naves separated by a
line of columns, and
light streamed through
rows of windows.

skin-clad Goths and to the Burgundians, who stank of the rancid butter they smeared on their tow-haired skulls.

The Romans generally imposed on these new, unwelcome, and disconcerting neighbors a kind of spiritual and social apartheid. They set them apart, beyond a wall of contempt. Only Aetius, if he had lived, might have reversed the general trend, for he knew the Germans well, and handled them with tact. But what happened instead was painfully displayed by the rise of Gaiseric the Vandal. Far from talking of coexistence and partnership within the empire, he raised his north African state to virulently hostile independence. And at the same time, King Euric of the Visigoths (466-484/5 A.D.) was making his people in Gaul and Spain into another wholly independent nation. His legal Code (475 A.D.) rejected any kind of amalgamation between the German and Roman peoples in his kingdom. It was dramatically appropriate that the last emperor of the West was forced to abdicate in the year immediately following the publication of Euric's code.

TEACHING SCENE
(Funerary monument, 4th century) The deceased, a grammaticus, is depicted practicing his profession. Seated on a bench, his feet slightly raised, he holds an open scroll, which one of his students seems to be reading.

Christians and pagans

Church and state were bound in a close alliance, established by Constantine the Great. The state was, at first, the controlling partner, but when the imperial court moved elsewhere, the bishops of Rome, the popes, were left free to become great men on their own account. Popes Innocent I (401–17 A.D.) and Leo I (440–61 A.D.) treated with Alaric and Attila respectively, the latter with triumphant success. And in the same period, mighty Roman churches were under construction.

It was Pope Leo's view that collaboration between state and the Catholic Church was uniquely capable of binding the disunited Western world together. But in fact

ROMAN EDUCATION

The Roman educational system was traditionally built around the family. The mother kept the children at her side until age 8. At that point, the father took over, preparing them to be citizens by taking them with him to the Forum and Senate before training them for military life. However, perhaps as early as the 4th century B.C., schools provided basic education, and this phenomenon grew after contact with Greek culture. The teaching of literature continued to prevail, with science (that is, mathematics and music) emphasized only on occasion.

Until age 11, boys and girls alike were taught how to read, write, and add by a teacher called a *litterator;* the wealthiest were accompanied by a slave, the *pedagogue.* From ages 12 to 16, children were entrusted to the *grammaticus,* who taught grammar and literature—in Greek, then in Latin, starting in the 2nd century B.C., when a national literature emerged. From ages 16 to 18, boys were taught rhetoric (first in Greek, then in Latin) by a *rhetor.* In large families, it was customary to have the boys undertake higher education in Greece, Gaul, or Asia.

Education was a paramount concern of the emperors, who founded municipal primary schools and saw to it that respected Greek teachers made their way to Rome.

the alliance turned out to have the opposite effect. This was because of the excessive, violent zeal with which the civil leaders, acting upon the requests of their spiritual partners, pressed conformity upon the pagans. There was a great symbolic moment in the war against paganism when Gratian expelled the pagan statue of Victory from the Senate house (382 A.D.). And then Theodosius I passed a whole series of laws endeavoring to obliterate paganism altogether. In north Africa, however, religious riots broke out among the pagans because their temples had been closed, but this only spurred the bishops of the region to demand even more hostile legislation.

One of the ecclesiastics who took the lead in this was Augustine, the outstanding churchman and intellectual and writer of his age. Augustine was born at Thagaste (Souk-Ahras in Algeria) in 354 A.D. The young man received a careful education in north Africa and became professor of rhetoric at Mediolanum. After passing through a variety of religious convictions, recaptured in his passionately introspective and self-critical *Confessions*, he was ordained a priest at Hippo Regius (Annaba), where he became bishop four years later, in 395 A.D. And now he came out in favor of coercing pagans—for Christ, he declared, like a general, must use military methods to recall deserters to his army.

Imperial repression against the pagans continued well on into the 440s. These coercive measures did in the end almost succeed in extirpating paganism. Yet during the crucial years of the earlier fifth century, this persecution had intensified the very disunities it was designed to eliminate; it had thus played its part in the destruction of the Western Roman Empire. Moreover, the psychological attitudes of pagans and Christians alike were equally unhelpful to the government. The pagans relied too complacently on the glories of the past, and the Christian theologians deprecated the importance of serving the state.

CHRISTIAN SARCOPHAGUS
Strigils (reliefs undulating like waves) decorate this sarcophagus. Its shape, a vat perched on lion feet, was typical of late antiquity. The central motif—a young shepherd carrying a lamb on his shoulders—symbolizes the Good Shepherd, a traditional theme in Christian art.

The pagans' ancient educational habits were very far from dead. Indeed, their purveyance of the classical tradition still held the field virtually unopposed. And in the great universities of Rome and Mediolanum and Carthage, the professors adhered to the classical pattern of the Seven Liberal Arts—or rather, since four of them were no longer much taught (arithmetic, geometry, astronomy, music), they concentrated on the remaining three—grammar, rhetoric, and dialectic. As the middle class decayed the pursuit of such studies became increasingly limited to the aristocracy, whose attitudes, as revealed in their poems and letters, remained fixed in an almost uniform sterility.

These works display a romantic, nostalgic feeling for Eternal Rome—the "Invicta Roma Aeterna" of coins and medallions. The trouble

about this veneration of the past was that it tempted people to see every contemporary event in terms of *previous* Roman happenings. Yet this propensity led to catastrophes. When, for instance, the pagan historian Ammianus writes of the recent defeat of the Romans by the Visigoths at Hadrianopolis (376 A.D.), he compares the disaster to German invasions half a millennium earlier; his point is that such tribulations had been overcome before, so there is no reason why they should not be overcome once again. Yet the German invasions five centuries previously had never offered the slightest threat to the Empire's survival, whereas now the degree of magnitude had altogether changed. The complacent nostalgia of Roman education made it impossible to face up to such novel situations with any adequate or constructive response. "Your power is felt wherever the sun's light shines," declared the poet Rutilius about Rome. But he was wrong, since the Roman West was approaching collapse; countermeasures were urgently required, and attitudes such as his distracted attention from this necessity.

The great Christian theologians, on the other hand, were often guilty of a different but equally serious disservice to the state, namely, the discouragement of Christians from working on its behalf, either in a peaceful or a warlike capacity. St. Martin of Tours, founder of monasteries in Gaul, asked to be released from the Roman army because he was Christ's soldier and could not fight for his country. When such views took hold of the population, the power of the Empire to resist its foes was weakened.

It was sapped further by Augustine. He was not, it is true, a pacifist. But the massive twenty-two books of his *City of God* undermined patriotism by more insidious means. For in this supreme literary masterpiece of the later Roman Empire, he made a sharp distinction between the earthly city and its counterpart in heaven. Plato and Paul had told of such ideal cities before, but Augustine, writing soon after Alaric's sack of Rome, described the concept with a vividness that was altogether new. And he infused it with a distinct unhopefulness about the future of any terrestrial state. It seemed to him that Christianity was the crop coming just before the icy frosts of winter—frosts which would freeze the nations of the world to death.

True, his "earthly city," which contains not only the sinners of this world but unrighteous men and women anywhere in the universe, is a wider concept than the Roman Empire. But this pessimism carries gloomy implications for the future of Rome's civilization.

Augustine had cut Rome firmly down to size. Its interests could no longer be held paramount: "Please pardon us if *our* country, up above, has to cause trouble to *yours...*" As he grew older, Augustine came more than ever to reject any identification between Christianity and Empire. In terms of world politics, he did not prevail. But his influence was widespread, and his refusal to believe in a Christian Empire was part of the West's failure to stave off its own collapse.

The successor states in the West

When Rome's rule crumbled in the West, it left the Visigoths ruling the southwest of Gaul as well as Spain and the Burgundians in control of southeastern Gaul, while another group of German communites, the Franks, had established themselves in the north of the country. The Visigoths and Burgundians, however, were overcome in 507 A.D. by the Franks, whose pagan chief and founder of the Merovingian dynasty, Clovis (ca. 482–511 A.D.), had embraced Christianity. Clovis and his successors extended this Frankish dominion both to the east and to the south, where Mediterranean Gaul gave them strength and culture.

Later Merovingian monarchs gradually became puppets of their mayors of the palace, of whom one, Pepin the Short, finally deposed his overlord and founded the Carolingian dynasty (751 A.D.), named after his father, Charles Martel. Then a ruler of that house, Charlemagne (772–814 A.D.) broke with his family's policy of peaceful missionary penetration by undertaking military campaigns and forcible conversions throughout northern Europe. Permanent inspectors were dispatched to the three hundred counties of his realm, and a legislative assembly was summoned twice a year. Finally, Charlemagne declared himself Roman emperor and had himself crowned at Rome by Pope Leo III (800 A.D.).

In Spain, Euric (466–85 A.D.) and Alaric II (485–507 A.D.) had fully established the power of the Visigoths; after the collapse of the Gallic portion of their empire to Clovis, this Visigothic kingdom assumed a more national, Spanish character. But Islamic power, spreading explosively across north Africa after the death of the Prophet Mohammed (632 A.D.), soon impinged forcibly on Spain.

In 711 A.D., the country was invaded by the Mohammedan prince Tarik, whose

BAPTISMAL POOL
(6th century A.D.) This mosaic-covered pool comes from the region around Kelibia , in Tunisia. Used to baptize the first Christians through immersion, it bears an inscription in honor of the bishop Cyprian.

successors asserted Mos-lem control throughout the southern part of the peninsula, relegating the Christian Spanish monarchy to its northern regions for centuries.

Meanwhile, in Italy, after Odoacer had asserted virtual independence of Constantinople, his Ostrogothic successor, Theoderic (493–526 A.D.), brought unaccustomed peace and prosperity to the land. He retained the Roman civil administration, and Latin literature flourished, producing such writers as Boethius and then Cassiodorus, who served as bridges between the past and the medieval civilization which was dawning. Moreover, although the Ostrogothic regime was not Catholic but Arian, the Roman church continued to gain power.

The survival of Byzantium

It was in Zeno's reign that the Eastern Empire, named Byzantine after the original name of Constantinople, remained very much in existence after the Western Empire became extinct. It nominally assumed control of the West, though in practice, Zeno refrained from interfering. But one of the chief events of his time was a quarrel between the ecclesiastical authorities in Rome and Constantinople; it would eventually result in the permanent division between Catholic and Orthodox.

THE EMPEROR
TRIUMPHANT
*(Central leaf of diptych
named the Barberini Ivory,
6th century A.D.) Here, the
image of the triumph of the
emperor (center) corresponds
to the image of Christ (top).
To the left, a general carries
victory while the conquered
people (bottom) carry
their tribute.*

would eventually result in the permanent division between Catholic and Orthodox. On Zeno's death, his widow gave the throne to a rich nobleman, Anastasius I (491–518 A.D.), who shored up a difficult financial situation.

Then Justin 1 (518–527 A.D.), in whose time the Slavs appeared as a major threat in the Balkans, became the founder of a new dynasty and elevated his nephew, Justinian I, to the throne (527–565 A.D.). The guiding spirit of one of the most creative epochs in human history, Justinian also built some of the world's greatest buildings; at Constantinople, his church of the Holy Wisdom (Santa Sophia), still stands. The last emperor to speak Latin better than Greek, Justinian instigated the compilation of a Latin Corpus of Civil Law which summed up and adapted the whole legal experience of Rome.

The Eastern Roman or Byzantine Empire continued to exist until its capital fell to the Ottoman Turkish sultan Mohammed II in 1453. Throughout almost the entire period, Constantinople was the most splendid and most learned city in Europe. Although its culture was Greek, the Byzantine emperors saw themselves as the heirs of ancient Rome and called themselves "Kings of the Romans."

Why did this eastern monarchy outlast its western counterpart? For one thing, the western realm was far more vulnerable to attack owing to its location. In Europe, it had to guard the long frontiers of the Upper and Middle Danube and the Rhine, whereas the Byzantine empire had only the lower Danube to cover.

Furthermore, the Eastern Empire possessed a sounder social and economic structure than the West, embodying fewer glaring disunities. It did not, for example, suffer in the same way from enormously wealthy noblemen, who grudged both men and money to the government and the army. The East was also both more populous and better cultivated than the West, and its provinces had survived the ravages of the third-century invasions with greater resilience. During a whole century and a half from 365 A.D., its internal peace was broken by only five usurpers, a remarkable contrast to the proliferation of such rebels in the West. Constantinople had its troubles, but it could weather them, owing to its inherently superior situation in other respects.

That was why it was the West which fell, whereas the East was able to survive for another thousand years.

Epilogue

The Roman Empire rose from a few villages founded along the Tiber. From this point on, it gradually expanded until it formed a huge, multiracial society that was sustained for a long time before dividing into separate entities, which were to become future modern nations. Although history doesn't repeat itself exactly—i.e., circumstances always differ, on both the cultural and political level—the Roman adventure is undeniably filled with lessons and warnings, even though defining them is sometimes difficult.

The modern world doesn't necessarily want to relive this adventure. Although certain aspects of the work accomplished by Rome are admirable and respectable, many are nevertheless detestable—namely the preponderance of violence. The culture that it passed down to us, with its unique masterpieces, could only exist and survive through violence—violence that our modern societies cannot and will not tolerate.

But how, then, are we to resolve the clashes of ethnic and religious groups that are still as harmful, if not more, than those of ancient Rome? And how do we do so without falling back on the unacceptable methods of the ancient Romans? The question remains. Here we have to ponder the annexation process used by the Romans: After the military phase came a political phase, during which legal advisors were extremely cunning. It would be pointless to seek an equivalent in another era, ours included.

Therefore, through the different stages of its history—and despite the changes that occurred through the centuries—Rome was able to essentially preserve its language, institutions, laws, religion, literature, arts, mores, and customs. Since that time, Western civilization has been continuously conscious of the persistent and widespread presence of this Roman influence, regularly honoring, celebrating, and reviving it.

VOLUBILIS *(Morocco) Despite successive invasions and despite its destruction in the 2nd century, Rome left its mark in a far-reaching empire. These monuments in north Africa speak to its power and glory.*

Glossary

Alba Longa Town located near the revered Alban Mount, in Latium

Anthropomorphic Adjective form of anthropomorphism, the attribution of human characteristics to a god, animal, or inanimate object

Barbarians Collective term for invaders of Rome, including the Visigoths and Gauls

Consul One of two annually elected chief magistrates who exercised supreme authority in the Roman Republic

Cult A form of worship with particular rites and ceremonies

Decemvir Member of a council of ten magistrates who drew up the first Roman code of law

Equestrian Member of a specially privileged class of citizens, from whom the Roman cavalry was formed

Fibula Buckle or clasp for fastening garments

Gnomic Wise and pithy; of a writer of aphorisms

Hellenism The character, culture, thought, and ethical system of ancient Greece

Hypogeum (pl. hypogea) Underground burial chamber

Inhume To bury a dead body

Invicta Roma aeterna Latin for "Rome remains eternal."

Massif Mass of peaks forming the backbone of a mountain range

Necropolis Cemetery in an ancient city

Patrician(s) Member of the original senatorial aristocracy

Peristyle A row of columns, or colonnade, surrounding a temple or other building

Philhellenic Adjectival form of philhellene, a friend of supporter of the Greeks

Plebeian(s) Roman commoner, a member of the Plebs

Praetors Elected magistrate charged with the administration of civil justice

Proconsul Officer who acted as governor or military commander in a province, discharging the duties of a consul

Procurator Officer in a province who collected taxes, paid troops, and managed the imperial treasury

Quadriga(s) Two-wheel chariot drawn by four horses abreast

Quinquereme(s) Ship with five banks of oars

Serried Adjective describing files or ranks of armed men who are close together

Tribune Magistrate, especially one appointed to protect the rights of plebeians

Tribute Rent or tax paid by a subject to a sovereign

Triumph Ceremonial, Senate-authorized entrance into Rome of a victorious commander and his troops

Triumvir Member of a triumvirate

Triumvirate Any group of three administrators who shared authority equally

Trompe l'oeil Visual deception in paintings, often involving perspective; French for "break the eye"

Sard A type of quartz with a deep orange-red color

Sumptuary law Regulation outlawing extravagance, based on moral or religious grounds

Index

Note: Page references in *italic* indicate photographs.

Picture credits